Ancient Views on
the Natural World

Books by David Whitwell

The Sousa Oral History Project
The Art of Musical Conducting
The Longy Club: 1900–1917
La Téléphonie and the Universal Musical Language
Extraordinary Women
A Concise History of the Wind Band
Essays on the Modern Wind Band
Essays on Performance Practice
A New History of Wind Music
The College and University Band
The Early Symphonies of Mozart
Music of the French Revolution
Stories from the Podium

On Composers
Wagner on Bands
Berlioz on Bands
Chopin: A Self-Portrait
Liszt: A Self-Portrait
Schumann: A Self-Portrait in His Own Words
Mendelssohn: A Self-Portrait in His Own Words

On Education
Philosophic Foundations of Education
Foundations of Music Education
Music Education of the Future

Aesthetics of Music
Aesthetics of Music in Ancient Civilizations
Aesthetics of Music in the Middle Ages
Aesthetics of Music in the Early Renaissance
Aesthetics of Music in Sixteenth-Century Italy, France and Spain
Aesthetics of Music in Sixteenth-Century Germany, the Low Countries and England
Aesthetics of Baroque Music in Italy, Spain, the German-Speaking Countries and the Low Countries
Aesthetics of Baroque Music in France
Aesthetics of Baroque Music in England

The History and Literature of the Wind Band and Wind Ensemble Series

Volume 1 The Wind Band and Wind Ensemble Before 1500
Volume 2 The Renaissance Wind Band and Wind Ensemble
Volume 3 The Baroque Wind Band and Wind Ensemble
Volume 4 The Wind Band and Wind Ensemble of the Classical Period (1750–1800)
Volume 5 The Nineteenth-Century Wind Band and Wind Ensemble
Volume 6 A Catalog of Multi-Part Repertoire for Wind Instruments or for Undesignated Instrumentation before 1600
Volume 7 Baroque Wind Band and Wind Ensemble Repertoire
Volume 8 Classical Period Wind Band and Wind Ensemble Repertoire
Volume 9 Nineteenth-Century Wind Band and Wind Ensemble Repertoire
Volume 10 A Supplementary Catalog of Wind Band and Wind Ensemble Repertoire
Volume 11 A Catalog of Wind Repertoire before the Twentieth Century for One to Five Players
Volume 12 A Second Supplementary Catalog of Early Wind Band and Wind Ensemble Repertoire
Volume 13 Name Index, Volumes 1–12, The History and Literature of the Wind Band and Wind Ensemble

Ancient Voices

Ancient Views on Music and Religion
Ancient Views on the Natural World
Ancient Views on What Is Music
Contemporary Descriptions of Early Musicians
Early Views of Music and Ethics

Renaissance Voices

Essays on Renaissance Philosophies of Music
Renaissance Men on Music

www.whitwellbooks.com

David Whitwell

Ancient Voices
Views on Music by Ancient and
Medieval Writers

Ancient Views on the Natural World

Edited by Craig Dabelstein

WHITWELL PUBLISHING • AUSTIN, TEXAS, USA

Ancient Voices: Views on music by ancient and medieval writers
Ancient Views on the Natural World
Dr. David Whitwell

WHITWELL PUBLISHING
AUSTIN, TX 78701
WWW.WHITWELLPUBLISHING.COM

© 2013 by David Whitwell
All rights reserved.

Composed in Bembo Book.
Published in the United States of America.
All images used in this book are in the public domain except where otherwise noted.

ISBN-13: 978-1-936512-73-7
ISBN-10: 1936512734

Cover design by Daniel Ferla

Contents

	Foreword	ix
	Acknowledgement	xi
1	The Ancient Voice of Pythagoras	1
2	On the Music of the Spheres, 'the Sacred Madness'	15
3	Early Views on Music Therapy	41
4	'to soothe a savage breast'	55
5	Ancient Views on Music and Movement	77
6	Ancient Views on Music and Oratory	95
7	Ancient Voices Wonder: Are Musicians Born or Made?	113
8	Ancient Voices Wonder: Is Music Genetic?	125
9	Ancient Views on Geography and Music	139
10	Weird Science	163
	Bibliography	177
	About The Author	189
	About the Editor	191

Foreword

IT IS IMPOSSIBLE TO DOCUMENT how old Music is, but all philologists agree that it is older than speech. That seems a reasonable idea and so it would follow that as man developed language it would have been natural for him to try to explain music in terms of the physical world around him. Thus in the most ancient extant literature of Western civilization one finds Music at the center of the development of mathematics, astronomy, medicine and religion.

The purpose of this book is to bring to the reader's attention some of the early views of music and the physical world. We begin with Pythagoras (570–495 BC) for history credits him with the association of music with the beginnings of mathematics, astronomy and music therapy. But we also consider the association of music with movement, another idea which would seem very ancient.

With so much of the physical world thus related to music, it is no wonder that ancient views also wondered if music was then genetic. To frame this as a question: Are musicians born or made? And if they are born musicians, does then geography influence their development?

Looking back we are amazed how often early thinkers, without the body of scientific evidence available to us, found the correct explanations. Sometimes they did not, however, and so we close with a chapter we call, Weird Science, for the reader's interest.

David Whitwell
Austin, Texas

Acknowledgments

I am indebted to my friend and colleague, Craig Dabelstein, for his help in preparing this book for publication.

David Whitwell
Austin, Texas

The Ancient Voice of Pythagoras

*Pythagoras ... one of the most outstanding mathematicians
of all times [and] an eminent idealistic philosopher ...*
Walther Kirchner, 1960 AD[1]

Pythagoras is the chief captain of swindlers.
Heraclitus, ca. 500 BC[2]

THESE TWO DISSIMILAR ASSESSMENTS OF PYTHAGORAS (580–500 BC) reflect the centuries old difficulty in trying to evaluate the contribution of this man. Nothing is more symbolic of the confusion surrounding the man's importance than the famous legend of how he discovered that the lower tones of the overtone series could be represented by numbers. Even though the entire story passed down about this is physically impossible, nevertheless whatever he did resulted in his inadvertently making man's first step toward higher mathematics. While our information from 2,500 years ago is so terribly flawed and incomplete, one must nevertheless admit that his is the oldest voice which has reverberated strongly until the present day.

The most fundamental problem we have in judging the man is that we possess not a single word actually written by him. What we have instead are mostly accounts by his disciples and followers, who often picture him as a mythological figure with powers above those of normal men. They said of him, for example, that he had the ability to be seen in different cities at the same time, that he gave predictions of earthquakes, chased away a pestilence, suppressed violent winds and hail and calmed storms on the seas, for the comfort and safe passage of his friends.[3] They portrayed him as a figure like Jesus (six centuries *before* Jesus), saying that he restored life to a dead woman and that he vanished bodily from the world to become a god.[4] Like Jesus, he sometimes spoke in parables, for example (here together with one scholar's deduction of their presumed meaning[5]):

Do not poke the fire with a sword.
　　(*Do not further inflame the quarrelsome*).

---

[1] Walther Kirchner, *Western Civilization to 1500* (New York: Barnes & Noble, 1960), 40.

[2] Fragment 81a, quoted in T. M. Robinson, *Heraclitus* (Toronto: University of Toronto Press, 1987). In the *Encyclopedia Britannica* (1951), XVIII, 802, we are also told that Heraclitus nevertheless admitted that 'Phythagoras was the most assiduous enquirer.'

[3] Porphyry (ca. 233–305 AD), 'Life of Pythagoras,' in Kenneth S. Guthrie, *The Pythagorean Sourcebook* (Grand Rapids: Phanes Press, 1987).

[4] Empedocles, quoted in Stuart Isacoff, *Temperament* (New York: Vintage Books, 2001), 29.

[5] Guthrie, *The Pythagorean Sourcebook*, 159–161.

Suffer no swallows around your house.
  (*Associate not with those who chatter vainly*).

Wear not a narrow ring.
  (*Seek freedom, avoid slavery*).

Abstain from beans.
  (*Avoid democratic voting*).

Abstain from eating animals.
  (*Have no conversation with unreasonable men*).

Never break the bread.
  (*When giving charity, do not pare too closely*).

Do not urinate against the sun.
  (*Be modest*).

Never sing without lyre accompaniment.
  (*Make of life a whole*).

Pick not up what is fallen from the table.
  (*Always leave something for charity*).

Place not the candle against the wall.
  (*Persist not in enlightening the stupid*).

Reading these examples, the reader will perhaps understand the frustration of Erasmus, who, in a letter to Henry VIII in 1523, cried, 'Who gives a fig for those puzzling precepts of Pythagoras?'

Porphyry wrote of Pythagoras that 'none was allowed to become his friend or associate without being examined in facial expression and disposition.'[6]

Who was this man? He was a Greek, a native of Samos and said to have been a pupil of Pherecydes, although Porphyry tells us that Pythagoras' first study was with a lyre player, a gymnast and a painter. He apparently traveled widely throughout the Mediterranean, including Egypt, according to Isocrates. Another biographer tells us he spent twelve years in Egypt where he studied 'arithmetic, music and all the other sciences.'[7]

Driven from Samos by the evil Polycrates, he arrived in Croton, a Dorian community in southern Italy, in about 529 BC. It was here that he developed his 'school,' a kind of religious brotherhood which aimed at the moral reformation of society. When the members of this school became actively involved in politics, in mid sixth century, its meeting houses were sacked and burned. One account, of the 'house of Milo' in Croton, tells of more than fifty Pythagoreans being surprised and slain. A number of his followers fled to Thebes, but as a

---

[6] Ibid.

[7] Iamblichus (ca. 250–325 AD), 'The Life of Pythagoras,' in Ibid.

school of philosophy it did not survive the fourth century. Some of the individual contributions of Pythagoras, especially in the field of mathematics, remain valid today. Aurelian of Reome, in his *Musica Disciplina* of 843 AD, begins his treatise with a poem:

> Whoever reads this, composed in the line of great authority,
> Will know that the most wholesome authors are here;
> Here is the musician Pythagoras, the fountain head of the Greeks ...

And if the school of philosophy did not survive, the model did. As Marrou, in his *History of Education in Antiquity*, describes,

> This ... was no longer a simple 'hetairia' of the ancient type, with the master and his pupils all on the same level; it was a real school, taking charge of the whole man and forcing him to adopt a particular way of life. It was an organized institution, with its own buildings and laws and regular meetings—a kind of religious brotherhood devoted to the cult of the Muses and, after the death of its founder, to the cult of the apotheosized Pythagoras. And it set the type: modeled on it later were Plato's Academy, Aristotle's Lyceum and the school of Epicurus, and it was always to remain the standard pattern of the Greek school of philosophy.[8]

Everything we know of the 'School of Pythagoras' is second-hand, passed down by his followers. Perhaps it was for this reason that Aristotle never referred to Pythagoras, only to Pythagoreans. Of the many anecdotes told of this school, some are very attractive, as for example his idea that one should preserve what one has learned from a teacher with the same sense of value that one saves a gift of money. Another thing he got right was his imposition of a term of five years of silence upon new students who came to study with him[9] before they were allowed to talk! Porphyry summarized the general nature of his teaching in this passage:

> He taught the following. A cultivated and fruit-bearing plant, harmless to man and beast, should neither be injured nor destroyed. A deposit of money or of teachings should be faithfully preserved by the trustee.
> There are three kinds of things that deserve to be pursued and acquired: honorable and virtuous things, those that conduce to the use of life, and those that bring pleasures of the blameless, secure and solemn kind, and not the vulgar intoxicating kinds. Of pleasures there are two kinds: one that indulges the stomach and lusts by a profusion of wealth, which he compared to the murderous songs of the Sirens; the other kind consists of things honest, just, and necessary to life, which are just as sweet as the first, without being followed by repentance, and these pleasures he compared to the harmony of the Muses.
>
> ......
>
> His utterances were of two kinds, plain or symbolical. His teaching was twofold: of his disciples some were called Students (*mathematikoi*), and other Hearers (*akousmatikoi*). The Students learned the fuller and more exactly elaborate reasons of science, while the Hearers heard only the summarized instructions of learning, without more detailed explanations.

---

8 H.I. Marrou, *A History of Education in Antiquity* (New York: The New American Library, 1964), 77.
9 'Of Inquisitiveness into Things Impertinent.'

There seem to have been several main areas of interest discussed by the members of this school. One was an emphasis on the kinship of men and beasts. Another was the divine application given to transmigration. Montaigne, in the sixteenth century, had heard that the idea of the after-life taking the form of another animal on earth was an idea attributed to Pythagoras, and for which he found some credibility in the observation of the transformation of the butterfly.[10] Somewhat related to this subject, the idea of Pythagoras about the body being the house of the soul continues to be of interest even by the much later Christians.

The scientific areas of interest appear to have been kept separate from the moral and divine discussions. He is given credit for making geometry a part of liberal education.

First and foremost the school devoted itself to a study of numbers and it might be said that Pythagoras was the first to remove numbers from their mere commercial utility and to make them the subject of formal study. They soon arrived at the idea that all things are inseparable from numbers, that numbers are the essence of things. In the fragments of Philolaus things are spoken of, not as being numbers, but as having number and thereby becoming knowable, the basis of Reason, one might say. Aristotle mentions this fundamental essence which the school gave to numbers.

> The so-called Pythagoreans, who were the first to take up mathematics, not only advanced this study, but also having been brought up in it they thought that its principles were the principles of all things. And since of these principles *numbers* are by nature the first, and in numbers they seemed to see many resemblances to the things that exist and come into being—more than in fire and earth and water ... since again, they saw that the modifications and the ratios of the musical scales were expressible in numbers—since, then, all other things seemed in their whole nature modeled on numbers, and numbers seemed to be the first things in the whole of nature, *they supposed the elements of numbers to be the elements of all things, and the whole heaven to be a musical scale and a number.*[11]

Thus placing numbers at the essence of things, it followed that for this school numbers soon became mixed up with metaphysics. The number one was identified with the point, which was thus a unit having position and magnitude, two was identified with line, three with surface and four with solid. The Odd and Even and the Limit and Unlimited were the first two of a set of ten fundamental oppositions postulated by the Pythagoreans, the remaining eight being: One and the Many, Right and Left, Male and Female, Rest and Motion, Straight and Curved, Light and Darkness, Good and Evil, Square and Oblong.[12]

Similarly, they found the number five to be equated with marriage, because it is the union of the first masculine and the first feminine numbers (3+2). The number one is identified with Reason, because it is unchangeable; two with opinion and four with Justice, because it is the first square number, the product of equals.

They also found relationships between numbers and the long tradition of Greek gods. For example, the number one, the monad, was regarded with mystical adoration.

---

[10] Michel de Montaigne, *Essays*, trans. M. A. Screech (London: Penguin, 1993), II, xii, 579. Montaigne also wonders here what grounds the gods have for rewarding or punishing man after death, when they have created him.

[11] *Metaphysics*, quoted in Reale, *A History of Ancient Philosophy* (Albany: State University of New York Press, 1987), 61.

[12] *Encyclopedia Britannica*, 803.

> In her resides all that is intellectual and uncreated; she is the nature of Ideas, she is God, the Mind, the Beautiful, the Good and every intellectual essences ... The number Seven was Athena, the goddess who was no one's mother and no one's daughter—for seven is the only number that cannot produce any of the other numbers of the decade [the first ten] and cannot be produced by them.[13]

This focus on the fundamental nature of numbers led also to the connection of numbers with geometry. They made note of the fact that if one places a dot on paper, and centered underneath it 2 dots, and then 3 and then 4, one has a triangle of dots not only representing the normal sequence of numbers (1+2+3+4), but the sum of 10, a number given special significance by the school. Also, tradition attributes to Pythagoras the theorem of the square of the hypotenuse of a right-angled triangle and that he proved that the sum of the 3 angles of any triangle is equal to 2 right angles. And there is much more.

The Pythagoreans created a new interest in astronomy. Pythagoras, apparently, was one of the first to hold that the earth and the universe are spherical in shape. His followers contribute more ideas, some of a metaphysical nature and others which lead to Copernicus. The best-known of Pythagoras' contributions to astronomy were his findings based on his study of musical sounds.

Pythagoras' interest in music was a subject which becomes inseparable from many of his other pursuits. Porphyry suggests that as an adult, Pythagoras continued his activity as a musician on a daily basis.

> He himself held morning conferences at his residence, composing his soul with the music of the lyre, and singing certain ancient paeans of Thales. He also sang verses of Homer and Hesiod, which seemed to soothe the mind. He danced certain dances which he thought conferred on the body agility and health.

Regarding his school, Aristides quotes something of Pythagoras which is not found elsewhere.

> This was also the sense of the advice Pythagoras is said to have given his disciples: that if they heard the aulos they should wash out their ears because the breath had defiled them,[14] but that they should use well-omened melodies sung to the lyra to cleanse their souls of irrational impulses. The aulos, he said, serves the thing that is master of our worse part, while the lyra is loved and enjoyed by that which cares for our rational nature.[15]

Martianus Capella, writing in the fifth century AD, knew of no such distinction between winds and strings.

---

13 Theon of Smyrna, 'Of the Mathematical Knowledge Necessary in Order to read Plato,' *Arithmetic*, 40ff.

14 Many philosophers at the time of Pythagoras considered the player himself to be of the lower class, 'sordid persons,' as Plutarch called them. The suggestion here is that it is the breathe of the aulos player, rather than sound waves, which travels through space to the ear of the listener, hence 'defiling them.'

15 Aristides, in Andrew Barker, trans., *Greek Musical Writings* (Cambridge: Cambridge University Press, 1989), II 457ff.

> The Pythagoreans too assuaged the ferocity of men's spirits with pipes and strings and taught that there is a firmly binding relationship between souls and bodies.[16]

Iamblichus gives us a very interesting, and more detailed, account of Pythagoras' use of music in relationship to health. There are some, no doubt, who would consider Pythagoras as 'the Father of Music Therapy.'

> Pythagoras conceived the first attention that should be given to men should be addressed to the senses,[17] as when one perceives beautiful figures and forms, or hears beautiful rhythms and melodies. Consequently he laid down that the first erudition was that which subsists through music's melodies and rhythms, and from these he obtained remedies of human manners and passions, and restored the pristine harmony of the faculties of the soul. Moreover, he devised medicines calculated to repress and cure the diseases of both bodies and souls. Here is also by Zeus, something which deserves to be mentioned above all: namely, that for his disciples he arranged and adjusted what might be called 'preparations' and 'touchings,' divinely contriving mingling of certain diatonic, chromatic and enharmonic melodies, through which he easily switched and circulated the passions of the soul in a contrary direction, whenever they had accumulated recently, irrationally, or clandestinely—such as sorrow, rage, pity, over-emulation, fear, manifold desires, angers, appetites, pride, collapse or spasms. Each of these he corrected by the rule of virtue, at tempering them through appropriate melodies, as through some salutary medicine.
>
> In the evening, likewise, when his disciples were retiring to sleep, he would thus liberate them from the day's perturbations and tumults, purifying their intellective powers from the influxive and effluxive waves of corporeal nature, quieting their sleep, and rendering their dreams pleasing and prophetic. But when they arose again in the morning, he would free them from the night's heaviness, coma and torpor through certain peculiar chords and modulations, produced by either simply striking the lyre, or adapting the voice.[18]

One of Pythagoras' followers, Euryphamus, continued the association of music and health by making an analogy with the lyre.

> Human life resembles a properly tuned and cared for lyre. Every lyre requires three things: apparatus, tuning, and musical skill of the player. By apparatus we mean preparation of all the appropriate parts: the strings, the plectrum and other instruments cooperating in the tuning of the instrument. By tuning we mean the adaptation of the sounds to each other. The musical skill is the motion of the player in consideration of the tuning. Human life requires the same three things. Apparatus is the preparation of the physical basis of life, riches, renown, and friends. Tuning is the organizing of these according to virtue and the laws. Musical skill is the mingling of these according to virtue and the laws, virtue sailing with a prosperous wind and no external resistance.[19]

---

[16] *Martianus Capella and the Seven Liberal Arts*, trans. William Harris Stahl and Richard Johnson (New York: Columbia University Press, 1977), II, 356ff.

[17] This seems very different from the comment by Plutarch, six centuries after Pythagoras:

> Pythagoras, that grave philosopher, rejected the judging of music by the senses, affirming that the virtue of music could be appreciated only by the intellect. And therefore he did not judge of music by the ear, but by the harmonical proportion. ('Concerning Music')

[18] Iamblichus, 'The Life of Pythagoras.'

[19] Quoted in Guthrie, *The Pythagorean Sourcebook*, 245.

Another disciple of Pythagoras, Diotogenes, in a fragment entitled, 'Concerning a Kingdom,' gives the same analogy, but on a larger scale.

> The king should therefore organize the well-legislated city like a lyre, first in himself establishing the justest boundary and order of law, knowing that the people's proper arrangement should be organized according to this interior boundary, the divinity having given him dominion over them.[20]

Pythagoras, as well, believed that since music was an important key to maintaining the balance of health in the individual, so must the same idea be valid for the larger society. When consulted by Crotonian civic leaders, Iambilichus relates that Pythagoras responded as follows.

> His first advice was to build a temple to the Muses, which would preserve the already existing concord. He observed to them that all of these divinities were grouped together by their common names, that they subsisted only in conjunction with each other, that they specially rejoiced in social honors, and that the choir of the Muses subsisted always one and the same. They comprehended symphony, harmony, rhythm, and all things breeding concord. Not only to beautiful theorems does their power extend, but to the general symphonious harmony.[21]

Among musicians today, of course, Pythagoras is remembered as the person who is credited with working out the numerical ratios of the dependence of musical intervals on certain arithmetical ratios in lengths of string held at the same tension, 2:1 producing the octave, 3:2 the fifth and 4:3 the fourth, in other words, the lower portion of the overtone series. This was a far-reaching discovery of great influence, as we can see, for example, in St. Augustine insisting that in the construction of cathedrals the heights, lengths and depths were to form the proportions 1:1, 1:2, 2:3 and 3:4.[22]

But here again, since we do not have an account by Pythagoras in his own words, we are deprived of everything we would like to know about his historic discovery. The story that has been passed down to us, by one of his disciples, is a story which is improbable with respect to the physics of sound.

> Once as he was intently considering music, and reasoning with himself whether it would be possible to devise some instrumental assistance to the sense of hearing, so as to systematize it, as sight is made precise by the compass, rule, and telescope, or touch is made reckonable by balance and measures—so thinking of these things Pythagoras happened to pass by a brazier's shop where he heard the hammers beating out a piece of iron on an anvil, producing sounds that harmonized, except one. But he recognized in these sounds the concord of the octave, the fifth, and the fourth. He saw that the sound between the fourth and the fifth, taken by itself, was a dissonance, and yet completed the greater sound [the octave] among them.
>
> Delighted, therefore, to find that the thing he was anxious to discover had by divine assistance succeeded, he went into the [blacksmith's shop], and by various experiments discovered that the difference of sound arose from the magnitude of the hammers, but not from the force of the strokes,

---

[20] Ibid., 223.
[21] Iambilichus, 'The Life of Pythagoras.'
[22] Isacoff, *Temperament*, 76.

nor from the shape of the hammers, nor from the change of position of the beaten iron. Having then accurately examined the weights and the swing of the hammers, he returned home, and fixed one stake diagonally to the walls, lest some difference should arise from there being several of them, or from some difference in the material of the stakes.

From this stake he then suspended four gut-strings, of similar materials, size, thickness, and twist. A weight was suspended from the bottom of each. When the strings were equal in length, he struck two of them simultaneously, he reproduced the former intervals, forming different pairs. He discovered that the string stretched by the greatest weight, when compared with that stretched by the smallest weight, had the interval of an octave. The weight of the first was twelve pounds, and that of the latter, six. Being therefore in a double ratio, it formed the octave, which was made plain by the weights themselves. Then he found that the string from which the greatest weight was suspended compared with that from which was suspended the weight next to the smallest, and which weight was eight pounds, produced the interval known as the fifth. Hence he discovered that this interval is in a ratio of one and a half to one, or three to two, in which ratio the weights also were to each other.

This story of Pythagoras and the blacksmith had a charm which attracted later writers for centuries. Plutarch, for example, in his 'Conjugal Precepts,' carried the logic of the overtone series into the domestic environment.

As in musical concords, when the upper strings are so tuned as exactly to accord, the base always gives the tone; so in well-regulated and well-ordered families, all things are carried on with the harmonious consent and agreement of both parties, but the conduct and contrivance chiefly redounds to the reputation and management of the husband.

Galileo Galilei, was the first to point out the mathematical and physical impossibility of the account of Pythagoras' discovery of the overtone series by listening to a blacksmith—a story which had been unchallenged for two thousand years! By the seventeenth century, at least in England, this story appears to have become confused with the biblical account, in Genesis 3:21, of the birth of musical instruments by the family Cain, 'Zillah bore Tubal-cain; he was the forger of all the instruments of bronze and iron.' For example in the long poem, 'Britannia's Pastorals,' by William Browne (1591–1643), we read,

Fondly have some been led to think, that Man
Musiques invention first of all began
From the dull Hammers stroke; since well we know
From sure tradition that hath taught us so.[23]

And in the *Spectator* of 1 September 1712, is a similar confusion of Pythagoras and the biblical account, although here the newspaper has the wrong brother. Jubal created the lyres and double-reeds, it being his brother, Tubal-cain, who worked with hammer and anvil.

---

[23] Book II, Song 4.

> Musick indeed may plead another original, since Jubal by the different falls of his hammer on the anvil, discovered by the ear the first rude Musick that pleased the Antediluvian fathers; but then the *sight* has not only reduced those wilder sounds into artful Order and Harmony, but [through notation] conveys that Harmony to the most distant parts of the world without the help of sound.[24]

Regardless of the curious particulars of the earliest account of Pythagoras' discovery, because his discovery itself is so frequently mentioned by earlier writers there is little reason to doubt that he in fact did somehow arrive at the numerical ratios of at least the lower part of the overtone series. Ironically, his great contribution to science was not in this discovery itself, but in the realization which followed. That is, that numbers could represent abstract thought. This might be called, in fact, the beginning of all higher mathematics.

Certainly this discovery, however it happened, of the ability to express the lower tones of the overtone series in numerical terms has had greater and more far reaching discussion than anything else attributed to Pythagoras. The great Isaac Newton, as an example, found an entirely different significance in this discovery of Pythagoras.

> Newton believed that Pythagoras knew that when varying the weights attached to the ends of the strings, rather than the string length, the proportions had to be squared and inverted. To Newton, the Pythagoras story was a parable; its true intent was to reveal 'that the weights of the planets towards the sun were reciprocally as the squares of their distances from the sun.'[25]

In any case, we must assume that the discovery of the numeric ratios between the lower tones of the overtone series led to Pythagoras' conclusion that these same ratios could be found among the planets. From this, in turn, he developed his concept of the 'Music of the Spheres.'[26] For some this concept was very fundamental indeed, as we can see in the very influential sixth-century writer, Cassiodorus, who seemed to believe it was connected with creation itself.

> The sky and the earth and everything which is accomplished in them by the supernal stewardship are not without the science of music; for Pythagoras is witness to the fact that this world was founded through the instrumentality of music and can be governed by it.[27]

According to Porphyry, Pythagoras claimed the sole ability to actually hear this music of the spheres, his students not being developed enough to be able to do so.

---

[24] The last sentence may be a satirical reference to a debate during the seventeenth century regarding the senses. Voltaire, for example, humorously observed that the blind were the best judges of art and the deaf the best judges of music. Here the Spectator seems to be suggesting that music has become famous as something for the eye, not the ear.

[25] Isacoff, *Temperament*, 192.

[26] Essay II in this series is devoted to the music of the spheres.

[27] Cassiodorus, 'On Music,' in *An Introduction to Divine and Human Readings*, trans. Leslie Jones (New York, Octagon Books, 1966).

> He himself could hear the Harmony of the Universe, and understood the universal music of the spheres, and of the stars which move in concert with them, and which we cannot hear because of the limitations of our weak nature ...
>
> Pythagoras affirmed that the Nine Muses were constituted by the sounds made by the seven planets, the sphere of the fixed stars, and that which is opposed to our earth, called the 'counter-earth.' He called Mnemosyne, or Memory, the composition, symphony and connection of them all, which is eternal and unbegotton as being composed of all of them.[28]

Aristotle, again, provides us with the thought process of this Pythagorean view of the universe.

> Some think it necessary that noise should arise when so great bodies are in motion, since sound does arise from bodies among us which are not so large and do not move so swiftly; and from the sun and moon and from the stars in so great number, and of so great size, moving so swiftly, there must necessarily arise a sound inconceivably great. Assuming these things and that the swiftness has the principle of harmony by reason of the intervals, they say that the sound of the stars moving on in a circle becomes musical. And since it seems unreasonable that we also do not hear this sound, they say that the reason for this is that the noise exists in the very nature of things, so as not to be distinguishable from the opposite silence; for the distinction of sound and silence lies in their contrast with each other, so that as blacksmiths think there is no difference between them because they are accustomed to the sound, so the same things happen to men. What occasions the difficulty and makes the Pythagoreans say that there is a harmony of the bodies as they move, is a proof. For whatever things move themselves make a sound and noise; but whatever things are fastened in what moves or exist in it as the parts in a ship, cannot make a noise, nor yet does the ship if it moves in a river.[29]

Plutarch provides us with the development of this concept among some of the followers of Pythagoras.

> For some there are who seek these proportions in the swift motions of the spheres of the planets; others rather in the distances, others in the magnitude of the stars; others, more accurate and nice in their inquiry, seek for the same proportions in the diameters of the epicycles; as if the Supreme Architect, for the sake of these, had adapted the soul, divided into seven parts, to the celestial bodies. Many also there are, who hither transfer the inventions of the Pythagoreans, tripling the distances of bodies from the middle. This is done by placing the unit next the fire; three next the Antichthon, or earth which is opposite to our earth; nine next the Earth; 27 next the Moon; 81 next to Mercury; 243 upon Venus; and 729 upon the Sun. The last (729) is both a tetragonal and cubical number, whence it is, that they also call the sun a tetragon and a cube.
>
> ......
>
> Others there are, who fancy the earth to be in the lowest string of the harp, called proslambanomenos; and so proceeding, they place the moon in hypate, Mercury and Venus in the diatoni and lichani; the sun they likewise place in mese, as in the midst of the diapason, a fifth above the earth and a fourth from the sphere of the fixed stars.

---

[28] Porphyry, 'Life of Pythagoras.'

[29] de Caelo, II, quoted in Milton C. Nahm, *Selections from Early Greek Philosophy* (New York: Appleton-Century-Crofts, 1964), 58.

> But neither doth this pleasant conceit of the latter come near the truth, neither do the former attain perfect accuracy. However, they who will not allow the latter to depend upon Plato's sentiments will yet grant the former to partake of musical proportions; so that there being five tetrachords, and in these five distances they place all the planets; making the first tetrachord from the Moon to the Sun and the planets which move with the Sun, that is, Mercury and Venus; the next from the Sun to the fiery planet of Mars; the third between this and Jupiter; the fourth from thence to Saturn; and the fifth from Saturn to the sphere of the fixed stars. So that the sounds and notes which bound the five tetrachords bear the same proportion with the intervals of the planets.
>
> ......
>
> So it is most probable that the bodies of the stars, the distances of spheres, and the swiftness of the motions and revolutions, have their sundry proportions, as well one to another as to the whole fabric, like instruments of music well set and tuned, though the measure of the quantity be unknown to us.[30]

We should digress a moment to mention that one of the members of the Pythagorean School, Archytas, correctly (if circuitously) arrived at the observation that higher frequencies travel with more energy.

> Of the sounds that fall within the range of our senses, some—those that come quickly from the bodies struck—seem shrill; those that arrive slowly and feebly, seem of low pitch. In fact, when one agitates some object slowly and feebly, the shock produces a low pitch; if the waving is done quickly, and with energy, the sound is shrill. This is not the only proof of the fact, which we can prove when we speak or sing; when we wish to speak loud and high, we use a great force of breath. So also with something thrown; if you throw them hard, they go far; if you throw them without energy, they fall near, for the air yields more to bodies moved with much force, than to those thrown with little. This phenomenon is also reproduced in the sound of the voice, for the sounds produced by an energetic breath are shrill, while those produced by a feeble breath are weak and low in pitch. This same observation can be seen in the force of a signal given from any place: if you pronounce it loud, it can be heard far; if you pronounce the same signal low, we do not hear it even when near. So also in the aulos, the breath emitted by the mouth and which presents itself to the holes nearest the mouthpiece, produces a shriller sound, because the impulsive force is greater; farther down, they are of lower pitch. It is therefore evident that the swiftness of the movement produces shrillness, and slowness, lower pitch.[31]

The idea of the music of the spheres was another idea too interesting to die, and so would be debated, pro and con, for more than two thousand years after Pythagoras, a debate we follow in a later chapter.[32] We might just quote here, however, an interesting passage in a manuscript by the great seventeenth-century English poet, Milton, for it documents the respect which Pythagoras still held among some thinkers so many centuries after his death. It is particularly interesting here that Milton seems to criticize Aristotle for not defending Pythagoras on the question of the music of the spheres.

---

30   'Of the Procreation of the Soul.'

31   Fragment 15, quoted in Guthrie, *The Pythagorean Sourcebook*, 184.

32   Essay II.

For what sane man would have thought that Pythagoras, that god of the philosophers, at whose name all mortals of his age stood up in very sacred veneration;—who, I say, would have thought that he would ever have expressed in public an opinion so uncertainly founded? Surely, if indeed he taught the harmony of the spheres and that the heavens revolved with melodious charm, he wished to signify by it, in his wise way, the very loving and affectionate relations of the orbs and their eternally uniform revolutions according to the fixed laws of necessity. Certainly, in this he imitated either the poets or, what is almost the same thing, the divine oracles, by whom no secret and hidden mystery is exhibited in public, unless clad in some covering or garment. That most skillful interpreter of Mother Nature, Plato, has followed him, since he affirms that certain sirens sit one upon each of the circles of the heavens and hold spell-bound gods and men by their most honey-sweet song. And finally, this agreement of things universal and this loving concord, which Pythagoras secretly introduced in poetic fashion by the term Harmony, Homer likewise suggested significantly and appropriately by means of that famous golden chain of Jove hanging down from heaven.

Aristotle, the envious and perpetual calumniator of Pythagoras and Plato, desiring to pave a way to renown on the shattered opinions of these great men, imputed to Pythagoras the unheard symphony of the heavens and tunes of the spheres. But if either fate or necessity had decreed that your soul, O Father Pythagoras, should have been translated into me, there would not have been lacking one who would easily have come to your rescue, however great the infamy under which you were laboring at the moment. Indeed, why should not the celestial bodies during their everlasting courses evolve musical sounds? Does it not seem fair to you, O Aristotle? Truly, I hardly believe your intelligences would be able to endure with patience that sedentary toil of the rolling heavens for so many ages, unless that ineffable song of the stars had prevented your departure and by the charm of its melody had persuaded a delay. It would be as if you were to take away from heaven those beautiful little goddesses and should deliver the ministering gods to mere drudgery and to condemn them to the treadmill. Nay indeed, Atlas himself long ago would have withdrawn his shoulders from a heaven that was about to fall, had not that sweet song soothed, with its most delightful charm, him, gasping and sweating under his great burden.[33]

Finally, because of the relatively instant fame which Pythagoras achieved through the retelling of the stories of his discovery of the numerical ratios of the overtone series and his notion of the music of the spheres, along with all the philosophical commentary there have also been satirical contributions. Athenaeus, in *Deipnosophistae*, III, 103, provides a satire on the Pythagoreans' tendency to find music as the organizational principle of nearly everything.

A: For myself, I never enter the kitchen.
B: Why, what do you do?
A: I sit near by and watch, while others do the work; to them I explain the principles and the result. 'Softly! the mincemeat is seasoned sharp enough.'
B: You must be a musician, not a cook!
A: 'Play fortissimo with the fire. Make the tempo even. The first dish is not simmering in tune with the others next to it.'
B: Save us!
A: It's beginning to look like an art to you, what? You see, I serve no course without study mingle all in a harmonious scale.
B: What does that mean?

---

[33] 'On the Music of the Spheres,' in *The Works of John Milton*, ed. Frank Patterson (New York: Columbia University Press, 1931–1938), XII, 149ff.

A: Some things are related to each other by fourths, by fifths, or by octaves. These I join their own proper intervals, and weave them into a series of appropriate courses.

Another example of humor in early dialog form is found in Lucian, of the second century. He touches all the bases on Pythagoras, mentioning the music of the spheres, transmigration and the five years' silence demanded by Pythagoras of his new students. The scene is an 'Auction of Philosophers' and Pythagoras, who remained an object of interest and curiosity among all the later Greeks, is put on the block first.

Hermes: Gentlemen! I have here for sale a live philosopher, the best of the lot, and with the most imposing presence. Who'll buy? Who wants to be more than a man? Who wants to understand the music of the spheres and return to life again?
A Customer: He's not a mean looking fellow. But what does he know best?
Hermes: Oh — arithmetic, astronomy, jugglery, geometry, music and witchcraft....

...

Customer: Well, if I purchase you, what will you teach me?
Pythagoras: I shall teach you nothing. I shall merely rub up your memory.
Customer: Why, how will you do that?
Pythagoras: By first cleansing your soul and washing off the filth there is on it.
Customer: Well, suppose now that I am already cleansed — what is your method of refreshing the memory?
Pythagoras: In the first place, one must lead a quiet life for a long time and observe silence — not uttering a word for five entire years.... Then you shall practice music and geometry.
Customer: That's a clever suggestion of yours — that I must first learn to play the harp before I can be wise.[34]

---

34 'Dialogues of the Gods,' trans. Winthrop D. Sheldon in *A Second Century Satirist* (Philadelphia: Drexel Biddle, 1901), 399.

On the Music of the Spheres, 'The Sacred Madness'

To thee, the heaven and its stars make music,
Sun and moon sing praises to thee,
The whole earth is making music for thee.[1]

'Hymn to Hathor'
Temple of Dandera

IN GENERAL THE LITERATURE OF ANCIENT GREECE attributed the concept of the Music of the Spheres to Pythagoras (580–500 BC), but as the reader can see in the above ancient Egyptian hymn some form of the concept of 'music of the spheres,' the notion that musical sounds are produced by the movements of the planets, was known in Egypt long before the beginning of European literature.

How could such a an idea occur to ancient man? The answer we suppose lay in the sounds of ordinary life. The sounds of trees responding to wind, the sound made by the fast movement of a whip, etc., could have made the association of movement and sound an observed experience at some very remote age. It would then be not so implausible a leap to imagine that if sound is created by movement, then the movement of the planets must *ipso facto* create sound. But in this case there was a problem because no one could hear these sounds. The ancients did not yet understand the role of air in carrying the sounds of music, nor did they understand there was no air in outer space. They only knew they could not hear the music of the spheres and the efforts of those who felt obligated to explain this makes for interesting reading.

The basic concept of the music of the spheres had much to recommend for itself to the later ancient Greeks, who became very interested in the relationship of man and nature. As mentioned above, surviving ancient Greek literature tends to associate this concept with Pythagoras and his discovery of the numerical ratios of the lower part of the overtone series. Believing everything in nature must be related, they presumed that the ratios representing the separation of the lower tones of the overtone series must be the same ratios as those representing the distances separating the planets. We cannot know exactly what Pythagoras himself believed on this subject for he has left no extant writing. His association with this idea is found only in the writings of his followers and students. Thus it was that even Aristotle, writing some two hundred years later seemed to identify the notion of the music of the spheres with Pythagoras and his school.

---

[1] Quoted in Lise Manniche, *Music and Musicians in Ancient Egypt* (London: British Museum Press, 1991), 12. Hathor was a dual god, an Egyptian god of love and music.

> The so-called Pythagoreans, who were the first to take up mathematics, not only advanced this study, but also having been brought up in it they thought that its principles were the principles of all things. And since of these principles *numbers* are by nature the first, and in numbers they seemed to see many resemblances to the things that exist and come into being—more than in fire and earth and water … since again, they saw that the modifications and the ratios of the musical scales were expressible in numbers—since, then, all other things seemed in their whole nature modeled on numbers, and numbers seemed to be the first things in the whole of nature, they supposed the elements of numbers to be the elements of all things, and *the whole heaven to be a musical scale* and a number.[2]

According to Porphyry (third century AD), Pythagoras claimed to be the only person who could hear the music of the spheres, his students not being developed enough to be able to do so.

> He himself could hear the Harmony of the Universe, and understood the universal music of the spheres, and of the stars which move in concert with them, and which we cannot hear because of the limitations of our weak nature …
> Pythagoras affirmed that the Nine Muses were constituted by the sounds made by the seven planets, the sphere of the fixed stars, and that which is opposed to our earth, called the 'counter-earth.' He called Mnemosyne, or Memory, the composition, symphony and connection of them all, which is eternal and unbegotton as being composed of all of them.[3]

Perhaps Pythagoras could hear the music of the spheres, but Aristotle could not and as a result for him this subject never made sense. In the following passage he points out that the difficulty is in the absence of proof.

> Some think it necessary that noise should arise when so great bodies are in motion, since sound does arise from bodies among us which are not so large and do not move so swiftly; and from the sun and moon and from the stars in so great number, and of so great size, moving so swiftly, there must necessarily arise a sound inconceivably great. Assuming these things and that the swiftness has the principle of harmony by reason of the intervals, they say that the sound of the stars moving on in a circle becomes musical. And since it seems unreasonable that we also do not hear this sound, they say that the reason for this is that the noise exists in the very nature of things, so as not to be distinguishable from the opposite silence; for the distinction of sound and silence lies in their contrast with each other, so that as blacksmiths think there is no difference between them because they are accustomed to the sound, so the same things happen to men. What occasions the difficulty and makes the Pythagoreans say that there is a harmony of the bodies as they move, is a proof. For whatever things move themselves make a sound and noise; but whatever things are fastened in what moves or exist in it as the parts in a ship, cannot make a noise, nor yet does the ship if it moves in a river.[4]

---

[2] *Metaphysics*, quoted in Giovanni Reale, *A History of Ancient Philosophy* (Albany: State University of New York Press, 1987, 61.

[3] Porphyry, 'Life of Pythagoras.'

[4] 'De Caelo,' II, quoted in Milton C. Nahm, *Selections from Early Greek Philosophy* (New York: Appleton-Century-Crofts, 1964), 58.

In the end, Aristotle stated his belief without qualification: this concept is not true.

> It is clear that the theory that the movement of the stars produces a harmony, i.e., that the sounds they make are concordant, in spite of the grace and originality with which it has been stated, is nevertheless untrue.[5]

Aristotle was, of course, one of the most brilliant and rational minds of all time, a man who's thought had enormous influence on the following centuries. Nevertheless, even with his clear rejection, the Music of the Spheres was an idea apparently too attractive to let die.

Plutarch (first century AD), one of the last of the ancient Greek philosophers and a writer with a keen ear for good stories, provides some additional information on the beliefs regarding the music of the spheres held among the followers of Pythagoras. It appears that many new claims had been superimposed on the original concept of Pythagoras during the three centuries after Aristotle.

> For some there are who seek these proportions in the swift motions of the spheres of the planets; others rather in the distances, others in the magnitude of the stars; others, more accurate and nice in their inquiry, seek for the same proportions in the diameters of the epicycles; as if the Supreme Architect, for the sake of these, had adapted the soul, divided into seven parts, to the celestial bodies. Many also there are, who hither transfer the inventions of the Pythagoreans, tripling the distances of bodies from the middle. This is done by placing the unit next the fire; three next the Antichthon, or earth which is opposite to our earth; nine next the Earth; 27 next the Moon; 81 next to Mercury; 243 upon Venus; and 729 upon the Sun. The last (729) is both a tetragonal and cubical number, whence it is, that they also call the sun a tetragon and a cube.
>
> ......
>
> Others there are, who fancy the earth to be in the lowest string of the harp, called proslambanomenos; and so proceeding, they place the moon in hypate, Mercury and Venus in the diatoni and lichani; the sun they likewise place in mese, as in the midst of the diapason, a fifth above the earth and a fourth from the sphere of the fixed stars.
>
> But neither doth this pleasant conceit of the latter come near the truth, neither do the former attain perfect accuracy. However, they who will not allow the latter to depend upon Plato's sentiments will yet grant the former to partake of musical proportions; so that there being five tetrachords, and in these five distances they place all the planets; making the first tetrachord from the Moon to the Sun and the planets which move with the Sun, that is, Mercury and Venus; the next from the Sun to the fiery planet of Mars; the third between this and Jupiter; the fourth from thence to Saturn; and the fifth from Saturn to the sphere of the fixed stars. So that the sounds and notes which bound the five tetrachords bear the same proportion with the intervals of the planets.
>
> ......

---

5 'De Caelo,' 290b.13.

> So it is most probable that the bodies of the stars, the distances of spheres, and the swiftness of the motions and revolutions, have their sundry proportions, as well one to another as to the whole fabric, like instruments of music well set and tuned, though the measure of the quantity be unknown to us.[6]

Plutarch's Roman contemporary of the 1st century, Pliny the Elder, also mentions the music of the spheres but he does not take it seriously since he cannot hear these sounds.

> The world thus shaped then is not at rest but eternally revolves with indescribable velocity, each revolution occupying the space of 24 hours: the rising and setting of the sun have left this not doubtful. Whether the sound of this vast mass whirling in unceasing rotation is of enormous volume and consequently beyond the capacity of our ears to perceive, for my own part I cannot easily say—any more in fact than whether this is true of the tinkling of the stars that travel round with it, revolving in their own orbits; or whether it emits a sweet harmonious music that is beyond belief charming. To us who live within it, the world glides silently alike by day and night.[7]

Nevertheless, we are indebted to Pliny the Elder for providing us with information not found in earlier literature on Pythagoras, the latter's correspondence of the ratios of the tones of the scale with the order of the planets. Pliny cannot help observing that he found this more entertaining than believable.

> But occasionally Pythagoras draws on the theory of music, and designates the distance between the earth and the moon as a whole tone, between Mercury and Venus the same, between her and the sun a tone and a half, between the sun and Mars a tone, between Mars and Jupiter half a tone, between Jupiter and Saturn half a tone, between Saturn and the zodiac a tone and a half; the seven tones thus producing the so-called diapason, i.e. a universal harmony; in this Saturn moves in the Dorian mode, Jupiter in the Phrygian, and similarly with the other planets—a refinement more entertaining than convincing.[8]

Another first-century Roman, Quintilian (30–96 AD), also mentions the music of the spheres and the school of Pythagoras. One gets the feeling he was not prepared to contest six centuries of commentary on the music of the spheres, as he confesses he is 'ready to accept the verdict of antiquity.'

> Pythagoras and his followers popularized the belief, which they no doubt had received from earlier teachers, that the universe is constructed on the same principles which were afterwards imitated in the construction of the lyre, and not content merely with emphasizing that concord of discordant elements which they style harmony, attributed a sound to the motions of the celestial bodies.[9]

---

[6] 'Of the Procreation of the Soul.' Plutarch, himself, in 'Conjugal Precepts,' carried the logic of the overtone series into the domestic environment.

> As in musical concords, when the upper strings are so tuned as exactly to accord, the base always gives the tone; so in well-regulated and well-ordered families, all things are carried on with the harmonious consent and agreement of both parties, but the conduct and contrivance chiefly redounds to the reputation and management of the husband.

[7] Pliny the Elder, *Natural History*, II, iii.

[8] Ibid., II, xx.

[9] Quintilian, *The Education of an Orator (Institutio Oratoria)*, trans. H. E. Butler (London: Heinemann, 1938), I, x, 12.

During the early years of the Christian Era the credibility of the concept of music of the spheres increased, especially by the fourth century or so when most of the works of Aristotle were now unknown to Church philosophers.[10] St. Ambrose described the music of the spheres not only as something real, but as something he could hear.

> By the impact and motion of these spheres there is produced a tone full of sweetness, the fruit of consummate art and of the most delightful modulation, inasmuch as the air, torn apart by such artful motion, combines in even and melodious fashion high and low notes to such a degree that it surpasses in sweetness any other musical composition.[11]

An important book on music by a 'pagan' philosopher of the fifth century is the allegorical description of 'The Marriage of Philology and Mercury,' by Martianus Capella. This work is a defense of the importance of the seven liberal arts, which were by this time established in the Roman schools. These were the *Trivium*, consisting of Grammar, Dialectic, and Rhetoric, and the *Quadrivium*, consisting of Geometry, Arithmetic, Astronomy, and Music.[12] The book was written at a time when Christianity had not yet won its final battle against the 'pagans' and might well be thought of as an attempt to fight back against the efforts of the new Church to shut down traditional education and knowledge. Thus this book represents one of the efforts which helped keep the liberal arts alive during the 'Dark Ages.' Music for its own sake had been rejected by the Church and it could only find its place in the Church schools as a branch of mathematics. This is what Capella refers to when he writes,

> Having long since taken her departure from earth, music has rejected mortals and their desolated academies.[13]

Capella makes reference to the music of the spheres after 'Harmony' [music] has sung at the allegorical wedding which his book describes. Some of the guests wondered at the 'pains and labor involved in the production of the music and the effort and unabated concentration that must have gone into the mastery and attainment of harmonies so soft and caressing as to enthrall the innermost emotions of their hearts.' It was a subject much discussed in ancient literature. The answer provided by 'Harmony' begins with reference to the disinterest by the Church and mentions the music of the spheres.

---

10 In its effort to rid the world of pagan ideas, the new Church, among other things, made a determined effort to burn the books of the ancient philosophers, including Aristotle.

11 Saint Ambrose, 'Six Days of Creation: Two,' in *Hexameron, Paradise, and Cain and Abel*, trans. John J. Savage (New York: Fathers of the Church, 1961`), 50.

12 Capella used the word, 'Harmony,' but his meaning was music.

13 *Martianus Capella and the Seven Liberal Arts*, trans. William Harris Stahl and Richard Johnson (New York: Columbia University Press, 1977), 349.

> A loathsome and detestable creature to earthborn mortals, I have been striking against the star-studded heavenly spheres, where I am forbidden to discourse on the precepts of my art — this despite the fact that the swirling celestial mechanism, in the swiftness of its motion, produces a harmony which it recognizes as concordant with the gamut of all proportions.[14]

Cassiodorus (480–573 AD), one of the great philosophers of the sixth century mentions the music of the spheres in a letter to the famous Boethius (475–524 AD). He recalls that earlier philosophers had found the lyre in the constellations and points out that while Nature has not prepared us to hear the music of the spheres, Reason assures us it must exist. In any case, he offers the consolation that we will finally hear this music in Heaven!

> Yet, the harmony of heaven cannot be fittingly described by human speech, as nature has not revealed it to human ears, but the soul knows it through reason only. For they say that we should believe that the blessedness of heaven enjoys those pleasures which have no end, and are diminished by no interruption. They maintain, indeed, that things above are absorbed by that same perception, that heavenly beings enjoy those same pleasures, and that those who are engrossed by such contemplations are constantly enfolded in blessed delights.[15]

His great contemporary, Boethius, in *De institutione musica*, divided music into three kinds, in an apparent descending order of importance: Cosmic Music (which included the music of the spheres), Human music (meaning vocal music) and Instrumental Music. It was a definition which would be followed for centuries, as we can see, for example, in the *Musica Disciplina* by Aurelian of the ninth century who faithfully copies the three divisions of music by Boethius. While Aurelian admits that man cannot actually hear the music of the spheres, he finds evidence for it in a mistranslation of a passage from the Old Testament book, Job 38:37, 'or who can make the harmony of heaven to sleep.'[16]

A tenth-century nun, Hrotswitha, also carries on the three divisions of music by Boethius in a very interesting play, *Paphnutius*. The character of the title is a monk, a teacher, who carries on an extensive dialog on the subject of music with a group of students, who have asked, 'What *is* music?'[17] Paphnutius answers with a brief description of the place held by music among the liberal arts. The Disciples beg for more information and Paphnutius relents, 'since it is knowledge which monks don't have.'

Paphnutius, following the definition by Boethius, begins by telling the students that music is divided into three species: the celestial, the human, and that made with instruments.

> DISCIPLES. What does celestial music consist of?
> PAPHNUTIUS. Of the seven planets and the celestial sphere.

---

[14] Ibid., 356ff.

[15] Letter to Boethius, in *Variae*, trans. Thomas Hodgkin (London: Frowde, 1886), II, xl.

[16] Modern translations, such as the *Revised Standard Version*, make no inference to music.
> Who has put wisdom in the clouds, or given understanding to the mists?
> Who can number the clouds by wisdom?

[17] *The Plays of Hrotswitha of Gandersheim*, trans. Larissa Bonfante (New York: New York University Press, 1979), 108ff.

DISCIPLES. How do you mean that?
PAPHNUTIUS. Because, you see, they produce the same harmonious music as the strings of stringed instruments; For just as in the case of instruments, we find the same concordances and intervals of like number and length.
DISCIPLES. And what are these 'intervals' you speak of?
PAPHNUTIUS. They are the distances which exist between the planets, as between the notes of strings.

Upon further questions about the 'notes' just mentioned, Paphnutius begins to speak in the complex mathematical language of Boethius. The students object to this conceptual language and respond, 'What has this got to do with *music*?,' implying, we presume, that music has instead to do with feelings and emotions, not mathematics. The teacher's answer, like that of so many theory teachers today, is, 'But that is how you *talk* about music!'

After some discussion of music theory, the students now ask the difficult question, 'Why can't we hear the music of the spheres?' Of all early philosophers, this monk, Paphnutius, now gives the most complete answer, indeed four possible explanations.

DISCIPLES. Well, why can't we hear them, then?
PAPHNUTIUS. Many different reasons are given to explain why we can't hear the music of the heavenly spheres. Some assert it can't be heard because the music never stops, and we become accustomed to its sound. Others say it is the density of the air, while there are some who claim that a sound of such grand volume cannot physically be taken in by the narrow passages of our human ears. And there are some who say that the spheres give forth a sound so sweet, of such great joy, that if men ever heard it, they would all join together, of one common accord, forget about themselves and any other interest, and be intent only on following this sound as it led them from the East to the Western regions.

The now well-known Hildegard, of the twelfth century, mentions the music of the spheres briefly in the context of a description of the voices of the angels in heaven. She appears to have understood the necessity of air to hear musical sounds and seems to suggest it was the wind of earth which made possible hearing the music of the spheres. After describing the host of angels as having 'a richer harmony than all the sounds living creatures have ever produced,' she concludes,

> More wonderful is this sound than the music of the spheres that arises from the blowing of the winds that sustain the four elements and are well adjusted to them.[18]

The thirteenth-century French poem, 'Romance of the Rose,' mentions the music of the spheres in a passage reflecting the ancient Greek emphasis on the unity of man and nature. Moreover, the poem maintains that the music of the spheres is the source of all earthly music.

> Sweet harmonies they make,
> Which are the source of all the melodies
> And divers tunes that we in concord set

---

[18] 'Vision Six: 4,' in *The Book of Divine Works*, ed. Matthew Fox (Santa Fe: Bear & Company, 1987), 181ff.

> In all our sorts of song. There is no thing
> That would not chant in unison with them.[19]

Johannes de Grecheo, in his *De Musica* (ca. 1300) proves himself to be a man far ahead of his time. He was the earliest philosopher, in our view, whose descriptions regarding the nature of music seem to ring true with readers of our own time. Taking up the traditional classification of music into Music of the Spheres, Human Music and Instrumental Music, a classification which theorists had accepted without comment for half a millennium, Grocheo now blasts Boethius into oblivion. He courageously attacks the faulty logic, the pseudo-science, the beliefs of the Church and the nonsense which Boethius had put forth.[20]

> Those who make this kind of division either invent their opinion or they wish to obey the Pythagoreans or others more than the truth, or they are ignorant of nature and logic. First of all, they say universally that music is a science concerning numbered sound. Nevertheless, celestial bodies in movement do not make a sound, although our ancestors believed this.[21]

During the early Renaissance there were two Italian intellectuals who took the characteristics of the music of the spheres and transposed them onto the soul. Marsilio Ficino (fifteenth century), for example, in his commentary on Plato's 'Timaeus,' carries over the concept of circular motion.

> Musical consonance occurs in [air] and reaches the ears through motion, spherical motion: so that it is not surprising that it should be fitting to the soul, which is both the mean of things, and the origin of circular motion. In addition, musical sound, more than anything else perceived by the senses, conveys, as if animated, the emotions and thoughts of the singer's or player's soul to the listeners' souls; thus it preeminently corresponds with the soul.

Similarly, another fifteenth-century Italian, Franchino Gaffurio, in his *De harmonia*, finds the soul organized in correspondence with the ratios of sound and the planets.

> The intellective part corresponds to the octave, the sensitive to the fifth, and the habitual to the fourth. The species of fourth are analogous to the motions of the habitual soul—increase, stasis, and decrease; the species of fifth, to the powers of the sensitive soul—sight, hearing, smell, and taste; the species of octave, to the function of the intellective soul—imagination, intellect, thought, reflection, opinion, reason and knowledge.[22]

---

[19] Guillaume de Lorris and Jean de Meun, 'The Romance of the Rose,' trans. Harry Robbins (New York: Dutton, 1962), LXXXI, 187.

[20] Grocheo substitutes a new division of music into Civic, Regular and Church.

[21] Johannes de Grocheo, *De Musica*, trans. Albert Seay (Colorado Springs: Colorado College Music Press, 1967), 10.

[22] Quoted in Claude V. Palisca, *Humanism in Italian Renaissance Musical Thought* (New Haven: Yale University Press, 1985), 177.

The above mentioned Ficino, who was also founder of the famous Florentine Academy, contributed a new definition of the purpose of music. Music, he believed, served man's 'spirit' in the same way medicine serves the body and theology the soul. The music one hears provokes a memory in the soul of the divine music found in the mind of God and in the music of the spheres. He also found correlations between the music of the spheres and the signs of the zodiac and with the tones of the scale.

The great fifteenth-century theorist, Tinctoris, followed the lead of Aristotle and declared that the heavenly spheres do not make sound. Music, he says, is of the earth, not the heavens.

> But although, as Boethius says, some assert that Saturn is moved with the deepest sound and, taking the remaining planets in proper order, the moon with the highest, while others, however, conversely attribute the deepest sound to the moon and the highest to the stars in their movement, I adhere to neither position. On the contrary, I unshakably agree with Aristotle ... together with our more recent philosophers, who most clearly prove that there is neither real nor potential sound in the heavens. For this reason I can never be persuaded that musical consonances, which cannot be produced without sound, are made by the motion of heavenly bodies.
>
> Concords of sounds and melodies, therefore, from whose sweetness, as Lactantius says, the pleasure of the ears is derived, are brought about, not by heavenly bodies, but by earthly instruments with the cooperation of nature.[23]

Leonardo da Vinci declared that the spheres moving through the heavens do not make a sound. In his ever inquiring way, he also wondered if, in Pythagoras' famous story, it were the hammer or the anvil which created the pitch.[24]

The two best-known English writers of the early Renaissance were poets, and for poets it was much nicer to cling to the imagery of the past. Chaucer (fourteenth century) finds the music of the spheres to be the original source for melody and harmony in the world.

> And after shewede he hym the nyne speres,
> And after that the melodye herde he
> That cometh of thilke speres thryes thre,
> That welle is of musik and melodye
> In this world here, and cause of armonye.[25]

Lydgate (fifteenth century) also concludes that the planets are, 'the mother of music.'

> How the seuene planetes in ther cours hem dresse,
> Meuyng of sterris, sparklyng in ther brihtnesse,
> With reuolociouns of the speeris nyne,
> Moodres of musik, as auctours determyne.[26]

---

23 *The Art of Counterpoint*, trans. Albert Seay (American Institute of Musicology, 1961), 14.

24 Stuart Isacoff, *Temperament* (New York: Vintage Books, 2001), 86.

25 'The Parliament of the Birds,' 59ff.

26 John Lydgate, *Fall of Princes*, ed. Henry Bergen (London: Oxford University Press, 1967), IV, 1166ff.. This work is ostensibly a translation of Giovanni Boccaccio's *De Casibus Virorum Illustrium*, although Lydgate freely engages in his own commentary and philosophy.

During sixteenth-century Italy we also find writers who are still willing to believe in the music of the spheres. The great theorist, Gioseffo Zarlino, in his *Le Istitutioni Harmoniche*, takes the position that we may not hear the music of the spheres but we can understand it on the basis of Reason.

> Every reason persuades us to believe at least that the world is composed with harmony, both because its soul is a harmony (as Plato believed), and because the heavens are turned around their intelligences with harmony, as may be gathered from their revolutions, which are proportionate to each other in velocity. This harmony is known also from the distances of the celestial spheres, for these distances (as some believe) are related in harmonic proportion, which, although not measured by the sense [of hearing], is measured by the reason.[27]

This relationship between the music of the spheres and the soul, mentioned by Zarlino, is found again in Castiglione's famous book, *The Courtier*. Here Signor Gaspare questions whether music is something appropriate to 'real' men and the Count answers,

> Do not say that, or I shall launch into oceans of praise for music and remind you how greatly it was honored in the ancient world, and held to be sacred, and that the wisest of philosophers held the opinion that the universe was made up of music, that the heavens make harmony as they move, and that as our own souls are formed on the same principle they are awakened and have their faculties, as it were, brought to life thorough music.[28]

Among the sixteenth-century French writers we find two more explanations why we cannot hear the music of the spheres. First, the important theorist, Pontus de Tyard, in his book, *Solitaire second*, a character named 'le Curieux,' speaks of the ancient Greek notion of the universe being a kind of harmony, in which all of its parts have some comparable relationship with the harmony found in music. He mentions the music of the spheres, offering the explanation for man's inability to hear it that, taken together, its effect is that of silence. Then he contends that the basic elements of the earth are related as the tones of the tetrachord, earth being as the lowest pitch, then water, air and fire.

For Montaigne, it is the constant, never ending quality of the music of the spheres which makes them unnoticeable to us.

> ... that those solid material circles rub and lightly play against each other and so cannot fail to produce a wondrous harmony (by the modulations and mutations of which are conducted the revolutions and variations of the dance of the stars) yet none of the creatures in the whole Universe can hear it, loud though it is, since our sense of hearing has been dulled by the continuity of the sound.[29]

This is comparable, he says, to how blacksmiths become able to tolerate the noise of their shops.

---

[27] Quoted in Palisca, *Humanism in Italian Renaissance Musical Thought*, 179.
[28] *The Courtier*, trans. George Bull (New York: Penguin Books, 1967), I, 94ff.
[29] *Essays*, trans. M. A. Screech (London: Penguin, 1993), I, xxiii, 123.

Francisco de Salinas (1513–1590), an important Spanish writer, rejected the Boethius division of music into Cosmic, Human and Instrumental and instead divided music into that which moves only the sense, the intellect, or both. With regard to the music of the spheres, Salinas took the position that God would not have wasted his time on anything superfluous.

> We do not believe that celestial motions yield any sounds at all, whether as subject or as efficient cause, as it pleases the physicists. Now aside from the reasons of Aristotle, which we did not wish to translate here, lest we seem to want to teach physics rather than music, it appears certainly probable that the creator of the universal framework would not have made anything superfluous any more than he would have failed to provide the necessities. For such would have been that celestial sound which could not be heard by anyone.[30]

One of the most curious philosophical books of sixteenth-century Germany which is worthy of some attention is Henry Agrippa's three volume *De occulta philosophia*,[31] written in 1509–1510 before the appearance of Luther on the German scene. In spite of the title, 'Occult Philosophy,' Agrippa was at this time a philosopher in the old mold of Catholic Scholasticism. In a chapter, 'Concerning the Agreement of them with the Celestial Bodies, and what Harmony and Sound is Correspondent of every Star,' he goes far beyond any earlier philosopher by adding emotional qualities to the celestial sounds. This can only be understood as being the result of Humanism thought.

> But understand now, that of the seven planets, Saturn, Mars, and the Moon have more of the voice than of the harmony. Saturn hath sad, hoarse, heavy and slow words, and sounds, as it were pressed to the center; but Mars, rough, sharp, threatening, great and wrathful words; the Moon observeth a mean between these two.
> But Jupiter, the Sun, Venus and Mercury, do possess harmonies; yet Jupiter hath grave, constant, fixed, sweet, merry, and pleasant consorts; the Sun venerable, settled, pure and sweet, with a certain grace; but Venus lascivious, luxurious, delicate, voluptuous, dissolute and fluent; Mercury hath harmonies more remiss, and various, merry and pleasant, with a certain boldness: but the tone of particulars, and proportionate consorts obeys the nine Muses. Jupiter has the grace of the octave, and also the quinte, viz. the diapason with the diapente: the Sun obtains the melody of the octave voice, viz. diapason: in like manner by fifteen tones, a disdiapason: Venus keeps the grace of the quinte or diapente: Mercury has diatessaron, viz. the grace of the quarte.

Then quoting some unnamed 'ancients,' he associates particular pitches with the planets, as well as the 'humors' and the modes.

> Moreover, they that followed the number of the elements, did affirm, that the four kinds of music do agree to them, and also to the four humors, and did think the Dorian music to be consonant to the Water and phlegm, the Phrygian to choler and Fire, the Lydian to blood and Air, the mixed-Lydian to melancholy and Earth: others respecting the number and virtue of the heavens, have attributed

---

[30] 'De musica libri septem,' I, 1, p. i, quoted in Palisca, *Humanism in Italian Renaissance Musical Thought*, 186.

[31] Henry Cornelius Agrippa, *De occulta Philosophia*, I, x. The best modern edition, which is highly recommended, is Donald Tyson, *Three Books of Occult Philosophy* (St. Paul: Llewellyn Publications, 1993).

the Dorian to the Sun, the Phrygian to Mars, the Lydian to Jupiter, the mixed-Lydian to Saturn, the hypo-Phrygian to Mercury, the hypo-Lydian to Venus, the hypo-Dorian to the Moon, the hypo-mixed-Lydian to the fixed stars …

Moreover there are some who find out the harmony of the heavens by their distance one from another. For that space which is between the Earth and the Moon, viz. an hundred and twenty-six thousand Italian miles,[32] makes the interval of a tone; but from the Moon to Mercury being half that distance, makes a half-tone; and from Mercury to Venus another half-tone; but from there to the Sun, as it were three tones and a half, and that makes a diapente; but from the Moon to the Sun, a twofold diatessaron with a half; again from the Sun to Mars is the same space as from the Earth to the Moon, making a tone; from there to Jupiter half of the same making a half tone; so much likewise from Jupiter to Saturn, consisting of an half tone; from whence to the starry firmaments is also the space of an half tone.

He concludes,

Hence there are not any songs, sounds, or musical instruments more powerful in moving man's affections, or introducing magical impressions, than those which are composed of numbers, measures, and proportions, after the example of the heavens.[33]

Agrippa makes no attempt to explain why we cannot hear any of this music of the spheres, but in Book III he offered a unique explanation for the source of music's ability to soothe. He begins with a discussion of 'divine frenzy,' which is so often mentioned by the ancient poets. This comes from the Muses, he says, and the Muses, in turn, are the souls of the separate planets. Of these only the Sun is given a musical soul.

The fourth degree belongs to the sphere of the Sun; this possesses voices, words, singing and harmonic sounds, by the sweet consonance whereof it drives forth of the mind any troublesomeness therein, and cheers it up.[34]

Johannes Cochlaeus, in his *Tetrachordum Musices* of 1511, keeps the division of music into Cosmic, Human and Instrumental, after Boethius, but he expands the Cosmic to now include the calendar, the seasons and the phases of the moon as well.

Andreas Ornithoparchus, in *Musice active micrologus*, of 1517, begins by dividing music into Mundane, Human and Instrumental Music. Mundane music, he finds in the 'harmony caused by the motion of the stars and the violence of the spheres,' which he also relates to elements and climate. Here he quotes a nice phrase, from a lost work by the philosopher, Dorilaus, 'The world is God's organ.' Even, as he admits, if we cannot hear the music of the spheres, one has to admit that God has created in all things number, weight, and measure. Since these are also the principal properties of music, therefore it is reasonable to believe that the music of the spheres exists.

---

32   Or about 116,000 English miles, whereas the correct distance is 240,000 miles.

33   *De occulta philosophia*, II, xxvi.

34   Agrippa, *De occulta philosophia*, III, xxxii.

Heinrich Glarean, in *Dodecachordon*, of 1547, mentions the theory of the music of the spheres as argued by Servius, that the planets existed in an order of decreasing volume, ranging from Saturn, Jupiter, Mars, the Sun, Venus, Mercury to the moon which was the softest. Glarean expresses some doubts about this, adding that his mention of the music of the spheres is necessary only because so many great early writers had discussed it. As for himself, he agrees with Aristotle that there is no basis in fact for this theory.

> But this indulgence is allowed to antiquity, which has thought that the human mind must be raised in every possible way to the contemplation of heavenly objects.[35]

In Elizabethan England we find the poets still calling upon the imagery of the music of the spheres. Humphrey Gifford doubts that we could live without this music.

> The planets and celestial parts
> Sweet harmony contain,
> Of which if creatures were deprived
> This world could not remain.[36]

His contemporary, Fulke Greville, in his romance, 'Caelica,' makes a lovely reference to the music of the spheres.

> Atlas upon his shoulders bare the sky,
> The load was heavy, but the load was fair;
> His sense was ravished with the melody,
> Made from the motion of the highest sphere.[37]

Shakespeare also seems to have been well read with respect to earlier theories on music, as we can see in his several references to the ancient Greek notion of the 'music of the spheres.' The most extended of these is found in *The Merchant of Venice*, where Lorenzo reflects,

> How sweet the moonlight sleeps upon this bank!
> Here will we sit, and let the sounds of music
> Creep in our ears; soft stillness and the night
> Become the touches of sweet harmony.
> Sir, Jessica: look, how the floor of heaven
> is thick inlaid with [patinas] of bright gold:
> There's not the smallest orb which thou behold'st
> But in his motion like an angel sings,
> Still choiring to the young-eyed cherubins;
> Such harmony is in immortal souls;

---

35 Glarean, *Dodecachordon*, trans. Clement Miller (American Institute of Musicology, 1965), I, 136ff.
36 Humphrey Gifford, 'In the praise of music.'
37 Fulke Greville, 'Caelica,' XLVII.

> But, whilst this muddy vesture of decay
> Doth grossly close it in, we cannot hear it.[38]

Finally, we should mention that Thomas Nashe, in his famous fictional work, *The Unfortunate Traveller* (1594), claims to have visited an estate in Rome where there was a banquet house with a mechanical illustration of the music of the spheres and in this case it was music which could be heard!

> The heaven was a clear overhanging vault of crystal, wherein the Sun and Moon and each visible Star had his true similitude, shine, situation, and motion, and, by what enwrapped art I cannot conceive, these spheres in their proper orbits observed a kind of soft angelical murmuring music in their often windings and going about; which music the philosophers say in the true heaven, by reason of the grossness of our senses, we are not capable of hearing.[39]

With the dawn of the seventeenth century we still find persons who express belief in the music of the spheres. The poet, Giambattista Marino, writes that whoever does not feel the power of the 'charming melody' of voices and the lyre,

> must have a spirit dissonant, that for
> the music of the spheres is out of tune.[40]

The Spanish playwright, Molina, in *Tamar's Revenge* has Amnon rhapsodize,

> Break forth, celestial harmony
> that kindles love and voice alone …[41]

One of the most important studies on music of the seventeenth century was the monumental *Harmonie universelle* (1636), in five treatises, by Marin Mersenne. Mersenne begins his discussion of this subject by stating that he will not attempt to prove the existence of the music of the spheres, and then devotes many pages to doing precisely that.[42] First he offers some possibilities why we cannot hear this music:

> Of course, we shall not be able to show whether the planets and stars make any sound. If the air extends as far as the firmament or infinity, as some people believe, having no doubt that God created it infinite …

---

[38] *The Merchant of Venice*, V, i, 61ff. Additional references to the 'Music of the Spheres,' can be found in *As You Like It*, II, vii, 6; *Henry VIII*, IV, ii, 85ff and *Twelfth Night or What You Will*, III, i, 109.

[39] *The Works of Thomas Nashe*, ed. Ronald McKerrow (Oxford: Blackwell, 1966), II, 282ff.

[40] Giambattista Marino, *L'Adone* (1623), trans. Harold Priest (Ithaca: Cornell University Press, 1967), VII, 1–2, 10. Athanasius Kircher (1601–1680) also discusses the music of the spheres in Vol. 10 of his *Musurgia Universalis*.

[41] *Tamar's Revenge*, I, lines 649ff. Molina was a nom de plume for Fray Gabriel Tellez.

[42] Most of his discussion is found in Book II, v.

> It is probable that the stars and planets make some sound, inasmuch as they do move in the air. We do not hear the sound, for we are accustomed to it from the wombs of our mothers. Sometimes the sound is too far from us, too low, too high, or too great to be heard, as happens with certain other phenomena. We are, for example, unable to hear the sound or noise which ants and other little animals make when they walk, run, crawl, or fly, inasmuch as the sound is too little and too feeble.
>
> It may be concluded that sound has too imperceptible extremities. It may be too strong or too violent. It may be too feeble or too small. It may be made by too slow movement or too small movement. It may be made by a too swift, too large, or too precipitous movement. Both extremities exceed the sphere which the ear has for its activity and understanding.
>
> Now, if the celestial bodies do make sounds, one may ascertain what their qualities are by considering the size and movement of the celestial bodies.

Mersenne next paraphrases the conclusions of the ancient Greek Pythagorean school of philosophy (not a single word of which is extant in the writings of Pythagoras himself).

> The seven planets contain not only the consonances, but also the dissonances. Orpheus invented his heptachord or lyre of seven strings, each of which represented one of the planets, but the Pythagoreans added the *Proslambanomenos* from the Earth up to the Moon in order to create their lyre with eight strings. There was a whole-tone from the first acquired string up to the principal, which they called *Hypate*; there was a semitone from *Hypate* to *Parhypate*, which represented the distance from the Moon to Mercury. From *Hypate* up to *Lichanos* there was a whole-tone, which represented the distance from Mercury to Venus. From *Lichanos* to *Mese*, or from Venus to the Sun, there was another whole-tone. From there to Mars, or from *Mese* to *Paramese*, there was a semitone. Finally, from the *Paranete* or from Jupiter there was a whole-tone, and from Jupiter to *Nete* or Saturn there was another whole-tone. Consequently they placed the octave from the Earth to Saturn, the perfect fifth from the Earth to the Sun, the perfect fourth from the Moon to the Sun, the perfect fifth from Venus to Saturn, and the perfect fourth from the Sun to Saturn. Thus they based their music on planetary movement from east to west, for the movement of the lowest planets is the slowest, and that of the highest planets is the quickest, since the latter make a greater journey in the same time.
>
> If, however, we tune a lute according to planetary movement from west to east, it is necessary to change the order of the names and give the *Proslambanomenos* to Saturn, the *Hypate* to Mars, etc.

Mersenne quotes at length another contemporary who believed in the music of the spheres, the German astronomer Johann Kepler (1571–1630), from whom he borrows the notion that,

> if the planets produce harmony, 'it would be necessary to make Saturn and Jupiter the bass, Mars the tenor, the Earth and Venus the alto, and Mercury the soprano, because Mercury has a greater range and is livelier than the others.'

In another place, Mersenne cites Gosselin and Guy Aretin relative to their theories that the musical intervals and the voice can be related to the planets, concluding that Jupiter is the root, Saturn is the second, the Moon is the third, Mercury is the fourth, Venus is the fifth, the Sun is the sixth, Mars is the seventh and Jupiter again the octave. Mersenne, however, finds this knowledge not necessary for practical musicianship, although he observes that if there really is music of the spheres, the musical instruments should be tuned to these pitches.

One of the greatest continental scientists of the seventeenth century, Christian Huygens, left a treatise entitled, *The Celestial Worlds Discovered: or, Conjectures Concerning the Inhabitants, Plants and Productions of the Worlds in the Planets* (1698). We remind the reader that even by the 17th century telescopes were not powerful enough to determine if there were life on the moon, not to mention the other planets. Assuming they were all inhabited, and noticing that the same animals are found, generally, in both America and Europe, Huygens speculates on the nature of the music to be heard on the other planets and concludes it would be about the same as on Earth.

The English physicist and physician, Robert Flud (1574–1637) imagined that the Earth and the other planets constituted a cosmic musical instrument, which he called a Mundane Monochord. His book devoted to this, *De Musica Mundana* (1617), includes the following:

> But it is to be considered that in this mundane monochord the consonances, and likewise the proper intervals, measuring them, cannot be otherwise delineated than as we divide the instrumental monochord into proportional parts; for the frigidity, and also the matter itself, of the earth, as to the thickness and weight thereof, naturally bears the same proportion to the frigidity as the matter of the lowest region, in which there is only one fourth part of the natural light and heat, as 4 to 3, which is the sesquitertia proportion; in which proportion a diatessaron consists, composed of three intervals, namely, water, air, and fire; for the earth in mundane music is the same thing as the fundamental in music, unity in arithmetic, or a point in geometry; it being as it were the term and sound from which the ratio of proportional matter is to be calculated. Water therefore occupies the place of one tone, and the air that of another interval more remote; and the sphere of fire, as it is only the summit of the region of the air, kindled or lighted up, possesses the place of a lesser semitone. But in as much as two portions of this matter are extended upwards as far as to the middle heaven to resist the action of the supernatural heat; and the same number of parts of light, act downwards against these two portions of matter, these make up the composition of the sphere of the sun, and naturally give it the attribute of equality, and by that means the sesquialtera proportion is produced, in which three parts of the lower spirit or matter of the middle heaven are opposed to the two parts of the solar sphere, producing the consonant diapente: for such is the difference between the moon and the sun, as there are four intervals between the convexity of this heaven and the middle of the solar sphere, namely, those of the entire spheres of the moon, Mercury, and Venus, compared to full tones, and the half part of the solar sphere, which we have compared to the semitone ...

The great Francis Bacon hardly mentions the music of the spheres, but one sardonic comment speaks for itself.

> The heavens turn about in a most rapid motion, without noise to us perceived; though in some dreams they have been said to make an excellent music.[43]

---

[43] *The Works of Francis Bacon*, ed. James Spedding (Cambridge: Cambridge University Press, 1869) VII, 389, Section 115.

In a catalog of projected histories, Bacon includes a 'History of Sounds in the Upper Region (if there be any).'⁴⁴ Finally, we might mention that in his *History of Dense and Rare*, Bacon, while discussing 'motion of dilatation and contraction in the air by heat,' mentions without further identification a musical instrument 'played by the rays of the sun.'⁴⁵

Christopher Simpson, in his *Division-Violist* (1654) finds significance in the number seven, there being seven pitch names, seven days of the week, creation fulfilled in seven days, the seven strings of the lyre of Orpheus and the (then known) seven heavenly bodies.

> Within the circumference of this great universe, be seven globes or spherical bodies in continual motion, producing still new and various figures, according to their diverse positions one to another. When with these I compare my seven gradual sounds, I cannot but admire the resemblance of their harmonies, the concords of the one so exactly answering to the aspects of the other; as an unison to conjunction, an octave to an opposition; the middle consonants to a diapason, to the middle aspects of an orb; as a third, fifth, sixth, in music, to a trine, quartile, sextile in the Zodiac.⁴⁶

The English poet, John Donne, suggests the music of the spheres cannot be heard but can be felt.

> Make all this All, three Choirs, heaven, earth, and spheres,
> The first, Heaven, hath a song, but no man hears,
> The Spheres have Musick, but they have no tongue,
> Their harmony is rather danced than sung.⁴⁷

Richard Crashaw makes the same assertion in his Hymn, 'The Name of Jesus,' in which he mentions the Music of the Spheres 'which dull mortality more feels than hears.'⁴⁸

The greatest English poet of the seventeenth century, Milton, devoted much attention to the Music of the Spheres. He mentions this frequently in his poetry, beginning with the music of creation.

> … up he rode
> Followed with acclamation and the sound
> Symphonious of ten thousand Harps that tuned
> Angelic harmonies: the Earth, the Air
> Resounded, (thou remember'st, for thou heardst)

---

44 'Catalog of Particular Histories,' in Ibid., VIII, 374.

45 *History of Dense and Rare*, in Ibid., X, 265.

46 Christopher Simpson, *Division-Violist* (1654), here (London: Curwen, 1965, facsimile of 1665 edition, 1965), 23ff.

47 'Upon the translation of the Psalmes by Sir Philip Sydney,' *The Complete Poetry of John Donne*, Op. cit., 389. Donne also mentions the 'Spheares Musick' in 'Valediction of the booke,' [Ibid., 117] and in his 'Obsequies to the Lord Harrington' [Ibid., 260].

48 'The Name of Jesus,' in *The Complete Poetry of Richard Crashaw*, 32. Crashaw mentions the music of the spheres again in his 'Upon the Kings Coronation,' lines 21ff; 'Hymn in the Glorious Epiphanie,' lines 131ff and in 'The Teare' [Ibid., 51]. Henry Vaughan refers to the music of the spheres in his 'The Tempest,' in *The Works of Henry Vaughan*, 461. Lovelace mentions the music of the spheres in *The Poems of Richard Lovelace*, ed. C. H. Wilkinson (Oxford: Clarendon Press, 1930), 26, 92, 114, 160, 187.

> The Heavens and all the Constellations rung,
> The Planets in their station listening stood.[49]

Several poems speak of the music of the spheres being in nine-parts, representing the seven known planets, the sun and our moon. In the poem, 'The Hymn,' we find,

> Ring out ye Crystal spheres,
> Once bless our humane ears,
> (If ye have power to touch our senses so)
> And let your silver chime
> Move in melodious time;
> And let the Base of Heavens deep Organ blow,
> And with your ninefold harmony
> Make up full consort to the Angelike symphony.[50]

And again in 'Arcades,'

> But else in deep of night when drowsiness
> Hath locked up mortal sense, then listen I
> To the celestial Sirens harmony,
> That sit upon the nine enfolded Spheres.[51]

Why, even God listens to the music of the spheres.

> And in their motions harmonie Divine
> So smooths her charming tones, that Gods own ear
> Listens delighted.[52]

In several places, such as in his masque composed for a performance at Ludlow Castle in 1634, Milton refers to the music of the spheres as 'the Starry Quire.'[53] One of these 'starry choir' references provides the only attempt by Milton to describe the actual music, 'a never-dying melody, a song beyond all describing.'[54]

Eventually, Milton left a lengthy discussion, 'On the Music of the Spheres,' which appears to have been intended as his contribution to a debate on this subject. In this work he summarizes the history of comments by various philosophers and includes the following:

---

[49] 'Paradise Lost,' VII, 557, in *The Works of John Milton*, ed. Frank Patterson (New York: Columbia University Press, 1931–1938), II, 231. In the same poem [V, 178] there is a reference to stars that move 'in mystic Dance not without Song.'

[50] 'The Hymn,' in Ibid., I, 6.

[51] 'Arcades,' in Ibid., I, 74.

[52] 'Paradise Lost,' in V, 625ff, Ibid., II, 166.

[53] 'A Masque,' in Ibid., I, 89. A song in this masque also mentions 'all Heaven's Harmonies.' [Ibid., I,94].

[54] 'Ad Patrem,' line 35.

But supposing no one on earth had ever heard this symphony of the stars, does it therefore follow that all has been silent beyond the circle of the moon, and lulled to sleep by the benumbing silence? Nay rather, let us blame our feeble ears which are not able, or are not worthy, to overhear the songs and such sweet tones …

But Pythagoras alone of mortals is said to have heard this song; unless that good man was both some deity and native of the sky, who perchance by direction of the gods had descended for the purpose of instructing the minds of men with holy knowledge and of calling upon them to improve. Certainly he was a man who combined in himself the whole gamut of virtues and who was worthy to converse with the very gods like unto himself and to enjoy the company of the celestials. Therefore, I do not wonder that the gods, loving him very much, permitted him to take part in the most secret mysteries of Nature …

But if we possessed hearts so pure, so spotless, so snowy, as once upon a time Pythagoras had, then indeed would our ears be made to resound and to be completely filled with that most delicious music of the revolving stars.[55]

Among the Restoration poets, Dryden mentions the music of the spheres, but cautions that upon the sounding of the trumpet on the Day of Judgment this music will end, 'Musick shall untune the sky.'[56]

James Thomson suggests that composers may find their inspiration in this celestial music.

> O yon high harmonious spheres,
> Your powerful Mover sing;
> To Him your circling course that steers,
> Your tuneful praises bring.
>
> Ungrateful mortals, catch the sound,
> And in your numerous lays,
> To all the listening world around,
> The God of nature praise.[57]

Alexander Pope, in his poem, 'An Essay on Man,' argues that God was wise in not making man's senses more sensitive than they are, as he would likely be miserable. Of music, he says,

> If nature thundered in his opening ears,
> And stunned him with the music of the spheres,
> How would he wish that heaven had left him still
> The whispering zephyr, and the purling rill?[58]

There are a number of references to the music of the spheres among the Jacobean playwrights, among them Marston's *The Insatiate Countess* (III, iv):

> Let sphere-like music breathe delicious tones.

---

55 'On the Music of the Spheres,' in Ibid., XII, 149ff.
56 *The Works of John Dryden*, ed. Edward Hooker (Berkeley: University of California Press, 1956), II, 109, 111.
57 'Hymn to God's Power,' in *The Poetical Works of James Thomson* (London: Bell and Daldy, ca. 1860), II, 141.
58 'An Essay on Man,' lines 201ff, in *The Works of Alexander Pope* (New York: Gordian Press, 1967), II, 363.

And in Dekker's *Old Fortunatus* (I, i), Fortune says,

> No more: curse on: your cries to me are Musicke,
> And fill the sacred roundure of mine ears,
> With tunes more sweet then moving of the Spheres.[59]

Among the Restoration playwrights we find in George Villiers, *The Rehearsal* (V, i), a person who can hear the music of the spheres. A stage direction reads, 'Soft Music,' which is followed by this dialogue.

> KING USHER. What sound is this invades our ears?
> KING PHYSICIAN. Sure 'tis the Musick of the moving Spheres.[60]

In George Farquhar's Comedy, *Love and a Bottle* (II, ii), the character, Rigadoon, comments,

> From a prodigious great bass-viol with seven strings, that played a Jig called the *Musick of the Spheres*: The seven Planets were nothing but fiddle-strings.[61]

In Mrs. Aphra Behn's *The Emperor of the Moon* (II, v) a character maintains she danced to the 'Musick of the Spheres.'

And now we come to Johannes Kepler (1571–1630), the last astronomer to take seriously the music of the spheres. One day, when teaching a geometry class in 1595, he was drawing on the blackboard a triangle inscribed within a circle, in the center of which there was yet another circle, whereupon he experienced a sudden insight—it seemed to him that the ratio between these two circles was the same as that between the orbits of Saturn and Jupiter. This led to a long period of study in which he attempted to prove that the organization of the planets followed basic geometric figures.

Another turning point for Kepler came when he realized that in his purely geometrical and mathematical explanations he had given no consideration to *time*. It was the realization that time must be a factor in planetary design which caused him to turn his attention to *musical* harmony (which also moves through time), eventually resulting in his *Harmony of the Universe* (1619).[62] He now began to feel that music might illustrate the logic of planetary geometry, as for example in a correspondence he saw between the overtones of a vibrating string and the division of a circle into equal arcs.

---

[59] For additional references to the 'music of the spheres' see: John Webster's *The Dutchesse of Malfy* (I, i); Thomas Dekker's *The Virgin Martyr* (V, ii) and *The Noble Spanish Soldier* (II, i); George Chapman's *The Blind Beggar* (Scene viii), a reference to the music of the spheres as a metaphor for a couple's feelings, 'To echo sweetly to our celestial tunes'; Beaumont and Fletcher's *The Prophetess* (II, i), Delphia, a prophetess, gives a speech which includes 'The Musick of the Spheres attending on us'; and Marston's *Antonio and Mellida*, Part II (III, i).

[60] In Swift's *Gulliver's Travels*, when Gulliver travels to 'Laputa,' he finds people who can hear the music of the spheres.

[61] Farquhar mentions the Music of the Spheres again in *The Inconstant* (IV, iii).

[62] We present only a few excerpts from this book, as the entire work is available in a fine English translation as part of the *Great Books of the Western World* (University of Chicago, 1990) found in all libraries. The reader will need to have an extensive background in math to turn these pages!

Music, Kepler contends, reveals to us an order which is the principle also of our own being. The task of the astronomer is to correlate the harmony within with the harmony without. In the same way, he believed mathematical insights are only discovered, not invented. It follows that God, when making man, implanted in him consciousness of the fundamental harmonies which served as a pattern in the creation of the world.

It is in Book Five, of the *Harmony of the Universe*, that Kepler summarizes his theories of the 'Music of the Sphere' and the relationship of this music to planetary mechanics. He begins by reflecting on the many years of study which have brought him to this understanding, not failing to pay due tribute to those past and present who deserved recognition. It is important to remember that Kepler was about to set forth in considerable mathematical detail theories which were most unorthodox, and at a time when the idea that the Earth moved, and was not the center of the universe, was as yet by no means commonly believed. It was for this reason that Kepler concludes his introductory remarks by saying that he had decided to get up his courage and publish the book anyway. It's OK, he says, if it goes neglected for another hundred years—after all, God waited six thousand years[63] for someone [Kepler] to come along to discover the musical relationships of the cosmos.

> As regards that which I prophesied two and twenty years ago (especially that the five regular solids are found between the celestial spheres), as regards that of which I was firmly persuaded in my own mind before I had seen Ptolemy's *Harmonies*, as regards that which I promised my friends in the title of this fifth book before I was sure of the thing itself, that which, sixteen years ago, in a published statement, I insisted must be investigated, for the sake of which I spent the best part of my life in astronomical speculations, visited Tycho Brahe, and took up resident at Prague: finally, as God the Best and Greatest, Who had inspired my mind and aroused my great desire, prolonged my life and strength of mind and furnished the other means through the liberality of the two Emperors and the nobles of this province of Austria-on-the-Anisana: after I had discharged my astronomical duties as much as sufficed, finally, I say, I brought it to light and found it to be truer than I had even hoped, and I discovered among the celestial movements the full nature of harmony, in its due measure, together with all its parts unfolded in Book III—not in that mode wherein I had conceived it in my mind (this is not least in my joy) but in a very different mode which is also very excellent and very perfect. There took place in this intervening time, wherein the very laborious reconstruction of the movements held me in suspense, an extraordinary augmentation of my desire and incentive for the job, a reading of the *Harmonies* of Ptolemy, which had been sent to me in manuscript by John George Herwald, Chancellor of Bavaria, a very distinguished man and of a nature to advance philosophy and every type of learning. There, beyond my expectations and with the greatest wonder, I found approximately the whole third book given over to the same consideration of celestial harmony, fifteen hundred years ago … But now since the first light eight months ago, since broad day[light] three months ago, and since the sun of my wonderful speculation has shone fully a very few days ago: nothing holds me back. I am free to give myself up to the sacred madness, I am free to taunt mortals with the frank confession that I am stealing the golden vessels of the Egyptians, in order to build of them a temple for my God, far from the territory of Egypt. If you pardon me, I shall rejoice; if you are enraged, I

---

63 Until the mid nineteenth century it was believed that God created the Earth in the year 4,004 BC.

shall bear up. The die is cast, and I am writing the book—whether to be read by my contemporaries or by posterity matters not. Let it await its reader for a hundred years, if God Himself has been ready for His contemplator for six thousand years.[64]

In the first three chapters, Kepler introduces and defines the terms and concepts which are fundamental to his theories which follow. Among these he finds it necessary to point out that he is working from the premise of Copernicus that it is the Earth which moves, and not the Sun. He admits this is a proposition still not generally accepted.

> But because the thing is still new among the mass of the intelligentsia [*apud vulgus studiosortum*], and the doctrine that the Earth is one of the planets and moves among the stars around a motionless sun sounds very absurd to the ears of most of them ...[65]

He reminds the reader of his study of the relationship of the five basic geometric figures and the planetary system and admits that he could not quite make them fit. Since Kepler admits the concept of geometric figures is not sufficient to explain the planetary organization, it follows there must be other principles at work. This, of course, will turn out to be music.

In Chapter Four, 'In What Things Having to do with the Planetary Movements have the Harmonic Consonances been Expressed by the Creator?,' Kepler first studies the distances from the sun, the periodic times, the diurnal eccentric arcs, the diurnal delays in those arcs, the angles at the sun and the diurnal arcs apparent to those as if one's point of view were from the sun. From this study, and in particular the aphelion and perihelion of each planet, he arrives at some preliminary, if not quite satisfactory, relationships with music.

> Therefore the extreme intervals of no one planet come near consonances except those of Mars and Mercury.
> But if you compare the extreme intervals of different planets with one another, some harmonic light begins to shine. For the extreme diverging intervals of Saturn and Jupiter make slightly more than the octave; and the converging, a mean between the major and minor sixths. So the diverging extremes of Jupiter and Mars embrace approximately the double octave; and the converging, approximately the fifth and the octave. But the diverging extremes of the Earth and Mars embrace somewhat more than the major sixth; the converging, an augmented fourth. In the next couple, the Earth and Venus, there is again the same augmented fourth between the converging extremes; but we lack any harmonic ratio between the diverging extremes: for it is less than the semi-octave (so to speak), i.e., less than the square root of the ratio 2:1. Finally, between the diverging extremes of Venus and Mercury there is a ratio slightly less than the octave compounded with the minor third; between the converging there is a slightly augmented fifth.[66]

---

[64] Johannes Kepler, *Harmonies of the World*, V, trans. Charles Glenn Wallis, in *Great Books* (Chicago: Encyclopaedia Britannica, 1939), XVI, 1009ff.

[65] Ibid., 1015.

[66] Ibid., 1026ff.

Before going farther, Kepler pauses to consider the fundamental problem which had engaged so many earlier philosophers who had written on the subject of the 'Music of the Spheres,' that is, if there are musical pitches produced by the planets, why can't we hear them? Of all the explanations offered by earlier philosophers, Kepler is unique in transferring the experience to another sense.

> But whose good will it be to have harmonies between the journeys, or who will perceive these harmonies? For there are two things which disclose to us harmonies in natural things: either light or sound: light apprehended through the eyes or hidden senses proportioned to the eyes, and sound through the ears. The mind seizes upon these forms and, whether by instinct (on which Book Four speaks profusely) or by astronomical or harmonic ratiocination, discerns the concordant from the discordant. Now there are no sounds in the heavens, nor is the movement so turbulent that any noise is made by the rubbing against the ether. Light remains. If light has to teach these things about planetary journeys, it will teach either the eyes or a sensorium analogous to the eyes and situated in a definite place; and it seems that sense-perception must be present there in order that light of itself may immediately teach.[67]

While in this formal work, written for posterity, Kepler seems to avoid admitting any possibility of hearing these pitches, in a private letter to Mastlin, in 1599, he adds, 'but fill the heavens with air and in very truth music will sound forth.'[68]

He now determines the pitch by the angle that the planet would appear to describe in one day as estimated by an observer located on the Sun. These angular velocities were severally divided by arbitrary powers of two so as to reduce them to the same order of magnitude and to bring the corresponding notes all within the compass of a single octave. The ratio between any two of these angular velocities, so reduced, determined the musical interval between the corresponding notes and indicated whether that interval represented one of the seven accepted concords.[69] Now he begins to achieve more satisfactory results (if we are willing to overlook some minor problems!).

> Accordingly, perfect consonances are found: between the converging movements of Saturn and Jupiter, the octave; between the converging movements of Jupiter and Mars, the octave and minor third approximately; between the converging movements of Mars and the Earth, the fifth; between their perihelial, the minor sixth; between the diverging or even between the perihelial, the double octave: whence … it seems that the residual very slight discrepancy can be discounted, especially in the movements of Venus and Mercury.
>
> But you will note that where there is no perfect major consonance, as between Jupiter and Mars, there alone have I found the placing of the solid figure to be approximately perfect, since the perihelial distance of Jupiter is approximately three times the aphelial distance of Mars, in such fashion that this pair of planets strives after the perfect consonance in the intervals which it does not have in the movements.

---

67 Ibid., 1030.
68 Quoted in Angus Armitage, *John Kepler* (New York: Roy Publishers, 1966), 150.
69 This summary is given in *Harmony*, 1030.

> You will note, furthermore, that the major planetary ratio of Saturn and Jupiter exceeds the harmonic, viz., the triple, by approximately the same quantity as belongs to Venus; and the common major ratio of the converging and diverging movements of Mars and the Earth are diminished by approximately the same. You will note thirdly that, roughly speaking, in the upper [most distant] planets the consonances are established between the converging movements, but in the lower planets, between movements in the same field. And note fourthly that between the aphelial movements of Saturn and the Earth there are approximately five octaves; for one thirty-second of 57'3' is 1'47', although the aphelial movement of Saturn is 1'46'.
>
> Furthermore, a great distinction exists between the consonances of the single planets which have been unfolded and the consonances of the planets in pairs. For the former cannot exist at the same moment of time, while the latter absolutely can; because the same planet, moving at its aphelion, cannot be at the same time at the opposite perihelion too, but of two planets one can be at its aphelion and the other at its perihelion at the same moment of time. And so the ratio of plain-song or monody, which we call choral music and which alone was known to the ancients, to polyphony—called figured song, the invention of the latest generations—is the same as the ratio of the consonances which the single planets designate to the consonances of the planes taken together ... In the following chapters, the planets taken together and the figured modern music will be shown to do similar things.[70]

Now satisfied that he had discovered a natural correspondence between planetary movement and the relationship of pitches in the overtone series, in Chapter Five Kepler turns his attention to the search for a natural cosmic scale. Before beginning to attempt to construct scale-like patterns, Kepler first makes two qualifications: he will make necessary adjustments to bring all notes into a single octave and he will ignore (for now) all pitch discrepancies less than a half-step. Working with the orbits at perihelion and aphelion, and turning a blind eye to some minor problems, he begins his first effort at scale building as follows,

> Now the aphelial movement of Saturn at its slowest, i.e., the slowest movement, marks G, the lowest pitch in the system with the number 1'46'. Therefore the aphelial movement of the Earth will make the same pitch, but five octaves higher, because its number is 1'47', and who wants to quarrel about one second in the aphelial movement of Saturn? But let us take it into account, nevertheless; the difference will not be greater than 106:107, which is less than a comma. If you add 27', one quarter of this 1'47', the sum will be 2'14', although the perihelial movement of Saturn has 2'15'; similarly the aphelial movement of Jupiter, but one octave higher....
>
> ......
>
> Accordingly all the notes of the major scale ... are marked by all the extreme movements of the planets, except the perihelial movements of Venus and the Earth and the aphelial movement of Mercury, whose number, 2'23', approaches the note *c* sharp. For subtract from the 2'41' of *d* one sixteenth or 10', and 2'30' remains for the note *c* sharp. Thus only the perihelial movement of Venus and the Earth are missing from this scale.

Kepler notates the above as the pitches for a G major scale, with both a C and C-sharp. In a following effort, beginning with G at 2'15', the aphelial movement of Saturn, he arrives at a scale based on G, but with two flats. From these two efforts he concludes:

---

70 *Harmonies of the World*, 1033ff.

> Accordingly you won't wonder any more that a very excellent order of sounds or pitches in a musical system or scale has been set up by men, since you see that they are doing nothing else in this business except to play the apes of God the Creator and to act out, as it were, a certain drama of the ordination of the celestial movements.[71]

Following a third attempt at scale construction, Kepler constructs scale fragments for each planet, based on the eccentricity of the orbit. He finds Saturn produces G, A, B, A, G; Jupiter, G, A, B♭, A, G; Mars, F, G, A, B♭, C, B♭, A, G, F; Earth, G, A♭, G; Mercury, a C major scale; the Moon, G, A, B, C, B, A, G; and Venus, which produces only E's. From this it was evident to Kepler that the Church modes must have had their origin in the heavens.

If the orbits of the planets produce pitches, scale patterns and implications of mode, then, Kepler suggests, it must follow that in the interaction of these orbits, harmony is produced. But some of the harmonies can only rarely be heard, as in the case of that produced by the coincidence of the apsides of Saturn and Jupiter, which occurs only once each eight hundred years. Indeed, perhaps the entire harmony was heard only at the moment of the creation of the universe. If that were the case, and one could analyze harmonically and mathematically back to this sound, one could discover the precise date of the creation.

For Kepler it followed logically that in this cosmic harmony, even if it were only an intellectual reality and not actually heard, could be found the origin of polyphony. Given this hypothesis of the origin of polyphony, it was natural for Kepler to next think of the planets in terms of the four traditional vocal ranges.

> I do not know why but nevertheless this wonderful congruence with human song has such a strong effect upon me that I am compelled to pursue this part of the comparison, also, even without any solid natural cause. For those same properties which ... custom ascribed to the bass, and nature gave legal grounds for so doing, are somehow possessed by Saturn and Jupiter in the heavens; and we find those of the tenor in Mars, those of the alto are present in the Earth and Venus, and those of the soprano are possessed by Mercury, if not with equality of intervals, at least proportionately.[72]

Eventually Kepler provides a step-by-step summary of his logic and his contentions, expressed in a series of very complicated axioms. One example:

> XXXVIII. Proposition. *The increment 243:250 to 2:3, the compound of the private ratios of Saturn and Jupiter, which was up to now being established by the prior reasons, was to be distributed among the planets in such fashion that of it the comma 80:81 should accede to Saturn and the remainder, 19,683:20,000 or approximately 62:63, to Jupiter.*

Finally, Kepler's concept of the 'Music of the Spheres' was based on a mathematical presumption of an observer based on the Sun. Because contemporary telescopes had not ruled out life even on the moon, much less the rest of the galaxy, he could not categorically rule out the possibility that some form of life existed there capable of hearing this cosmic music. And if

---

[71] Ibid., 1038.
[72] Ibid., 1049.

not, then there is still the possibility that God has merely prepared the 'seats' for future listeners, for even the Earth was created and existed before it was inhabited and thus for a time *its* 'seats were empty.' And as if proof were needed, he quotes a verse from Psalm 19:4,[73] 'He has placed His tabernacle in the sun.'[74]

The great philosopher, Benedict Spinoza (1632–1677) wrote very little about music. He does mention the music of the spheres, perhaps because someone of the stature of Kepler was still writing about the subject. Spinoza makes it quite evident that he will have nothing to do with this belief.

> Whatsoever affects our ears is said to give rise to noise, sound, or harmony. In this last case, there are men lunatic enough to believe that even God himself takes pleasure in harmony; and philosophers are not lacking who have persuaded themselves, that the motion of the heavenly bodies gives rise to harmony.[75]

And this is pretty much where two thousand years of discussion ends. After the seventeenth century, both philosophy and science generally abandoned the concept of the 'music of the spheres,' relegating it to the shelf reserved for those whom Spinoza identifies as those 'men lunatic enough' to be interested. One might say that with Kepler and what he called 'the sacred madness' the Age of Reason closed the door on this subject.

Oh, oh …

In 2002, NASA's Chandra X-ray Observatory found that a black hole in the Perseus cluster produces a B♭, fifty-seven octaves below middle C!

---

[73] The *Revised Standard Version* (1952), not wishing to suggest the impossible, has changed the meaning to read, 'He has set a tent for the sun.'

[74] Ibid., 1080.

[75] Spinoza, *The Ethics*, 'Concerning God,' Appendix.

Early Views on Music Therapy

IN THE PREVIOUS CHAPTER the reader noticed that Pythagoras was given credit by a number of later philosophers for originating the notion of the Music of the Spheres, even though it was actually a much earlier idea. In much the same fashion, many later writers, even to the present day, point to Pythagoras as the origin of music therapy even though it was again surely already a practiced discipline by his time. The fascination of later writers for this idea led them, as the reader will see below, to carry their discussions in many directions, bringing the planets back into the discussion, crediting melody, crediting modes, improvisation and of course introducing the role of dance. Common sense would suggest that the association of music and dance must be very ancient. This is certainly documented in some of the caves which contain the paintings by early man and in which can be found also musical instruments left behind as well as the footprints of dancers.

In any case, the association of music and medicine was an idea which has never died. One notices that the ancient Greek god, Apollo, was the god of *both* music and medicine. This association perhaps bears some relationship to the fact that when Antonio Lido, a fourteenth-century professor of *medicine* at the University of Padua died, his epitaph began, *Musicus Artista* … And one has to say that the most interesting research in the field of music today is being done in the field of medicine.

Although not understood by ancient philosophers, it is vibration which is the fundamental element of music, and also, subsequently the fundamental element in any notion of Music of the Spheres. So in the association of music, movement and medicine, vibration may once again be the little recognized fundamental element. This is conclusively proven in the contemporary work by Dr. Hans Jenny of Switzerland, and his fellow physicists, in their work in the association of vibrations and consequent pitch in the various body organs and the possible role of vibrations and pitch in improving the health of those organs.

We would therefore venture to guess that if there is any truth in the many tales by early writers about the role of music and dance in curing spider bites, that some credit for those cures may belong to vibration. We sense this, for example, in an account by Baldassare Castiglione (1478–1529), in his famous book, *The Courtier (Il Cortigiano)*, where in describing the subsequent cure caused by the music and dance, he speaks of the *agitation* caused the patient by the music and that the patient was *shaken* back into good health.

> They say in Apulia when someone is bitten by a tarantula many musical instruments are played and various tunes are tried until the humor which is causing the sickness all of a sudden responds to the sound with which it has a certain affinity and so agitates the sick man that he is shaken back into good health.

This reminds us that the great composer Arthur Honegger once recalled the report of an interview with a Dr. J. Niemack, one of the doctors who treated Beethoven for his deafness. Dr. Niemack found that the Cavatina of the *String Quartet*, Op. 130, in which the first violin, in a strangely broken rhythm, gives voice to a melodic line marked by Beethoven as '*Beklemmt*' (anguished). Dr. Niemack continues:

> Ask a cardiologist to listen to this passage and ask him if he recognizes this rhythm. 'Naturally,' he will answer, 'It is the heart-beat of an arteriosclerotic,' whose heart is affected by a compensatory insufficiency.[1]

Perhaps the most familiar of early references to music therapy are those which relate to the use of music and dance to cure the bite of the Tarantula. Vicenzo Giustiniani, who left valuable accounts of sixteenth-century Italian performance practices, mentions the use of music in Puglia and Naples for persons who have been bitten by Tarantulas and he assures us that the effect of the use of music 'is found to be greater than the remedies the doctors give.' It is particularly interesting that he suggests that not just any music will work, but only something rather specific.

> They received great solace and many times total relief from music or the sound of instruments; and what is even more amazing, from one particular kind of music or instrument.[2]

Athanasius Kircher (1601–1680), a German born scholar who spent most of his adult life in Rome, was the author of the *Musurgia Universalis* (Rome, 1650), a virtual encyclopedia of music. In Book Nine of this massive work, 'The Magic of Consonance and Dissonance,' Kircher discusses the effects of music on the mind and the use of music therapy, including the use of music to cure the bite of the Tarantula spider. Kircher cites several histories of this phenomenon, including a girl who was bitten and was cured by the music of only a drum. In another case, however, he reports a volunteer allowed himself to be bitten by two Tarantulas, of different colors. As the bite of one responded to music and dance, but the bite of the other was made worse, the patient died. Kircher's technical medical explanation reads,

> The poison is sharp, gnawing, and bilious and is received and incorporated into the medullary substances of the fibers. The music has the power to rarefy the air to a certain harmonic pitch; the air thus rarefied, penetrating the pores of the patient's body, affects the muscles, arteries, and minute fibers, and incites him to dance, which begets a perspiration, in which the poison evaporates.

In an earlier book, *Magnes siue De arte magnetica opus tripartitum* (Rome, 1641), Kircher also discusses 'the magnetic power and faculties of music' and 'the affections of the mind which music excites.' Here again, of particular interest is a special science which he calls 'Tarantism,' the study of the 'magnetism and amazing sympathy with music' of the Tarantula.

---

[1] Arthur Honegger, *I am a Composer* (Faber & Faber, 1966), 67.

[2] Vicenzo Giustiniani, *Discorso sopra la Musica* (ca. 1628), trans. Carol MacClintock (American Institute of Musicology, 1962), 74.

The great German commentator on Baroque performance practice, Johann Mattheson, cites a publication, *Quintessence des Novelles*, 1727, Nr. 18,[3] which contains the music of a Rondo recommended for use as a cure for the bite of the Tarantula spider.

Finally, we have a testimonial of a physician, the Jacobean English doctor, Sir Thomas Browne. He has no doubt that these ancient tales are true.

> Some doubt many have of the *tarantula*, or poisonous spider of Calabria, and that magical cure of the bit thereof by music. But since we observe that many attest it from experience; since the learned Kircherus has positively averred it, and set down the songs and tunes solemnly used for it; since some also affirm the *tarantula* itself will dance upon certain strokes, whereby they set their instruments against its poison, we shall not at all question it.[4]

The reference above to Kircher's study of 'the affections of the mind which music excites,' might today be thought of by everyone as the great purpose of music, the communication of the emotions. But to some, especially the early writers still under the shadow of the Roman Church's long condemnation of the emotions, there was a concern that music promoted madness. An important early reference in this regard is found in the most important book on music of the fifth century, the allegorical description of *The Marriage of Philology and Mercury*, by Martianus Capella. This work is a defense of the importance of the seven liberal arts, which were by this time established in the Roman schools. These were the *Trivium*, consisting of Grammar, Dialectic, and Rhetoric, and the *Quadrivium*, consisting of Geometry, Arithmetic, Astronomy, and Music (here called by an ancient synonym, 'Harmony'). The book was written at a time when Christianity had not yet won its final battle against the 'pagans' and might well be thought of as an attempt to fight back against the efforts of the new Church to shut down traditional education and knowledge. This book represents one of the efforts which helped keep the liberal arts alive during the 'Dark Ages.' Regarding madness, in this book the allegorical character, Music, speaks,

> I have frequently recited chants that have had a therapeutic effect upon deranged minds and ailing bodies; I have restored the mad to health through consonance, a treatment which the physician Asclepiades learned from me.[5]

The thirteenth-century philosopher Bartholomew Anglicus mentions the use of music in writing of the treatment of madness. Those suffering from madness must be tied up, so they will not hurt themselves or others, and then,

---

3   Johann Mattheson, *Der vollkommene Capellmeister* (1739), trans. Ernest Harriss (Ann Arbor: UMI Research Press, 1981), I, iii, 43

4   'Enquiries into Vulgar and Common Errors,' in *Sir Thomas Browne's Works*, ed. Simon Wilkin (London: Pickering, 1836), II, 536.

5   *Martianus Capella and the Seven Liberal Arts*, trans. William Harris Stahl and Richard Johnson (New York: Columbia University Press, 1977), 358.

be refreshed, and comforted, and withdrawn from cause and matter of dread and busy thoughts. And they must be gladded with instruments of music, and some what be occupied.[6]

The great Renaissance philosopher Erasmus (1466–1536) attributed the discovery that music could cure madness to the famous ancient Greek philosopher, Pythagoras.

Pythagoras, by playing spondees in the Phrygian mode, transformed a young man mad with love and restored his sanity. A similar story is told of Empedocles, who is said by the use of some particular musical modes to have recalled to his proper wits a young man already beside himself with rage and hell-bent on murder.[7]

The sixteenth-century Church philosopher, Jean Bodin, following the official Church view, arrives at a startling conclusion, that *improvisation* in music drives men mad!

Harmony weakened and overdone by excessive elaboration exerts an influence, for while one both simple and natural is wont to cure serious illness of the mind, on the contrary one contrived from a medley of sounds and rapid rhythms usually drives a mind insane. This happens to men too anxious to please their ears, who dislike the Doric mode and dignified measures. They affect the Ionian, so that it ought not to seem remarkable if many become insane.[8]

In another place, in writing of the 'Humors,' in particular the influence of blood and black bile, he reports how this cure is effected in Germany.

In Lower Germany there are almost none who are mad from black bile, but rather from blood; this type of lunacy the common man calls the disease of St. Vitus, which impels them to exultation and senseless dancing. Musicians imitate this on the lyre; afterwards they make use of more serious rhythms and modes, doing this gradually until by the gravity of the mode and the rhythm the madmen are clearly soothed.[9]

In English literature of the Renaissance we notice a line in a poem by Sir John Davies (1569–1626), 'Orchestra, or A Poem of Dancing,' which we also take as a reference to the reputation of music to alleviate madness. Here he calls music 'the sick mind's leech.'[10]

With this background on the fear of some that music causes madness, the reader will understand that this concept was often reversed and the word music was used as a metaphor for an unbalanced mind, a mind 'out of tune.' Some examples from Shakespeare illustrate this usage.

'my feeble key of untuned cares'
   Shakespeare, *The Comedy of Errors*, V, i, 315

---

[6] 'Medieval Medicine,' In *Medieval Lore*, trans. Robert Steele (London: Stock, 1893), 58.

[7] Letter to Adrian VI [1522], quoted in *The Collected Works of Erasmus* (Toronto: University of Toronto Press, 1992), IX, 145ff.

[8] Jean Bodin, *Method for the Easy Comprehension of History*, trans. Beatrice Reynolds (New York: Columbia University Press, 1945), 31.

[9] Ibid., 103.

[10] Sir John Davies (1569–1626), 'Orchestra or A Poem of Dancing,' in *The New Oxford Book of Sixteenth Century Verse*, ed. Emrys Jones (Oxford: Oxford University Press, 1991), 652ff.

> 'Do you speak in the sick tune?'
> Shakespeare, *Much Ado About Nothing*, II, iv, 35

> O what a noble mind is here overthrown!
> The courtier's, soldier's, scholar's eye, tongue, sword;
> ......
> And I, of ladies most deject and wretched,
> That sucked the honey of his music vows
> Now see that noble and most sovereign reason,
> Like sweet bells jangled, out of tune and harsh....
> Shakespeare, *Hamlet*, III, i, 155ff.

In another place, however, Shakespeare seems to suggest that music, instead, *causes* madness! In *Richard II*, the imprisoned king, having heard some music, says,

> This music mads me. Let it sound no more,
> For though it have helped mad men to their wits,
> In me it seems it will make wise men mad.[11]

By the seventeenth century, however, most writers are pointing to music's ability to alleviate various forms of 'madness.' One of the earliest books of the Baroque, *The City of the Sun* (1602), by Tommaso Campanella, describes a fictional, utopian society.[12] The uses of music found in this society include a brief reference to music therapy, for the cure of 'burning fevers.'

Robert Burton (1577–1640), in his famous book, *The Anatomy of Melancholy*, has an extended discussion regarding the use of music for the cure of madness. Here, however, like the cure of the spider bite, it is the combination of dance with music which he advocates. When he lists what he considers the basic 'diseases of the mind,' among 'Dotage, Phrenzy, Madness, Hydrophobia, and Llycanthropia,' we are surprised to find 'St. Vitus' Dance.' His discussion of this condition is rather interesting.

> S. Vitus' Dance; the lascivious dance, Paracelsus calls it, because they that are taken with it, can do nothing but dance till they be dead, or cured. It is so called, for that the parties so troubled were wont to go to S. Vitus for help, & after they had danced there a while, they were certainly freed. It is strange to hear how long they will dance, & in what manner, over stools, forms, tables; even great-bellied women sometimes (and yet never hurt their children) will dance so long that they can stir neither hand nor foot, but seem to be quite dead. Only in red clothes they cannot abide. Musick above all things they love, & therefore Magistrates in Germany will hire Musicians to play to them, and some lusty sturdy companions to dance with them. This disease hath been very common in Germany, as appears by those relations of Sckenkius, and Paracelsus in his book of Madness, who brags how many several persons he hath cured of it. Felix Platerus reports of a woman in Basle whom he saw, that danced a whole month together.[13]

---

[11] *Richard II*, V, v.
[12] Tommaso Campanella, *La Citta del Sole*, trans. Daniel Donno (Berkeley: University of California Press, 1981), 41.
[13] Robert Burton, *The Anatomy of Melancholy*, ed. Floyd Dell (New York: Tudor Publishing Company, 1938), 124.

His English contemporary, Abraham Cowley, also has left an interesting observation on the use of music to cure madness. He began by reviewing several of the more familiar anecdotes in ancient literature in which music affected behavior. But music therapy is more than this.

> Neither should we wonder, that passions should be raised or suppressed … But that [music] should cure settled diseases in the body, we should hardly believe, if we had not both human and divine testimony for it.[14]

Cowley then adds, in addition to the testimony in the Old Testament, the well-known and documented instances in which music had cured the poison left by the bite of the Tarantula spider. But how does one explain it? He arrives at the unusual explanation that it is not music *per se*, but, according to an earlier author, the instrument on which the music is performed which is the agent for the cure of madness.

> For the explication of the reason of these cures, the Magicians fly to their *Colcodea*; the Platonicks to their *Anima Mundi*; the Rabbis to Fables and Prodigies not worth the repeating. Baptista Porta in his *Natural Magick*, seems to attribute it to the *Magical Power of the Instrument*, rather than of the Musick; for he says, that Madness is to be cured by the Harmony of a Pipe made of Hellobore, because the juice of that plant is held good for that purpose.

His explanation for this cure reads like something which might have been written by the ancient Greek philosophers:

> That Musick moves the spirits to act upon the soul, as medicines do to operate upon the body, and that it cures the body by the soul, as medicine does the soul by the body.

It was also in this vein that Cassiodorus (480–573 AD), in a famous letter to Boethius, describes the process by which music heals. He then points to the effect of music on a host of mental illnesses, beginning with melancholy.

> The artist changes men's hearts as they listen; and, when this artful pleasure issues from the secret place of nature as the queen of the senses, in all the glory of its tones, our remaining thoughts take to flight, and it expels all else, that it may delight itself simply in being heard. Harmful melancholy he turns to pleasure; he weakens swelling rage; he makes bloodthirsty cruelty kindly, arouses sleepy sloth from its torpor, restores to the sleepless their wholesome rest, recalls lust-corrupted chastity to its moral resolve, and heals boredom of spirit which is always the enemy of good thoughts. Dangerous hatreds he turns to helpful goodwill, and, in a blessed kind of healing, drives out the passions of the heart by means of sweetest pleasures.[15]

Beginning with the late Renaissance one finds, in both the literature and in music of England, a surprising focus on melancholy. Actually what this represents is a harbinger of the Baroque Period's strong fascination with the role of music and the emotions. Given the

---

[14] Ibid., 67.

[15] Letter to Boethius, in *Variae*, trans. Thomas Hodgkin (London: Frowde, 1886)., II, xl.

frequent reference in literature to the fact that the English have difficult expressing their emotions, perhaps it is not to far off the mark to say that these English writers, now becoming more aware of strong emotions, gave 'melancholy' as a synonym for strong emotions in general.

Henry Peacham (1576–1643), in his book, *The Complete Gentleman*, declares that music is 'the best physic for many melancholy diseases.'[16]

Robert Burton (1577–1640), in his famous book, *The Anatomy of Melancholy*, devotes a brief chapter to music.[17] There have been many means by which philosophers and physicians have attempted to 'exhilarate a sorrowful heart,' he notes, but for him there is nothing so powerful as 'a cup of strong drink, mirth, musick, and merry company.'[18] After citing some high recommendations of music by ancient writers, Burton observes,

> Musick is a tonic to the saddened soul, a [powerful cannon] against melancholy, to rear and revive the languishing soul, affecting not only the ears, but the very arteries, the vital and animal spirits; it erects the mind, and makes it nimble. This it will effect in the most dull, severe, and sorrowful souls, expel grief with mirth, and if there be any clouds, dust, or dregs of cares yet lurking in our thoughts, most powerfully it wipes them all away, and that which is more, it will perform all this in an instant: cheer up the countenance, expel austerity, bring in hilarity, inform our manners, mitigate anger … Our divine Musick, not only to expel the greatest griefs, but it doth extenuate fears and furies, appeases cruelty, abates heaviness, and to such as are watchful it causes quiet rest; it takes away spleen and hatred, be it instrumental, vocal, with strings, or wind; it leads us by the spirit, it cures all irksomeness and heaviness of the soul.

Music accomplishes this, he maintains, because,

> In a word, it is so powerful a thing that it ravishes the soul, the Queen of the senses, by sweet pleasure (which is a happy cure) and corporal tunes, pacifies our incorporeal soul, and rules it without words, and carries it beyond itself, helps, elevates, extends it.

But now he warns there are some men *made* melancholic by music and in these cases more music can make their condition worse, escalating it from melancholy to madness! He concludes this passage by pointing out, on the other hand, that there is such a thing as 'pleasing melancholy,' which he seems not to consider dangerous.

> And what young man is not [pleased with music]? As it is acceptable and conducing to most, so especially to a melancholy man; provided always, his disease proceed not originally from it, that he be not some light Inamorato, some idle phantastick, who capers in conceit all the day long, and thinks of nothing else but how to make Jigs, Sonnets, Madrigals, in commendation of his mistress. In such cases Musick is most pernicious, as a spur to a free horse will make him run himself blind, or break his wind; for Musick enchants, as Menander holds, it will make such melancholy persons mad, and the sound of those Jigs and Horn-pipes will not be removed out of the ears a week after … Many men

---

[16] Henry Peacham, *The Complete Gentleman*, ed. Virgil Heltzel (Ithaca: Cornell University Press, 1962), 116.

[17] Burton, *The Anatomy of Melancholy*, 478ff.

[18] Ibid., 478ff.

are melancholy by hearing Musick, but it is a pleasing melancholy that it causes, and therefore to such as are discontent, in woe, fear, sorrow, or dejected, it is a most present remedy; it expels cares, alters their grieved minds, and eases in an instant.

In another reference to melancholy among the Jacobean plays, but in this case, in Thomas Dekker's (b. 1570) *The Wonder of a Kingdom* (III, ii), a nurse rejects the idea of music therapy.

THE DUKE OF FLORENCE. Call for the Musicke.
ANGELO. Makea no noise, but bring in de Fidlers, and play sweet—
NURSE. Oh out upon this Doctor; hang him, does he think to cure dejected Ladies with Fidlers—

Johann Mattheson not only reviews many of the anecdotes of the healing powers of music found in ancient literature, but he also provides some contemporary examples.[19] He says he received a letter from the queen of Spain in 1737 in which she testifies that her husband was completely cured of 'black melancholy' by her having organized a concert every evening before dinner. So impressed was the king, that he began to study music himself.[20] He also cites the *Leipziger Zeitungen von gelehrten Sachen* (1733, p. 626), which discusses his own father being cured of melancholy by music, all other remedies having been in vain.

Aside from the more conspicuous madness and melancholy, the early philosophers write of music's ability to help with a wide variety of other mental illnesses. Iamblichus (ca. 250–325 AD) records the techniques of Pythagoras in using music to alleviate a number of primarily emotional disorders. It is no doubt this passage which has caused some more recent scholars to regard Pythagoras as 'The Father of Music Therapy.'[21]

> Pythagoras conceived the first attention that should be given to men should be addressed to the senses, as when one perceives beautiful figures and forms, or hears beautiful rhythms and melodies. Consequently he laid down that the first erudition was that which subsists through music's melodies and rhythms, and from these he obtained remedies of human manners and passions, and restored the pristine harmony of the faculties of the soul. Moreover, he devised medicines calculated to repress and cure the diseases of both bodies and souls. Here is also by Zeus, something which deserves to be mentioned above all: namely, that for his disciples he arranged and adjusted what might be called 'preparations' and 'touchings,' divinely contriving mingling of certain diatonic, chromatic and enharmonic melodies, through which he easily switched and circulated the passions of the soul in a contrary direction, whenever they had accumulated recently, irrationally, or clandestinely—such as sorrow, rage, pity, over-emulation, fear, manifold desires, angers, appetites, pride, collapse or spasms. Each of these he corrected by the rule of virtue, attempering them through appropriate melodies, as through some salutary medicine.

---

[19] Johann Mattheson, *Der vollkommene Capellmeister* (1739), trans. Ernest Harriss (Ann Arbor: UMI Research Press, 1981), I, iii, 43.

[20] Ibid., I, iii, 45.

[21] Iamblichus, in Kenneth Guthrie, *The Pythagorean Sourcebook* (Grand Rapids: Phanes Press, 1987).

Capella (fifth century), whom we have mentioned above, points to examples of using music to work with mentally disturbed and insane patients, not to mention an extraordinarily diverse list of other kinds of patients.

> Have not I myself brought healing to diseased bodies by prolonged therapy? The ancients were able to cure fever and wounds by incantation. Asclepiades healed with the trumpet patients who were stone deaf, and Theophrastus used the flute with mentally disturbed patients. Is anyone unaware that gout in the hip is removed by the sweet tones of the aulos? Xenocrates cured insane patients by playing on musical instruments. Thales of Crete is known to have dispelled diseases and pestilence by the sweetness of his cithara playing. Herophilus checked the pulse of his patients by comparing rhythms.[22]

The rather extraordinary claim that music can cure the deaf was also argued by the very important English philosopher, Robert Grosseteste, Bishop of Lincoln (1170–1253). Indeed, he regarded healing as being music's highest purpose. McEvoy summarizes Grosseteste's explanation for the process by which music heals.

> The soul follows the body in the latter's affections, and the body follows the soul's actions. When, therefore, the body is affected by sounding numbers, the soul draws out of itself numbers which are of the same proportion, and the spirits adjust the proportions of the numbers to agreement. The wise doctor must therefore have a knowledge of the due proportion of the body as impressed on it by the stars, and must be acquainted with the proportions which induce concord among the elements and the humid parts of the principal spirits, and between the soul and the body. When these proportions are expressed in terms of musical sound, upon the numbers' reaching the soul everything in man returns to a proportioned state. The doctor must also have studied the behavior of the spirits prevailing in different emotional states, such as in joy, when they dilate, and sadness, when they contract; for the states of the soul too can be affected by the knowledgeable employment of musical sound.[23]

Not all observers could believe such extraordinary claims, especially the idea that music could cure the deaf. François Rabelais, in his fictional visit to the kingdom of 'Quint Essence,' makes fun of the entire idea. Here the visitors were told the queen cures all maladies just by playing an appropriate song. In the demonstration given the visitors, first lepers were brought in.

> She played them a tune, but what one I don't know. Instantly they were perfectly cured. Then the poisoned were brought in; she played them another tune, and they were on their feet. Then the blind, the deaf, the mute, treating them similarly, which terrified us, not wrongly, and we fell to the ground, prostrating ourselves as people in ecstasy and rapt in contemplation of the powers we saw emanating from the Lady; and it was not in our power to say a single word.[24]

---

[22] *Martianus Capella and the Seven Liberal Arts*, 358. Marchetto of Padua, fourteenth century, in his Lucidarium, also mentions that physicians judge the pulse by the aid of music.

[23] James McEvoy, *The Philosophy of Robert Grosseteste* (Oxford: Clarendon, 1982), 257ff.

[24] François Rabelais, *Pantagruel*, trans. Donald Frame (Berkeley: University of California Press, 1991), V, xix.

Some more rather general references to music therapy include a passage found in Giovanni Boccaccio (1313–1375). In the seventh story of the tenth day, in *The Decameron*, one sings a song, accompanied by a viol, to a girl with the result that,

> she was so rejoiced and so content that she straightaway showed manifest signs of great improvement.[25]

Johann Mattheson cites the *Observations de Medecine sur la maladie, appellee convulsions par un Medecine de la Faculte de Paris* (Paris, 1732, xii, 32), which contains 'examples of music helping sick people to health.'[26]

There is a rather unusual poem by Abraham Cowley (1618–1667) in which he describes the 'music of the spheres,' including this nice thought:

> And this is Musick; sounds that charm our ears,
> Are but one dressing that rich science wears.

He goes on to make the case that everything on earth is impacted by this celestial music, including his own poetry. This relationship, which he also compares to the sympathetic vibration of the strings on a lyre, he gives as a metaphor for how music cures the patient.

> Though no man heard it, though no man rehearse,
> Yet will there still be musick in my verse.
> In this great world so much of it we see;
> The lesser, man, is all over harmony.
> Storehouse of all proportions! single Choir!
> Which first God's breath did tunefully inspire![27]
> From hence blessed musick's heavenly charms arise,
> From sympathy which them and to man allies.
> Thus they our souls, thus they our bodies win.
> Not by their force, but party that's within.
> Thus the strange cure on our split blood applied,
> Sympathy to the distant wound does guide.
> Thus when two brethren strings are set alike,
> To move them both, but one of them we strike.
> Thus David's lyre did Saul's wild rage control,
> And tuned the harsh disorders of his soul.[28]

---

[25] *The Decameron*, trans. Mark Musa and Peter Bondanella (New York: Norton, 1977), 193. II, 740.
[26] Mattheson, *Der vollkommene Capellmeister*, I, iii, 43.
[27] 'Inspire,' at this time in England was a synonym for 'to blow,' as to inspire a flute.
[28] 'Davideis,' in *The Complete Works of Abraham Cowley*, ed. Alexander Grosart (New York: AMS Press, 1967), I, 49.

There is a nice passage in the most famous play by the English Jacobean playwrights, Beaumont and Fletcher, *The Knight of the Burning Pestle* (II, i), in which music's cure is of a distinctly psychological one. Here an old merchant predicts that one who laughs and sings will be protected from a wide variety of illness.

> Let each man keep his heart at ease
> No man dies of that disease,
> He that would his body keep
> From diseases, must not weep,
> But whoever laughs and sings,
> Never his body brings
> Into Fevers, Gouts, or Rhumes,
> Or lingeringly his Lungs consumes:
> Or meets with aches in the bone,
> Or Catarrhs, or griping Stone.

Another example of the result of music's cure being of a psychological nature is found in John Dryden's (1631–1700) *The Indian Queen* (III, ii), when Ismeron calls for music for the purpose of helping Zempoalla.

> You Spirits that inhabit in the Air,
> With all your powerful Charms of Musick try
> To bring her Soul back to its harmony.

A curious negative reference to music's affect on the body is found in a Restoration poem by William Wycherley (1641–1715):

> Your verse, like your prescriptions, is so mean,
> That, like bad Musick, it provokes the Spleen.[29]

This reference to such a specific organ as the spleen, calls to mind Theophrastus of Eresus, 372–287 BC, a disciple of Aristotle, who wrote that a person suffering from sciatica would always be free from attacks if one played the aulos in the Phrygian mode over the part of the body affected?[30] And in the passage quoted above by Abraham Cowley, he adds that 'the Sciatique nerve is helped by playing on a musical instrument made of Poplar, because of the virtue of the Oil of that tree to mitigate those kinds of pains.'

Finally, there are several interesting references in the early literature regarding the use of music for pain in general. For example in Edmund Spenser's *The Faerie Queen*, we read,

---

[29] 'To a Doctor of Physick, on his Writing a Satyr against Wit,' in *The Complete Works of William Wycherley* (New York: Russell & Russell, 1964), IV.

[30] *On Inspiration*, quoted in Athenaeus, *Deipnosophistae*, XIV, 624. Plutarch, in 'Concerning the Virtues of Women,' also tells of a sickly woman who was healed by the study of music.

> And all the while most heavenly melody
> About the bed sweet music did divide,
> Him to beguile of grief and agony …[31]

Another Englishman, George Wither (1588–1667), also was thinking of some remote time, writing of 'He that first taught his Musicke such a strain,'

> He in his troubles eased the body's pains,
> By measures raised to the souls ravishing …[32]

Johann Mattheson mentions two accounts of pain being treated by music. One of these regards a professor at Gottingen who attributed the alleviation of pain in limbs with the effect music has on muscles. A particularly interesting report is that the seventeenth-century native Americans (Indians),

> use no other means than their somewhat coarse method of playing, by means of which they occasionally suppress and alleviate difficult infirmities and pains if not heal them.[33]

We have quoted above a poem by the seventeenth-century poet, Abraham Cowley, which contains the lines,

> Thus when two brethren strings are set alike,
> To move them both, but one of them we strike.

This reference to the sympathetic vibrations between strings on a harp, the playing on one string causing an untouched adjacent string to vibrate, was something observed with great fascination by early writers. For the ancient philosophers this was a metaphor for the body and soul and by treating the soul through music you could treat the body. The Italian philosopher who founded the famous academy at the court of Lorenzo the Magnificant in fifteenth-century Florence, worked as a healer using certain musical proportions based on the lyre.[34] Similarly, Bartolomeo Ramos de Pareja, inspired by Arabic texts in Spain, was convinced that certain musical scales had the power to affect sluggishness and various emotions. 'Music works miracles,' he asserted.[35]

Today we are more likely to speak of the 'spirit,' rather than the soul. But, while 'spirit' may have meaning for musicians, it only makes doctors nervous. Medical doctors today do not deal with 'the spirit,' they deal with body parts. Because we do not speak their language is one reason why medical doctors give only polite respect to music therapy.

---

[31] Edmund Spenser, *The Faerie Queene*, Book I, Canto V, xvii.

[32] Wither, Spenser Society Nr. 10, 'The Shepheards Hunting,' 506.

[33] Mattheson, *Der vollkommene Capellmeister*, I, iii, 47. He quotes François La Mothe le Vayer, *Oeuvres de Francois de la Mothe le Vayer* (Paris, 1656), I, 521.

[34] Stuart Isacoff, *Temperament* (New York: Vintage, 2003), 112.

[35] Ibid.

But healing through music does occur. We know, first-hand, of some medical conditions in which a music therapist accomplished what a medical doctor could not. The field of music therapy itself must be much more active in the basic research which explains scientifically how music cures. Music therapists must not only continue beating doctors at their own game, that is effecting healing where the medical profession cannot, but these cases must be vigorously reported and the practitioners honored. Music therapy must argue its own case, for only in this way will music therapy ever become fully recognized by the medical profession. After all, the other branches of medicine also had, at some earlier time, to make their own case. If the discipline of surgery had not done this, for example, then surgery would still be conducted by barbers.

'to soothe a savage breast'

> *Sweet sound can tame the savage hearts of the barbarians*
> Cassiodorus (480–573)
>
> *Music hath charms to soothe a savage breast*
> William Congreve (1670–1729)
>
> *No one, in any condition of life, has yet been found
> who was not eager to soothe his cares with music.*
> Franchinus Gafurius, *Practica musicae*, 1496

ONE DAY I WAS PLAYING GOLF with a physician and while walking the course I was questioning him to see what he had been educated to understand about the effects of music on the physiology. He had no training in music, and seemed to have little curiosity about the subject, until at one point when he suddenly blurted out, 'But of course, everyone knows you can change your mood by putting on a different record.'

That observation is a very old one and is the subject of this chapter. It would seem a reasonable conclusion that this common experience was what, at some remote time, was the bridge to the idea of the investigation of music therapy.

The frequency with which this topic is mentioned by earlier writers clearly invites the idea that the use of music for its soothing effect was considered even more important in earlier societies than it would be in ours. Perhaps this is because today we have a broader range of electives to lessen our passions and sorrows and thus do not depend so much on music for this purpose. On the other hand, even though an objective person would have to conclude that our society is far from civilized, it is very possible that earlier societies were even less well mannered. This certainly seems a distinct possibility when one reads the famous medical authority, Galen (second century AD),

> Whenever a man becomes violently angry over little things and bites and kicks his servants, you are sure that this man is in a state of passion.
> ......
> I watched a man eagerly trying to open a door. When things did not work out as he would have them, I saw him bite the key, kick the door, blaspheme, glare wildly like a madman, and all but foam at the mouth like a wild boar.[1]

---

[1] Galen, 'On the Passions and Errors of the Soul,' trans. Paul W. Harkins (Columbus: Ohio State University Press), 29, 38.

If Galen's descriptions here of a 'passionate man' were typical, then perhaps we can understand how music could have been more important to earlier societies than ours—at least most of us have advanced to a point of cultivation where we do not bite each other or foam at the mouth like a wild boar!

If our premise is correct one can only imagine how in even earlier times great value would have been placed on the ability of music to soothe the passions. And indeed the references for the soothing power of music are very ancient. One of the oldest Sumerian art works, the Standard of Ur, which dates from 2,500 BC pictures a singer and a harpist whose purpose is to 'dispel gloom.'[2] A beautiful description of what art music must have been to these people is found on a clay cylinder from 2,400 BC and its focus is on the ability of music to soothe.[3]

> To fill with joy the Temple court
> And chase the city's gloom away,
> The heart to still, the passions calm,
> Of weeping eyes the tears to stay.

A final example from the most ancient world is an anecdote about a prince of Byblos who had sent a member of the court to obtain a load of precious wood from Lebanon, where he encountered endless problems and delay. When the prince heard of this he sent to him,

> two measures of wine and a sheep, as well as his songstress to sing to him and chase away his gloomy thoughts.[4]

One of the very earliest of the ancient Greek poets was Hesiod (ca. 800 BC), a near contemporary of Homer. Their works date from some period even before the development of the written form of the Greek language and were transmitted until that time by oral tradition. Hesiod offers a specific prescription, maintaining that singing of 'the praises of virtuous men' was the best means of 'shaking off the dark mood,'

> A man may have some fresh grief over which to mourn,
> and sorrow may have left him no more tears, but if a singer,
> a servant of the Muses, sings the glories of ancient men
> and hymns the blessed gods who dwell on Olympus,
> the heavy-hearted man soon shakes off his dark mood, and
> forgetfulness soothes his grief, for this gift of the gods diverts his mind.[5]

---

[2] Henry G. Farmer, 'The Music of Ancient Mesopotamia,' in *The New Oxford History of Music* (London: Oxford University Press, 1966), 236.

[3] Trans. Francis Galpin, in *Music of the Sumerians* (Westport: Greenwood Press, 1970), vii.

[4] Quoted in Lise Manniche, *Music and Musicians in Ancient Egypt* (London: British Museum Press, 1991), 126.

[5] Apostolos N. Athanassakis, trans., *Theogony, Works and Days, Shield* (Baltimore: Johns Hopkins University Press, 1983), *Theogony*, 98–103.

Quoting the great ancient Greek philosopher, Pythagorias (sixth century BC), whom we know only through later writers as not a single original word of his survives, Iamblichus (ca. 250–325 AD) wrote of the tradition of Pythagoras personally playing music at night to soothe his students in order to bring tranquil sleep.

> In the evening, when his disciples were retiring to sleep, he would thus liberate them from the day's perturbations and tumults, purifying their intellective powers from the influxive and exfluxive waves of corporeal nature, quieting their sleep, and rendering their dreams pleasing and prophetic.[6]

The fifth-century philosopher, Martianus Capella, also mentions,

> … the Pythagoreans too assuaged the ferocity of men's spirits with pipes and strings.[7]

The Greek lyric poet, Moschus (fl. 100 BC) also sings of the power of music to 'lull my sorrow to sleep.'[8]

The early Roman poet, Tibullus (5 –10 BC), attributed to Apollo the power to soothe the sick.

> Come near, Apollo, come and make me well—
> Heal me, Apollo of the flowing hair …
> Be near me, holy presence; bring your songs
> And all your delicacies that soothe the sick.[9]

Regarding the Christian era, the first-century Roman poet, Cyrus, wished for skill in music for this purpose.

> Would that my father had taught me to shepherd fleecy flocks, so that, sitting under the elms or piping under a rock, I might cheer my sorrows with music.[10]

Two important early Christian fathers contributed to this topic. St. Basil (329–379) advised that the chief value of singing psalms was 'to calm and soften the wicked spirits which trouble souls.'[11] Cassiodorus (480–573) in a famous letter written to Boethius refers to music as that 'sweet sound can tame the savage hearts of the barbarians.' In this same letter he says of music's ability, that it,

---

[6] Quoted in Kenneth Guthrie, *The Pythagorean Sourcebook* (Grand Rapids: Phanes Press, 1987).

[7] *Martianus Capella and the Seven Liberal Arts*, trans. William Harris Stahl and Richard Johnson (New York: Columbia University Press, 1977), 356.

[8] 'Idyll IX,' trans. A. Lang, *Theocritus, Bion and Moschus* (London: Macmillan, 1920), 210.

[9] Tibullus, *Poems*, III, x.

[10] *The Greek Anthology*, IX, 136.

[11] St. Basil, 'Homily 14,' in *Exegetic Homilies*, trans. Sister Agnes Way (Washington, D.C.: The Catholic University of America Press), 214. In Homily 21, Ibid., 341, Basil says the purpose of psalm singing is to 'correct the passions of the soul.'

weakens swelling rage; he makes bloodthirsty cruelty kindly ... and drives out the passions of the heart by means of sweetest pleasures.

Cassiodorus also makes reference to some specific modes with respect to their effectiveness in soothing the listener. In this same letter, for example, he mentions,

the Aeolian calms the storms of the soul, and gives sleep to those who are already at peace.[12]

In his book *Institutiones*, Cassiodorus refers to the Hypodorian mode, 'the lowest of all,' for its soothing influence on the state of the listener.

These tones ... have been shown to possess such great usefulness that they calm excited minds and cause even wild animals and serpents and birds and dolphins to approach and listen to their harmony.[13]

We know of nothing more on this topic by early Church writers until the Pre-Renaissance and Dante (1265–1321). In his *Purgatorio* we find music being used to 'untie the knots of rage,'

I now heard voices, each one of which
Seemed to be praying for pity and for peace
To the Lamb of God, who lifts our sins from us.
They all started with the *Agnus Dei*,
And kept together in both word and measure,
So that there seemed among them every concord.
'Those are spirits, master, that I hear?'
I said; and he to me: 'You are correct;
They go about untying knots of rage.'[14]

In a passage in *Paradiso*, we can see the effect of the soothing quality of music.

Singing *Ave Maria, gratia
Plena*, now opened wide his wings before her.
From every side the blessed court responded
To the celestial melody, so that
Every face looked more serene because of it.[15]

The secular music of this period also includes some interesting texts on this topic. In the German Goliard literature, Hugh of Orleans speaks of the ability of music to relieve grief, here the grief brought by Fate.

---

[12] Letter to Boethius, in *Variae*, trans. Thomas Hodgkin (London: Frowde, 1886), II, xl.
[13] In 'On Music,' in *An Introduction to Divine and Human Readings*, trans. Leslie Jones (New York, Octagon Books, 1966). 8.
[14] *Purgatorio*, XVI.
[15] *Paradiso*, XXXII.

> Let us endure what cannot be changed, let's bear it serenely!
> Only the lyre assuages the grief that smarts ever keenly.[16]

On the other hand, we should note there is a French troubadour song by Borneil which, while admitting that music is usually used to soothe pain, finds that on occasion it can make matters worse.

> I lament and sigh and weep and sing, but my song brings me no pleasure; for, instead, the more I sing, the more sad I become and the more I weaken my heart and my reason. And I do not wonder that a man who is saddened by song—which usually drives away pain and sorrow—should fear to see his mind and his affairs gravely altered![17]

During the Renaissance one finds much reference to music's ability to soothe the listener. The great fourteenth-century Italian poet, Petrarch (1304–1374), who as a musician sang his famous poems, left a nice tribute to this purpose of music in his fourth pastoral Eclogue. Here we have a debate between Gallus (France) and Tyrrhenus (Italy) as to whom the gift of poetic expression belongs. Petrarch declares the god Daedalus first makes a gift of music to Tyrrhenus and one of its primary purposes is to provide solace.

> TYRRHENUS: Bearing his lyre he drew near me. 'Take this, my lad,' so he bade me;
> 'Let it console your cares and beguile your long days of labor.'

Gallus desires to possess the virtues of music, represented by the lyre, and says,

> GALLUS: Fix yourself the price you would take for that little
>   Object, and high though it be I'll pay—and add something to it.
> TYRRHENUS: So for this 'little' thing you'd pay a great price? Nay, you know not
>   What it is worth or you'd call it a great thing. In troubles it soothes us,
>   Raises our weary spirits, affords our friends consolation,
>   Rids our heart of their sorrows, making them once more joyful,
>   Dries up our tears and appeases all our complaints and even
>   Banishes fear, brings hope to our hearts and calm to our faces.[18]

However, in one of Petrarch's lyric poems the music fails to soothe.

> Song, you do not quiet me, rather you inflame me to tell of
> what steals me away from myself.[19]

One of the songs in *The Decameron*, by Giovanni Boccaccio (1313–1375), also fails to soothe the young lady:

---

16 In 'Quid luges, lirice,' in *Vagabond Verse*, trans. Edwin H. Zeydel (Detroit: Wayne State University Press, 1966), 237.

17 'Plaing e sospir,' in Ruth Sharman, *The Cansos and Sirventes of the Troubadour Giraut de Borneil* (Cambridge: Cambridge University Press, 1989), 411.

18 *Petrarch's Bucolicum Carmen*, trans. Thomas Bergin (New Haven: Yale University Press, 1974), IV, 22, 41ff.

19 'Perchee la vita e breve,' in *Petrarch's Lyric Poems*, trans. Robert Durling (Cambridge: Harvard University Press, 1976), 160.

> ... and then sang her sundry songs, the which were fire and flame to the girl's passion, whereas he thought to solace her.[20]

In another place in *The Decameron*, the first story of the seventh day, there is a reference to a hymn attributed to St. Ambrose, the 'Te lucis,' sung at the end of the day to protect one from evil dreams.[21]

In fourteenth-century France, the famous poet and composer, Guillaume de Machaut (1300–1377), gave great weight to music's ability to soothe. In the Prologue to his collected works which he made at the end of his life, Machaut dwells on this at length. First, he promises the allegorical figure of Love not to write anything sad or difficult to understand, but only pleasant and sweet works which will soften and nourish hardened hearts.[22] Even if his subject is sad, the poet's manner must be gay, for a heart full of sadness cannot sing gaily. The very nature of music, says Machaut, requires the artist-lover to be joyful. 'Music is a science which asks that one laugh, and sing, and dance. It does not care for melancholy, nor for the man who is melancholy.'

> Et Musique est une science
> qui vuet qu'on rie et chante et dance.
> Cure n'a de merencolie
> Ne d'homme qui merencolie.[23]

In the closing section of the Prologue, Machaut says this is his mission: music and poetry are meant to enlighten and soothe troubled mankind, as one can see in the example of David and his harp and Orpheus.

In only one place does Machaut admit that music fails to solace. Although he is speaking of the music of birds, he echoes the thirteenth-century troubadours who often voiced the thought that even music cannot cheer the sad lover.

> I went there this morning to listen to their beautiful service and their merry singing, although my heart, which nothing can console, could take little pleasure in them.[24]

In fourteenth-century England we find some references to music's ability to soothe among the stage repertoire which begins to appear after the Dark Ages. For example, in the 'Drapers play,' we find Jesus calling for music to soothe his mother,

---

[20] *The Decameron*, trans. Mark Musa and Peter Bondanella (New York: Norton, 1977), II, 737.

[21] Ibid., II, 489, 491; see also, III, 881, 882.

[22] Prologue, IV, 21ff.

[23] Ibid., IV, 85ff.

[24] Guillaume de Machaut, 'Le Jugement du roy de Behaigne,' trans. James Wimsatt and William Kibler (Athens: The University of Georgia Press, 1988), 136.

> And bring me my mother to the highest of heaven,
> With mirth and with melody, her mood for to mend.[25]

And in the 'Second Shepherds' Play' three shepherds sing a three-part song to cheer (to 'mirth') them up during the long night.

> COLL. That is right. By the cross, these nights are long!
>   Yet I would, ere we went, one gave us a song.
> GIB. So I thought as I stood, to mirth us among.
> DAW. I grant.[26]

Among the works of Geoffrey Chaucer (1340–1400), in his famous 'The Romaunt of the Rose,' we find a singer specifically sings to 'solace the folk':

> To syngen first, folk to solace.[27]

In his 'Troilus and Criseyde,' Troilus begins a song which also has the purpose of overcoming sorrow.[28] On the other hand, sometimes sadness is so great that even music cannot 'gladden the heart.' When Criseyde was away, Troilus was so sad that he could not bear to hear (instrumental) music and thought no one should make music.

> Syn that he saugh his lade was aweye,
> It was his sorwe upon him for to sen,
> Or for to here on instruments so pleye.
> For she, that of his herte berthe the keye,
> Was absent, lo, this was his fantasie,
> That no wight sholde maken melodie.[29]

A similar thought is expressed in a poem known as 'A.B.C.,' in which a plea is addressed to the Virgin Mary for solace, as 'no music or song can aid us in our adversity.'

> We han noon oother melodye or glee
> Us to rejoyse in oure adversitee.[30]

---

[25] J. S. Purvis, *The York Cycle* (London: S.P.C.K, 1957), 358.
[26] Quoted in *The Norton Anthology of English Literature* (New York: Norton, 1968), 182.
[27] 'The Romaunt of the Rose,' 756.
[28] 'Troilus and Criseyde,' I, 389.
[29] Ibid., V, 456.
[30] 'A.B.C.,' 100.

Additional examples can be found in 'The Knight's Tale,' where even music cannot cheer up a sad lover,[31] and in 'The Book of the Duchess,' when a character tells us that not even Orpheus, the god of music, can make his sorrow pass.[32] And after these several illustrations of cases where Chaucer points out that music fails to soothe, in another place he says this is also true with animals. In 'Troilus and Criseyde,' where Pandarus observes that an ass hears the sound of a man playing the harp, but it, being a beast, does not hear the *music*, 'no melody can sink in to his mind to gladden him.'

> Or artow lik an asse to the harpe,
> That hereth sown whan men the strynges plye,
> But in his mynde of that no melodie
> May sinken hym to gladen, for that he
> So dul ys of his bestialite.[33]

The fifteenth-century Italian philosophers continued to stress the long held purpose of music to offer solace to the listener. Thus, in Poliziano's play, *Orpheus* (1471), Orpheus prays to the gods to teach him a new kind of music, that he might soothe the Cardinal of Mantua who was attending the first performance, 'one that may make serene my lord's brow, lighten his cares and charm his learned ears.'[34] Similarly, Franchino Gaffurio (1451–1518), in the final chapter of his *Theorica,* writes,

> Music soothes the human ears with wonderful sweetness derived as nowhere else from such measure, so much order, so much measured sonority.[35]

For the Florentine philosopher, Leon Battista Alberti (b. 1404), it was in particular the music of the Church which had a powerful soothing power.

> All other modes and kinds of singing weary with reiteration; only religious music never palls. I know not how others are affected; but for myself, those hymns and psalms of the Church produce on me the very effect for which they were designed, soothing all disturbance of the soul, and inspiring a certain ineffable languor full of reverence towards God. What heart of man is so rude as not to be softened when he hears the rhythmic rise and fall of those voices, complete and true, in cadences so sweet and flexible? ... I ponder what power music brings with it to soften us and soothe.[36]

---

31 'The Knight's Tale,' 1367.
32 'The Book of the Duchess,' 569.
33 'Troilus and Criseyde,' I, 731ff.
34 *Orpheus*, trans. Louis Lord (Oxford: Oxford University Press, 1931), I, 84ff.
35 Quoted in Claude V. Palisca, *Humanism in Italian Renaissance Musical Thought* (New Haven: Yale University Press, 1985), 197.
36 Quoted in John Addington Symonds, *Renaissance in Italy* (New York: Capricorn Books, 1964), I, 188.

When Alberti asks, above, what man is so rude as not to be softened by music, it reminds us of a line in Gaffurio's *Practica musicae* where he observes that 'no one, in any condition of life, has yet been found who was not eager to soothe his cares with music.'[37]

In the literature of fifteenth-century France, we find in the manuscript, 'Le Chevalier du Papegau,' a parrot, as a literary surrogate for a real singer, which offers the traditional purpose of music to soothe.

> The parrot … began to sing and to comfort his lord and all the others who were there with a song so fine and beautiful that they soon forgot the grief they had suffered.[38]

In a fifteenth-century English poem by John Lydgate we also find that it is birds who are the surrogates for real singers. Here a lover suffering the pains of love specifically leaves his room to go 'into the woods to hear the birds sing' in order to 'find succor' and 'some release' from his pain.

> As he, alas, that nygh for sorow deyde,
> My sekenes sat ay so nygh myn hert.
> But for to fynde socour of my smert,
> Or attelest sum relesse of [my] peyn
> That me so sore halt in euery veyn,
> I rose anon and thoght I wol[de] goon
> Vnto the wode to her the briddes sing.[39]

In Lydgate's 'Reson and Sensuallyte,' a concert by the gods, we are told, would comfort even the most sorrowful of men.

Among the fifteenth-century Spanish playwrights, Fernando de Rojas in his *Celestina* gives a typical instance of the use of music to provide solace. Melibea, says,

> But I pray you, Father, have some stringed instrument brought to me so that I can wile away my grief by singing and playing. For though my sufferings torment me, sweet sounds and harmonies will much abate it.

Juan Ruiz, however, suggests the solace brought by music is not permanent, in observing 'although the jongleurs comfort, they don't heal our agonies.'[40]

From sixteenth-century Italy we find a document by the famous Niccolo Machiavelli (1469–1527) which speaks of his own personal use of music to soothe feelings.

---

37 *The Practica musicae of Franchinus Gafurius*, trans. Irwin Young, (Madison: University of Wisconsin Press, 1969), 3.
38 Thomas E. Vesce, trans., *The Knight of the Parrot* (New York: Garland, 1986), 84.
39 'A Complaynt of a Loveres Lyfe,' 15ff, in *John Lydgate Poems* (Oxford: Clarendon Press, 1966).
40 Juan Ruiz, *The Book of True Love*, trans. Saralyn Daly (University Park: Pennsylvania State University Press, 1978), 649.

> By singing, then, I strive to take from my heart and to bridle that sorrow for my afflictions that madly pursues my soul.[41]

Vincenzo Galilei (1533–1591) also wrote of his personal use of music to soothe, when he speaks of the capacity of 'sweet and harmonious sounds [to] dissipate the melancholy in me, as has happened many times.'[42]

The mathematician and philosopher, Girolamo Cardano (1501–1576), seems to make a recommendation we find by others in the high Renaissance, that one should use somber music to soothe those who are most sad. Cardano writes this, but then adds that he does not necessarily recommend it.

> If there is an instrument appropriate to tranquility and also a relation of meter and poetry to it, the instrument will be a cithara and the song will be mournful and almost tragic. In this way we can lighten the cares that result from the misery of human misfortune, although I do not necessarily recommend this.[43]

Among the sixteenth-century French poets we find a special recommendation of music's ability to soothe by Joachim du Bellay (b. 1525). Here the focus is on soothing the working men.

> So workmen sing who do not like their job
> Or ploughmen when the furrows are too long
> Or travelers who cannot get back home,
> So young men who have trouble with their girls
> Or sailors when the oars are hard to pull
> Or prisoners desperate to be out of prison.[44]

An anonymous poem, 'Las, voules vous q'une personne chante,' which was set as a chanson by Lassus, speaks of the inability of music to sooth.

> My heart is sighing;
> Yet alas, you ask for song.
> Let those sing who are happy,
> And leave me to endure my single grief.[45]

---

[41] *Machiavelli, the Chief Works*, trans. Allan Gilbert (Durham: Duke University Press, 1965), II, 740. The poet, Pietro Aretino, mentions the use of music to soothe during the night (Letter to Domenico Bolani) and by those 'persons, who, frightened out of their wits by the shadows of the night' (Letter to Sinistro). Torquato Tasso, *Creation of the World*, trans. Joseph Tusiani (Binghamton: Center for Medieval & Early Renaissance Studies, 1982), III, 18, also wrote on music soothing those with sorrow.

[42] Vincenzo Galilei, *Fronimo* (1584), trans. Carol MacClintock (Neuhasen-Stuttgart: Hanssler-Verlag, 1985), 31.

[43] Quoted in Clement Miller, *Hieronymus Cardanus, Writings on Music* (American Institute of Musicology, 1973), 204.

[44] Joachim du Bellay, *The Regrets*, trans. C. H. Sisson (Manchester: Carcanet Press, 1984),. Nr. 12. There are several poems by Ronsard which mention the ability of music to soothe.

[45] Quoted in Jane Bernstein, *French Chansons of the Sixteenth Century* (University Park: Pennsylvania State University Press, 1985), 138.

Late in life, the Church philosopher, Jean Bodin (1530–1596), wrote his prose work, *Colloquium of the Seven* [*Colloquium heptaplomeres*], a dialogue among men of seven different faiths. At the end of most day's stressful discussions there was music designed to bring the day to a close with a feeling of harmony. At the end of the first day, for example, we read,

> He called the boys who were accustomed to soothe everybody's spirits by sweetly singing divine praises with a harmony of lyres, flutes, and voices.[46]

In sixteenth-century Spanish prose one find's a reference to music's ability to soothe in the famous *Don Quijote* by Cervantes.

> I had learned from experience that music settles a jangled soul and comforts all manner of spiritual troubles.[47]

On the other hand in Lope de Vega's play, *La Dorotea*, Fernando cries, 'But neither composing verse nor singing it will calm the stormy oceans of my thoughts.'[48]

Among the sixteenth-century German writers we are drawn to an interesting discussion by Martin Luther, wherein he recognized the traditional use of music to soothe the listener. He mentions this in a lecture based on 2 Samuel 23, where he discusses the first verse, 'the sweet psalmist of Israel.' He follows the medieval Church fathers in implying that the real message is in the words, so it is not necessary to actually sing them. In the end, however, as one who not only composed and performed, but also loved and understood music thoroughly, he seems impelled to add a line on the importance of the music itself.

> When David uses the word *sweet* he is not thinking only of the sweetness and the charm of the Psalms from a grammatical and musical point of view, of artistic and euphonious words, of melodious song and notes, of beautiful text and beautiful tune; but he is referring much more to the theology they contain, to the spiritual meaning. That renders the Psalms lovely and sweet, for they are a solace to all saddened and wretched consciences, ensnared in the fear of sin, in the torture and terror of death, and in all sorts of adversity and misery. To such hearts the Book of Psalms is a sweet and delightful song because it sings of and proclaims the Messiah even when a person does not sing the notes but merely recites and pronounces the words. And yet the music, or the notes, which are a wonderful creation and gift of God, help materially in this, especially when the people sing along and reverently participate.[49]

---

[46] Jean Bodin, *Colloquium of the Seven*, trans. Marion Kuntz (Princeton: Princeton University Press, 1975), 15.

[47] Miguel de Cervantes, *Don Quijote*, trans. Burton Raffel (New York: Norton, 1995), I, xxviii.

[48] Act III, i.

[49] 'Lectures on the Last Words of David,' in *Luther's Works* (St. Louis: Concordia, 1961), XV, 273ff. In a long poem he wrote in a publication of 1538 called, 'A Preface for All Good Hymnals,' Luther writes that 'Gone are through me [music] all sorrows.'

He returns to this theme in a conversation at dinner in his home,

> One of the most beautiful and most precious gifts of God is music. Satan is very hostile to it, since it casts out many scruples and evil thoughts. The devil does not remain near it, for music is one of the finest of all arts. Its notes instill life into its texts. Music drives away the spirit of sadness, as may be seen from the life of King Saul …
>
> For a person beset by grief music is the most effective balm, for through it the heart is made content, is inspired and refreshed.[50]

There are a great many references to music's power to soothe in sixteenth-century English literature. Here we find a reference to the most familiar example of using music to soothe, the singing of a lullaby to soothe a baby. In this passage, from Lodowick Bryskett's (1546–1612) *A Discourse of Civill Life,* the author provides several curious possible explanations for how music achieves its results in this case.

> Here may also be added the singing of nurses, whereby they commonly still [children], using [music], as taught by nature only: which some men think comes to pass, by reason that the soul is (as they say) composed of harmony, and therefore is delighted with that which is proper and natural to it. Others (happily of better judgment) say, that children are stilled by the singing of their nurses, because one contrary expels and drives away another, when it is the stronger: so as the nurse's singing is louder than the child's crying, therefore it prevails. But the most effectual reason is, that the vegetative power or faculty being of most force in that age, and it taking pleasure in things delightful, and abhorring those that are displeasing and noisome; when with crying it finds itself annoyed, it more willingly admits the nurse's singing, and becomes calm and still by hearing the notes [numbers] and sweetness of the voice delighting them.

Among the sixteenth-century English poets there is an interesting anonymous poem, set as a madrigal by William Byrd, which begs music for solace. As we see in other examples of the English literature it seems to suggest the use of mournful music for this purpose.

> Come, woeful Orpheus, with thy charming lyre,
> And tune my voice unto thy skilful wire;
> Some strange chromatic notes do you devise,
> That best with mournful accents sympathise;
> Of sourest sharps and uncouth flats make choice,
> And I'll thereto compassionate my voice.[51]

---

[50] Quoted in Walter Buszin, 'Luther on Music,' *The Musical Quarterly* 32, no. 1 (January, 1946): 91ff.

[51] Anonymous, 'Come, woeful Orpheus,' in John Williams, ed., *English Renaissance Poetry* (Fayetteville: The University of Arkansas Press, 1990), 271. Another sixteenth-century English poem which mention the soothing of music is Arthur Brooke's 'Romeus and Juliet' (1562).

Another example is found in Edmund Spenser's famous, *The Faerie Queen*:

> There many Minstrels make melody,
> To drive away the dull melancholy.[52]

One poem, 'In the praise of music,' by Humphrey Gifford, explains that music's secret power to soothe is based on taking the mind away from earthly things and turning the listener's thought to heaven.

> [Music] with her silver sounding tunes
> Revives man's dulled sprites;
> She feeds the ear, she fills the heart,
> With choice and rare delights.
> Her sugared descant doth withdraw
> Thy mind from earthly toys,
> And makes thee feel within thy breast
> A taste of heavenly joys.
> The planets and celestial parts
> Sweet harmony contain,
> Of which if creatures were deprived
> This world could not remain.
> It is no doubt the very deed
> Of golden melody
> That neighbors do together live
> In love and unity.
> Where man and wife agrees in one,
> Sweet music doth abound;
> But when such strings begin to jar,
> Unpleasant is the sound.

In Philip Sidney's prose masterpiece, *The Countesse of Pembrokes Arcadia*, a listener approaches a singer, hoping to find solace.

> But (as a lamentable tune is the sweetest music to a woeful mind) she drew near, in hope to find some companion of her misery.[53]

We are not told if the listener indeed found solace, but the musician, who certainly found none, is given a strangely gloomy description.

---

52 Edmund Spenser, *The Faerie Queene*, Book I, Canto V, iii. In Book II, Canto VI, iii, a lady sings for this purpose.

> And there sat a Lady fresh and fair,
> Making sweet solace to herself alone.

53 Sir Philip Sidney, *The Countesse of Pembrokes Arcadia*, I, Book II, i. In Book III, vi, a serenade is given outside a lady's window with music designed first to cause her to think of sorrow and then to 'think of it with sweetness.' In Robert Green's *Arbasto* (1584) a lady sings to soothe her own feelings and in his *Penelope Web* (1587) a madrigal is sung for this purpose.

> For the woeful person (as if the lute had evil joined with the voice) threw it to the ground with such like words: Alas, poor Lute, how much art thou deceived to think, that in my miseries thou could ease my woes, as in my careless times thou was wont to please my fancies? The time is changed, my Lute, the time is changed; and no more did my joyful mind then receive everything in a joyful consideration, then my careful mind now makes each thing taste like bitter juice of care. The evil is inward, my Lute, the evil is inward; which all thou doost doth serve but to make me think more freely of, and the more I think, the more cause I find of thinking, but less of hoping. And alas, what is then thy harmony, but the sweet meats of sorrow? The discord of my thoughts, my Lute, doth ill agree to the concord of thy strings.

In the plays of the Elizabethan theater one finds many scenes where music is called on to soothe a character. This has additional significance because scholars regard the plays of this period as having had the specific goal of being 'life-like.' Thus it is likely that the scene we find in Lyly's *The Woman in the Moone* represents ideas widely accepted.

> O then to sift that humor from her heart,
> Let us with Rondelays delight her ear:
> For I have heard that Music is a means,
> To calm the rage of melancholy mood.[54]

Shakespeare was certainly a playwright who carefully reflected every day life in London. In *Henry VIII* (III, i) the rejected queen Katherine calls for work to stop so she can have music to soothe her feelings.

> QUEEN. Take thy lute, wench; my soul grows sad with troubles;
>   Sing and disperse 'em, if thou canst. Leave working.

As always with Shakespeare the music used in the play cannot be identified, but in this case he gives us the lyrics for the song.

In *Romeo and Juliet* (IV, iv) music to soothe is called for but one of the musicians says it is an inappropriate time.

> PETER. O Musicians, because my heart itself plays 'My Heart is Full'—O play me some merry dump to comfort me.
> 1. MUSICIAN. Not a dump, we, 'tis no time to play now.

The style of music above called a 'dump' is a representative for that peculiar interest by the Elizabethans in the melancholic. Shakespeare gives us a more lengthy example of this interest in his *As You Like It*, where he creates a character, the cynical malcontent, Jaques, who is soothed by melancholy emotions. Amiens, a professional singer, sings a song which ends,

---

54 John Lyly, *The Woman in the Moone*, I, i. Other examples can be found in Lyly's *Campaspe*, V, iv; Christopher Marlowe's *Tamburlaine the Great*, Part I, IV, iv and Part II, II, iv. Examples where music does not work can be found in Lodge and Greene's *A Looking Glass for London and England* and in Kyd's *The Spanish Tragedy*.

> *Come hither, come hither, come hither!*
> *Here shall he see*
> *No enemy*
> *But winter and rough weather.*
>
> JAQUES. More, more, I prithee, more.
> AMIENS. It will make you melancholy, Monsieur Jaques.
> JAQUES. I thank it. More, I prithee, more. I can suck melancholy out of a song as a weasel sucks eggs. More, I prithee, more.
> AMIENS. My voice is ragged; I know I cannot please you.
> JAQUES. I do not desire you to please me; I do desire you to sing. Come, more: another stanzo. Call you 'em stanzos?
> AMIENS. What you will, Monsieur Jaques.
> JAQUES. Nay, I care not for their names; they owe me nothing. Will you sing?
> AMIENS. More at your request than to please myself.[55]

There are two instances in the Shakespeare plays where music is not effective in its capacity to soothe. In *Richard II* (III, iv) and in the *Merchant of Venice* (V, i), where Shakespeare provides the reason why music does not soothe. Jessica says, 'I am never merry when I hear sweet music.' Lorenzo answers, 'The reason is, your spirits are [in]attentive.'

In the Spanish stage repertoire there is a lengthy scene built around the use of music to soothe in Molina's Old Testament play, *Tamar's Revenge* (I, lines 320ff). One passage gives the theme:

> TAMAR. Oh, Dina, I am sick at heart.
> DINA. It gives respite to my sadness
>   when I start to sing.
> TAMAR. In that case,
>   give me your instrument to play …
>   Music was made to soothe our care.

And eventually, Dina tells us that the music has indeed soothed.

> Please go on; your music brings relief.
> It cools and tames this savage heat.

In Calderon's *The Constant Prince* (I, i) there is a rather bizarre scene in which a lady of the court of the King of Fez finds it soothing to hear the sad songs of the Christian captives. And in Calderon's *The Surgeon of Honor* (III) a shepherd musician, Tirso, makes this remarkable statement:

> Well, whatever it is, by God,
> We'll sing a little song for you

---

[55] *As You Like It*, II, v. References to music to soothe can also be found in the Witches scene in *Macbeth* [IV, i] ('Come, sisters, cheer we up his sprites') and to soothe survivors of a shipwreck in *The Tempest* [I, ii].

> and drive away your sorrows.
> There's nothing else that's worth a damn.[56]

On the French stage, among the plays of Moliere, one finds in the *Monsieur de Pourceaugnac* (I, viii) two doctors who recommend a series of draconian treatments for de Pourceaugnac, including bleeding (from a vein in the head) and that he should be 'purged, de-obstructed, and evacuated by suitable purgatives.' But first, one doctor recommends, the patient needs to be soothed:

> I think he ought to be cheered by pleasant conversation, songs, and instruments of music.[57]

In French literature of the Baroque we notice an interesting letter to the Earl of St. Albans in 1677, by Saint-Evremond (1610–1703), who writes of the familiar purpose of music to soothe the listener. He recommends, in this case, preparing for approaching death in the manner of Monsieur des Yveteaux of Paris.

> He died at eighty years of age, causing a saraband to be played to him, a little before he expired, that his soul, as he expressed himself, might slide away the easier.[58]

A similar reference can be found in a letter by the Duchesse d'Orleans, Elisabeth Charlotte, in a letter to the Electress Sophie, 24 May 1705, in which she mentions an interesting anecdote regarding the death of the Emperor Leopold (who was himself a composer).

> When the emperor, having received the sacraments, asked the doctors whether they knew of anything else that might help him. When they answered this question with 'No,' he called for all his musicians, sang hymns to their accompaniment, and thus died singing.

Voltaire mentions the use of music to soothe in his play, *The Prude* (IV, v), when Mme de Burlet says to Mme Dorfise, 'I have ordered him to get music, to purge your melancholy humors.' He also makes reference to this subject in several of his poems. A nice example is from his, 'The Nature of Pleasure.'

> That man is born to a propitious fate,
> Who to the muse his time can dedicate;
> He from the tuneful art derives repose,
> The Muse his anguish soothes, dispels his woes:

---

[56] Remarkable examples where music fails to soothe can be found in Molina's *Tamar's Revenge* (II, lines 170ff) and in Calderon's *Life is a Dream* (II, i),

> Sounds that only charm the ear
> Cannot soothe my sorrow's pain.

[57] In Scene Ten, two 'Italian Musicians dressed as grotesque doctors' attempt to soothe by singing.

[58] Quoted in *The Letters of Saint-Evremond*, ed. John Hayward (Freeport, NY: Books for Libraries Press, 1971), 189.

> He laughs at all the follies of mankind,
> And from his lyre a sure relief can find.[59]

In the Jacobean stage literature of the English Baroque there are many references to the use of music to soothe. In Beaumont and Fletcher's *The Lovers Progress* (III, i) a friar offers to have one of his novices sing to solace Clarange, who responds,

> And it will come timely,
> For I am full of melancholy thoughts,
> Against which I have heard with reason Musick
> To be the speediest cure, 'pray you apply it.'[60]

The novice's song begins,

> *A Dieu fond love, farewel you wanton powers,*
> *I am free again.*

Following the song,

> FRIAR. How do ye approve it?
> CLARANGE. It is a Heavenly Hymn, no ditty Father,
>   It passes through my ears unto my soul,
>   And works divinely on it.

And in Heywood's *A Woman Kilde with Kindnesse*,[61] a character is impatient and threatens,

> … quickly, if the Musicke overcome not my melancholly, I shall quarrell.

There are also several references to music *not* being able to soothe. These tend to be cases where somber music is played and it only makes the patient feel more gloomy. We find such a case in Beaumont and Fletcher's *The Coronation* (III, i), when the Queen complains,

> This is not Musick sprightly enough,
> It feeds the soul with melancholy.

Similarly, in these authors' *The Queen of Corinth* (III, ii), after the stage direction, 'A sad Song,'

> *Weep no more, nor sigh nor groan*
> *Sorrow calls no time that's gone …*

---

[59] 'The Nature of Pleasure,' in *The Works of Voltaire* (New York: St. Hubert Guild, 1901), XXXVI, 246. He mentions music soothing again in his poem 'The Henriade' and in his 'The Maid of Orleans' [Canto III].

[60] Other examples include Marston's *Antonio and Mellida* (III, ii) and his *What You Will* (II, i), Beaumont and Fletcher's *The Spanish Curate* (III, ii) and their *Thierry and Theodoret* (III, i).

[61] Heywood, *The Letters of Saint-Evremond*, II, 97.

> AGENOR. These heavy Ayres feed sorrow in her Lady,
>   And nourish it too strongly; like a Mother
>   That spoiles her Child with giving on't the will.

In Dekker's *Old Fortunatus* (III, i) a boy serenades Orleans with a lute, but the latter begs him to leave, saying, 'This musicke makes me but more out of tune.'[62]

The most interesting example from the later Restoration Theater repertoire is found in Thomas Otway's (1652–1685) *Alcibiades* (V, lines 108ff), where the king (just before he is murdered!) calls for his page:

> Boy take thy Lute, and with a pleasing Air
> Appease my sorrows, and delude my care.

Among the Jacobean poets there is a very unusual example by Milton found in 'Paradise Regained,' when Jesus says to Satan that 'I would delight my private hours with music or with poem' for the purpose of solace, provided it is in the Hebrew language.

In his poem, 'Halelviah,' George Wither (1588–1667) begs to learn the music which is so effective in soothing.[63]

> Teach me the skill,
> Of him, whose Harp assuaged
> Those passions ill,
> Which oft afflicted Saul.
> Teach me the strain
> Which calms mind's enraged;
> And, which from vain
> Affections, doth recall.

There are two more poems that we especially like, the first is an Epigram by Ben Jonson written for the publication of a book of music by Alphonso Ferrabosco.

> Which Musick had; or speake her knowne effects,
> That she removeth cares, sadness ejects,
> Declineth anger, persuades clemencie,
> Doth sweeten mirth, and heighten pietie.[64]

And we like a similar poem by Thomas Carew (1594–1639), in a poem inspired by the illness of a friend.

---

[62] Two additional example of this kind can be found in Middleton's *A Chaste Maid in Cheapside* (V, ii) and in his *The Iron Age*, Part II.

[63] Congreve's 'Hymn to St. Cecilia,' points out that music soothes immediately, whereas Reason is halted by [thinking about] 'Hopes or Fears betrayed.'

[64] *The Complete Poetry of Ben Jonson*, ed. William Hunter (New York: Norton, 1963), 65.

> Then let the God of Musick, with still charms,
> Her restless eyes in peaceful slumbers close,
> And with soft strains sweeten her calm repose.[65]

Another poet who wrote of the ability of music to soothe was George Herbert (1593–1633), a rector in the Church of England. In a poem entitled, 'Church Music,' he writes,

> Sweetest of sweets, I thank you! when displeasure
> Did through my body wound my mind,
> You took me hence, and in your house of pleasure
> A dainty lodging me assigned.[66]

Herbert also appears to have been a poet with considerable background in music. In his biography, by Izaak Walton, we find,

> During which time all, or the greatest diversion from his study, was the practice of music, in which he became a great master, and of which he would say, 'That it did relieve his drooping spirits, compose his distracted thoughts, and raised his weary soul so far above the earth, that it gave him an earnest of the joys of heaven before he possessed them.'[67]
>
> ......
>
> His chief recreation was music, in which heavenly art he was a most excellent master, and did himself compose many divine hymns and anthems, which he set and sung to his lute or viol; and through he was a lover of retiredness, yet his love to music was such, that he went usually twice every week on certain appointed days to the cathedral church in Salisbury; and at his return would say, that his time spent in prayer and cathedral music elevated his soul, and was his heaven upon earth. But before his return thence to Bemerton, he would usually sing and play his part at an appointed private music meeting; and, to justify this practice, he would often say, religion does not banish mirth, but only moderates and sets rules to it.

Walking once to such a chamber music rehearsal with his friends, Herbert apparently encountered a man with a horse in distress, whom he stopped to help. When his clergy friends suggested that he had 'disparaged himself by so dirty an employment,' he responded that,

> the thought of what he had done would prove music to him at midnight, and that the omission of it would have upbraided and made discord in his conscience … 'And now let us tune our instruments.'

Walton tells us that days before Herbert's death, he rose suddenly from his bed and couch, called for one of his instruments, took it into his hand, and cried,

> My God, my God!
> My music shall find Thee,
> And every string
> Shall have his attribute to sing.

---

[65] 'Upon the sickness of …,' in *The Poems of Thomas Carew*, ed. Rhodes Dunlap (Oxford: Clarendon Press, 1964), 31.
[66] 'Church Music,' in *The Poems of George Herbert*, ed. Ernest Rhys (London: Walter Scott, 1885), 59.
[67] Ibid., 260ff.

In general, the seventeenth century in England was rather somber, due to the very strong influence of the Puritans, a strict, fundamentalist religious movement. We sense this mood in a prose work by Thomas Browne (1605–1682), who points to those lucky enough to have music to help them sleep.

> Half our days we pass in the shadow of the earth; and the brother of death exacts a third part of our lives. A good part of our sleep is peered out with visions and fantastical objects, wherein we are confessedly deceived. The day supplies us with truths; the night with fictions and falsehoods, which uncomfortably divide the natural account of our beings. And, therefore, having passed the day in sober labors and rational enquiries of truth, we are fain to betake ourselves into such a state of being, wherein the soberest heads have acted all the monstrosities of melancholy, and which unto open eyes are no better than folly and madness.
>
> Happy are they that go to bed with grand music, like Pythagoras, or have ways to compose the fantastical spirit, whose unruly wanderings take off inward sleep.[68]

We turn now to the Puritan writers. John Donne (1573–1631) in one of his sermons explains that God gave man music to settle his emotions.

> And, to tune us, to compose and give us a harmonie and concord of affections, in all perturbations and passions, and discords in the passages of this life …[69]

The Reverend Joseph Hall (1574–1656) writes in several places of the special solace on hearing music at night. Other early philosophers mention this observation and one wonders if our tradition today of turning off the lights during concerts has its roots in these early ideas.

> How sweetly doth this music sound in this dead season! In the daytime it would not, it could not so much affect the ear. All harmonious sounds are advanced by a silent darkness.[70]

Hall finds a parallel in the glad tidings of salvation in the 'night of persecution of our private affliction.'[71] He expands on this idea in another work called 'Songs in the Night.'

> There is no time wherein [songs of praise] can be unseasonable: yea, rather, as all our artificial melody is wont to sound sweetest in the dark, so those songs are most pleasing to thee which we sing in the saddest night of our affliction …
>
> The night is a dismal season, attended with solitude and horror, and an aggravation of those pains and cares whereof the day is in any sort guilty … Songs in the night, are not, cannot be of nature's making, but are the sole gift of the heavenly Comforter.

---

68 *Sir Thomas Browne's Works*, ed. Simon Wilkin (London: Pickering, 1836), IV, 355.

69 John Donne, 'A Sermon preached at Pauls Crosse,' in *Five Sermons* (Menston: Scolar Press, 1970), 3.

70 'The Breathings of the Devout Soul,' in *The Works of Joseph Hall, D. D.*, ed. Philip Wynter (New York: AMS Press, 1969), VIII, 18ff.

71 'Occasional Meditations,' in Ibid., X, 142.

> And if we, out of the strength of our moral powers, shall be setting songs to ourselves in the night of our utmost disconsolation, woe is me, how miserably out of tune they are! how harsh, how misaccented, how discordous even to the sense of our own souls, much more in the ears of the Almighty, in whom dwells nothing beneath an infinite perfection!
>
> But the songs that thou, O God, puttest into the mouths of thy servants in the night of their tribulation are so exquisitely harmonious, as that thine angels rejoice to hear them, and disdain not to match them with their hallelujahs in heaven.[72]

Gervase Markham, in his *Countrey Contentments* (1615), makes it one of the characteristics of becoming a gentleman to be able to perform music, even for himself, when it is needed to soothe.

> A gentleman should not be unskillful in Music, that whensoever either melancholy, heaviness of his thoughts, or the perturbations of his own fancies, stirreth up sadness in him, he may remove the same with some godly Hymn or Anthem, of which David gives him ample examples.[73]

We conclude these many illustrations testifying to the ability of music to soothe with a nice poem by Abraham Cowley (1618–1667) which tells us that even birds benefit from music for this purpose.

> And when no Art affords me help or ease,
> I seek with verse my griefs to appease.
> Just as a bird that flies about
> And beats itself against the cage,
> Finding at last no passage out,
> It sits and sings, and so overcomes its rage.[74]

This, in turn, reminds us of a poem by George Wither in which a man thinks of his life as lived in a cage.

> But, though that all the world's delight forsake me,
> I have a Muse, and she shall Musicke make me:
> Whose airy notes, in spite of closest cages,
> Shall give content to me, and after ages.[75]

---

72 'Souls in the Night,' in Ibid., VII, 326.

73 Quoted in Robert Donnington, *The Interpretation of Early Music* (New York, 1964), 117.

74 'Friendship in Absence,' in *The Complete Works of Abraham Cowley*, ed. Alexander Grosart (New York: AMS Press, 1967), II, 139.

75 *Works of George Wither* (New York: Franklin, 1967), Spenser Society, Nr. 10, a Sonnet, in 'the Shepheards Hunting,' 529.

Ancient Views on Movement and Music

Music is invisible dance, as dancing is silent music.[1]
Jean Paul Richter

ONE MIGHT SUPPOSE THAT THE CLOSE RELATIONSHIP between movement and music begins in the fetus, where both hearing and movement develop in the inner ear. Therefore it should be no surprise to find the earliest of early men using movement as a form of communication long before the earliest speech. Lower animals, of course, also use movement as a means of communication, in particular with regard to mating ritual. Aristotle also found something very natural in the association of music and movement. 'Why,' he asks, 'do all men love music?'

> Is it because we naturally rejoice in natural movements? This is shown by the fact that children rejoice in [rhythm and melody] as soon as they are born. Now we delight in the various types of melody for their moral character, but we delight in rhythm because it contains a familiar and ordered number and moves in a regular manner; for ordered movement is naturally more akin to us than disordered, and is therefore more in accordance with nature.[2]

Curt Sachs, in his discussion of dance in primitive societies, also found this natural association.

> Whether we speak of individuals or of entire tribes, peoples, and races, their melodies and dances must always be closely related. For both are determined by the same impulse to motion.[3]

The association of music and dance is so close, and so ancient, that for centuries some writers remained unable to think of music without this association. Jean Paul Richter, the writer who so influenced nineteenth-century Romantic composers, considered that 'music is invisible dance, as dancing is silent music.'[4] Some early philosophers, focusing on the communicative nature of music, go even further. Agnolo Segni, in 1573, advanced the idea that music, language and dance are all imitations of each other.[5] Johannes Cochlaeus, in 1511, defined four categories of musician: orators, poets, mimes and (what *we* call) musicians.[6]

---

[1] *Levana* (1807).
[2] 'Problemata,' 920b.28.
[3] Curt Sachs, *World History of the Dance* (New York: Norton, 1937), 183.
[4] *Levana* (1807).
[5] 'Lezioni intorno alla poesia,' quoted in Claude V. Palisca, *Humanism in Italian Renaissance Musical Thought* (New Haven: Yale University Press, 1985), 401.
[6] *Tetrachordum Musices*.

The association between movement and music is documented in the oldest extant literature. For example, a stone relief from the Assyrian Empire (750–606 BC) pictures two male harpists who are dancing while playing. The lyric poets of ancient Greece, who flourished during the sixth and seventh centuries BC, were poets who sang their works in public performance. Athenaeus reports that while they performed with few facial expressions, they were active with their feet, 'both in marching and in dance steps.'[7]

The most interesting ancient medium which combined music and movement were the Greek choirs, because what we know of their movements suggests they were used specifically to express, or amplify, the emotions of the music they sang.[8] We first find reference to the Greek choral movements in a poem by the lyric poet, Alkman, in which he complains that he is too old and weak to *dance* with the chorus.

The historian, Xenophon (434–355 BC) suggests that a social value was placed on coordinated motions by the choir.

> There is nothing so convenient nor so good for human beings as order. Thus, a chorus is a combination of human beings; but when the members of it do as they choose, it becomes mere confusion, and there is no pleasure in watching it; but when they act and sing in an orderly fashion, then those same men at once seem worth seeing and worth hearing.[9]

Plato, in a lengthy discussion of music competitions (*Laws*, 659d) was concerned that the choirs not use the gestures of freemen and that the rhythms of the dance correspond with those of the melody.

After the rediscovery and republication of the ancient Greek treatises, Western European philosophers took note of the Greek's use of movement and music. Roger Bacon (b. ca. 1214) wrote of a category of music which he calls 'visual music,' which is of great significance. The ancient Greek philosophers never discussed this topic at length, but there are sufficient hints in their descriptions of choral performance to suggest that the inevitable movements by the singers were thought of not as a kind of dance, but as the part of music you could see. One must remember that the Greeks placed considerable significance in the fact that one cannot *see* music and it was for this reason that music was so closely associated with religion (whose principal mysteries also cannot be seen). Bacon's discussion supplies important insights into this ancient association of music and movement.

> Music, moreover, consisting in what is visible, is necessary; and that it is such is evident from the book on the Origin of the Sciences. For whatever can be conformed to sound in similar movements and in corresponding formations, so that our delight may be made complete not only by hearing, but by seeing, belongs to music. Therefore dances and all bendings of bodies are reduced to gesture,

---

7 Athenaeus, *Deipnosophistae*, I, 22.

8 Curt Sachs believed the development of choirs from the solo singers was begun by the Dorians, as a reflection on the higher emphasis on social order than on individual freedom, and that the Greek choral dance was used to vent youthful exuberance (*choreia*, which he believed came from *chara*, 'joy'). [*World History of the Dance*, 239, 237]

9 'Oeconomicus,' VIII, trans. E. C. Marchant, *Memorabilia and Oeconomicus* (Cambridge: Harvard University Press, 1953).

which is a branch of music, since these are conformed to sound in similar movements and corresponding formations, as the author of the aforesaid book maintains. Therefore Aristotle says in the seventh book of the Metaphysics that the art of dancing is not complete without another art, that is, without another kind of music to which the art of dancing is conformed.[10]

Girolamo Cardano (1501–1576) wrote that, 'In antiquity dancing was called a sixth part of music.'[11] He also adds an interesting observation on the relationship of ancient dance and music which we have not found in extant ancient literature, that the movements of Greek choral performances were patterned on even earlier statues.

> Dancing and gesticulation express the ample movements that were left from antique statues, and the movements were then transferred from the figures to choral dances, and from choral dances to wrestling schools.[12]

It does seem reasonable to assume that one of the very earliest physiological manifestations of music was dance. We know from the footprints in the caves of Spain that very ancient man danced to music. The ancient physiological connection between movement and music is easily understood if one, once again, reminds oneself that *real* music is something that occurs *live*. That is, live music travels through time, linking the listener with the performer lock-step in present tense. It is in this experience of music moving through time where you will find the ancient origin for musicians and listeners experiencing the urge to express themselves by physical movement while hearing the music. It was a form of acknowledgement of their being connected with their experience in the present tense.

The fundamental relationship between music and movement is the expression of feeling. Movement is also a kind of *visual* emotion and thus only a single character separates 'motion' from 'emotion' in our language. It is because of this relationship that the ancients often thought of dance as the part of music that you could see. It is for this reason that Socrates, in a discussion of the knowledge necessary to be a good musician,[13] maintains that a musician must understand how emotions are reflected in movement and that this movement ought to be called music.

> … when you have learned also how similar emotions appear and come to be in the movements of bodies, which when measured by numbers ought, as they say, to be called rhythms and measures …

There is one more important point to be made along these lines. First, the sole purpose of music is to communicate feeling and emotion; every listener understands that. Thus, it follows that it is because of this mirror-like relationship between music and dance, movements themselves are capable of communicating powerful emotions. It is because this understanding

---

[10] 'Mathematics,' XVI, in *The Opus Majus of Roger Bacon*, trans. Robert Burke (New York: Russell & Russell), I, 259.

[11] Quoted in Clement Miller, *Hieronymus Cardanus, Writings on Music* (American Institute of Musicology, 1973), 117.

[12] Ibid., 119.

[13] Plato, *Philebus*, 17c.

is also very ancient that we have one of the most frequently retold tales of ancient Greece. Herodotus, the great fifth century BC historian, tells this story of a great banquet during which a final group of suitors for the daughter of Cleisthenes were to compete with each other 'in music and in talking in company.'

> In both these accomplishments, it was Hippocleides who proved by far the doughtiest champion, until at last, as more and more wine was drunk, he asked the flute player to play him a tune and began to dance to it. Now it may well be that he danced to his own satisfaction; Cleisthenes, however, who was watching the performance, began to have serious doubts about the whole business. Presently, after a brief pause, Hippocleides sent for a table; the table was brought, and Hippocleides, climbing on to it, danced first some Laconian dances, next some Attic ones, and ended by standing on his head and beating time with his legs in the air. The Laconian and Attic dances were bad enough; but Cleisthenes, though he already loathed the thought of having a son-in-law like that, nevertheless restrained himself and managed to avoid an outburst; but when he saw Hippocleides beating time with his legs, he could bear it no longer. 'Son of Tisander,' he cried, 'you have danced away your marriage.'[14]

Thucydides, the fifth century BC historian, wrote of a tradition of the festival accompanying the Delian games which was already centuries old.

The cities brought choirs of dancers. Nothing can be clearer on this point than the following verses of Homer, taken from a hymn to Apollo:

> Phoebus, where'er thou strayest, far or near,
> Delos was still of all thy haunts most dear,
> Thiter the robed Ionians take their way
> With wife and child to keep they holiday,
> Invoke thy favor on each manly game,
> And dance and sing in honor of thy name.[15]

Another ancient tradition which we wish we knew more about, dating from the eighth century BC, is recorded by Livy. He writes of these choirs in processionals 'chanting their hymns to the triple beat of their ritual dance.'[16]

Based on the little literature which survives, it appears the use of movement by the ancient Greek choirs (*khoros*) was already common by the time of the lyric poets, seventh century BC. According to Athenaeus, at this time the singers used few facial expressions, but were active with the feet, 'both in marching and in dance steps.'[17] Pindar's (b. ca. 518 BC) 'Ode for Hieron of Aetna, Winner of the Chariot Race,' clearly implies the steps of the feet were specifically based on the music itself.

---

14 Herodotus, *The Histories*, VI, 128.

15 Thucydides, *The Peloponnesian War*, III, 103.

16 Livy, *The History of Rome*, I, 20.

17 *Deipnosophistae*, I, 22. One of these early poets, Alkman (ca. 640–600 BC) was a choral conductor.

> O glorious lyre, joint treasure of Apollo
> And of the Muses violet-tressed,
> Your notes the dancers' step obeys.[18]

Although we know little about the specific movements the ancient Greek choral groups used in their performances, or how they were specifically intended to underwrite the emotions of the song, it seems safe to say they were probably continuing very ancient traditions. Dance to music, of course, must be ancient far beyond literature. There are early pictures of dancers and music, such as a fragment of a Sumerian vase which dates from 3200 BC, which shows two lyre players accompanying a dance. But this may be considered relatively modern if one recalls the evidence of music and dancing in the cave paintings.

Among the tomb paintings of ancient Egypt we are attracted to an extraordinary painting from the more recent Graeco-Roman temple at Medamund, north of Thebes, which includes a complete hymn to the god Hathor. We see a group of female musicians, with harp, drum, and lute, beneath an hieroglyph description:

> The members of the choir take up their instruments and play them. The songstresses in full number adore the Golden Goddess and make music to the Golden Goddess: they never cease their chanting.

The lyrics of the hymn are written behind the lutanist and a singer. We take notice especially of the emotional aim of this music and movement, 'nourishment for the heart.'

> Come, O Golden Goddess, the singers chant
> for it is nourishment for the heart to dance the *iba*,
> to shine over the feast at the hour of retiring
> and to enjoy dance at night.[19]

We should also point out that there is one extraordinary hieroglyph from Amarna, dating 1,580 BC, which pictures a music school. In addition to illustrating various scenes of music instruction and store rooms for instruments, we see in one classroom a harpist and instructor teaching movement.

There is another important form of movement captured in the tomb paintings, and that is the early conductor. He was first named a *chironomist*, 'one who gestures with his hands,' by Marcus Fabius Quintilinus. One hieroglyph representation of him we particularly like for he is identified through two hieroglyph symbols as one who 'sings with the arm.' A perfect definition, it seems to us, of a good conductor's movements.

---

[18] Geoffrey S. Conway, *The Odes of Pindar* (London: Dent, 1972), 81.

[19] Quoted in Lise Manniche, *Music and Musicians in Ancient Egypt* (London: British Museum Press, 1991), 61.

Before we leave this brief survey of movement and music in the ancient worlds, there are two other rather interesting facets. First, examples of a dancer who sings at the same time are not rare.[20] This is a subject that Franz Liszt once reflected on.

> Dancing, being inseparable from music, lends itself naturally to singing; especially among primitive nations. Civilization eradicates and stifles this tendency by increasing the measure of what is expected from each art; and thus compelling it to adopt an isolated position, in order to become perfect. The union however always persists, until by degrees divorce becomes quite compulsory. Thus it happens that, in several countries (not by any means the least civilized) a custom survives of accompanying certain portions of the dance by choruses, interspersed with couplets, partly recited and partly sung by the principal dancer. In Poland, a neighboring country, the Krakowiaki and the Tropaki present examples, some of which have become quite celebrated in the history of national music.[21]

There are some early illustrations of a much more rare practice of instrumentalists who dance while they play. The most interesting of these, an ancient Assyrian stone-relief, shows a reception for Ashur-Idanni-Pal (668–626 BC) by the city of Susiana, in Elam. Here we see three male harp players, two of whom are dancing while playing; a man playing a kind of dulcimer, who is also dancing; a male aulos player; four female harp players; female players of an aulos and a drum; together with thirteen singers.

The association of music and dance also appears to have been a basic component in education in ancient Greece. The children were instructed in some instrumental music, the principal medium for music education in Plato's utopia was singing, which he seems to have envisioned as being coordinated with dance.

> AN ATHENIAN STRANGER. The whole choral art is also in our view the whole of education; and of this art, rhythms and harmonies form the part which has to do with the voice.
> CLEINIAS. Yes.
> AN ATHENIAN STRANGER. The movement of the body has rhythm in common with the movement of the voice, but gesture is peculiar to it, whereas song is simply the movement of the voice.
> CLEINIAS. Most true.
> AN ATHENIAN STRANGER. And the sound of the voice which reaches and educates the soul, we have ventured to term music.[22]

In another reference to this relationship, Plato also explains how accountability may be measured.

> AN ATHENIAN STRANGER. And the uneducated is he who has not been trained in the chorus, and the educated is he who has been well trained?
> CLEINIAS. Certainly.
> AN ATHENIAN STRANGER. And the chorus is made up of two parts, dance and song?

---

20 In *Euphues' Shadowe* (1592) by the Elizabethan playwright, Thomas Lodge, Philamis commands the cornets to play a 'Barginet,' to which he sings and dances. Similarly, in Moliere's *The Affected Ladies* (scene xiii) Mascarille sings and dances.

21 *The Gipsy in Music* [1859], (London: William Reeves, 1960), 292.

22 *Laws*, 672e.

CLEINIAS. True.

AN ATHENIAN STRANGER. Then he who is well educated will be able to sing and dance well?

CLEINIAS. I suppose that he will.

AN ATHENIAN STRANGER. Let us see; what are we saying?

CLEINIAS. What?

AN ATHENIAN STRANGER. He sings well and dances well; now must we add that he sings what is good and dances what is good?

CLEINIAS. Let us make that addition.

AN ATHENIAN STRANGER. We will suppose that he knows the good to be good, and the bad to be bad, and makes use of them accordingly: which now is the better trained in dancing and music—he who is able to move his body and use his voice in what he understands to be the right manner, but has no delight in good or hatred of evil; or he who is scarcely correct in gesture and voice and in understanding, but is right in his sense of pleasure and pain, and welcomes what is good, and is offended at what is evil?

CLEINIAS. There is a great difference, stranger, in the two kinds of education.

AN ATHENIAN STRANGER. If we know what is good in song and dance, then we truly know also who is educated and who is uneducated; but if not, then we certainly shall not know wherein lies the safeguard of education, and whether there is any or not.[23]

When the period of the ancient Greek drama arrives (fifth century BC), movement also plays an important role in the function of the chorus. According to Athenaeus, Thespis, Pratinas, Cratinus, and Phrynichus among older playwrights 'not only relied upon the dancing of the chorus for the interpretation of their plays, but, quite apart from their own compositions, they taught dancing to all who wanted instruction.'[24] Aethenaeus also notes that the first great playwright, Aeschylus, took a very personal interest in the movements of the chorus.

> Aeschylus was the first to give poses to his choruses, employing no dancing masters, but devising for himself the figures of the dance, and in general taking upon himself the entire management of the piece.[25]

Athenaeus also tells us that the great playwright, Sophocles, himself, was expert in both music and dancing.

> Sophocles, besides being handsome in his youth, became proficient in dancing and music, while still a lad, under the instruction of Lamprus. After the battle of Salamis, at any rate, he danced to the accompaniment of his lyre around the trophy, naked and anointed with oil. Others say he danced with his cloak on. And when he brought out the *Thamyris* he played the lyre himself.[26]

The ancient relationship between movement and music, particularly with respect to the communication of emotions, served as the foundation for later reflection on the more specific gestures used by actors and orators. In these writings we find ideas which have a very close

---

23 Ibid., 654b.

24 Athenaeus, *Deipnosophistae*, I, 22.

25 Ibid., I, 22.

26 Ibid., I, 20.

correspondence to the gestures of conducting. It was in Elizabethan England that modern theater had its revival and in *Hamlet* (III, ii) Shakespeare provides a brief discussion of the gestures of the actor, which of course came from his own experience on the stage. He seems primarily concerned that the gestures of the actor not communicate emotions at a higher level than the ordinary viewers can identify with. He pleas for natural gestures for which he advises the actor to 'hold, as it were, the mirror up to nature.'

From the early eighteenth century, Johann Mattheson (1681–1764) provides, under the title, 'On the Art of Gesticulation,'[27] an extraordinary discussion of the emotions as expressed by gesture. His frequent reference to music is typical of most early discussion of oratory.

The proper term for the art of gesticulation, according to Mattheson, is *Hypocritica*, which he says Cassiodorus defined as 'silent music.' Quintillian defined it as 'the science of hand gesticulation,' but used the term *chironomy*—a term which, as we shall see below, we specifically associate with the beginning of conducting.

But the word *Hypocritica*, for Mattheson, means more than chironomy, for *Hypo* (under) and *Crisis* (criticism) suggests the submission of one's thoughts for judgment. This should be thought of in a positive sense, as a form of stimulation, and not in the ill-meant 'hypocrisy.' The origin, and source of power, for gesture is found in its universality. First, Mattheson points out that language itself only developed as a shadow of action.[28] Second, he touches on a very important point.

> Words do not move a person who does not understand the language; discriminating words are good only for discriminating minds; but everyone understands the well-used facial expression, even young children with whom neither words nor beatings have as much effect as a glance.[29]

This observation is more important than Mattheson realized, with respect to universality, for modern research has shown that both facial expressions and the basic emotions are universal and the latter are formed before birth and are thus not learned, but genetic.

Mattheson classifies this subject under *oratorical*, which directs the movement of the body; the *histrionic*, which belongs to plays and requires much stronger gesturing than the first; and the *saltatorial*, which deals with all kinds of steps and leaps.

The oratorical he considered to be closely related to music, for music is 'an oratory in tones' and the ancient orators 'gleaned their best rules from music.' As he pauses at this point to discuss music, he seems to include under the concept of gesture the actions of the entire body. Regarding the singers in church he observes,

---

[27] Johann Mattheson, *Der Volkommene Capellmeister* (1739), trans. Ernest Harris (Ann Arbor: UMI Research Press, 1981), I, vi.

[28] Ibid., I, vi, 5.

[29] Ibid., I, vi, 6.

It would be desirable that if no proper gestures take place out of bad habit, at least nothing of a quite inappropriate, indecent, or cold and indifferent mien would occur: of which unfortunately! we are so little lacking that often the most serious and sacred pieces are sung and played in such a shameless manner, chattering, smirking, trifling, so that devout listeners are very annoyed.

I have attended many, many a Passion and Requiem which to my great chagrin evoked audible joking and laughter.[30]

Secular concert music is criticized for similar reasons.

If we go from the church to the concert room, one likewise encounters quite marvelous and diverse unseemly poses at Concerts which sometimes do not have anything in common with what is going on ... [Most players] seem to me like people who care only about filling their stomach and not about elegant taste.

Can the attentive listener be moved to pleasure if he is constantly disturbed by the noise of someone beating time, be it with his feet or hands? If he sees a dozen violinists who contort their bodies as if they are ill? If the clavier player writhes his jaw, wrinkles his brow, and contorts his face to such an extent that it could frighten children? If many of the wind instrumentalists contort or inflate their facial features so that they can bring them back to their proper shape and color in half an hour only with difficulty?[31]

Mattheson also provides some interesting national differences which he observed in performance.

If we turn from playing to singing, oh! that is when the misery really begins. Look at the fervor with which the French men and women singers present their pieces, and how they almost always seem really to feel what they are singing. Hence the reason that they strongly stir the emotions of the listeners, particularly their countrymen, and replace through gesticulation and mannerisms what they lack in thorough instruction, in strength, or in vocal ability.

The Italians carry this even further than the French; indeed, sometimes they even go a little too far: As in almost all their undertakings they frequently overstep the limits and love the extremes. Meanwhile they frequently have tears in their eyes when they perform something that is melancholy; and on the other hand, their heart is overjoyed when there is something enjoyable: for they are very emotional by nature ...

Only the cool Germans, although they have revealed to the Italians their great musical abilities through the three great H's, namely Händel, Heinichen and Hasse, on the one hand place their greatest merit in the fact that they look just as stiff and unemotional with the sad as well as the cheerful affections with which their music deals ... they sing very decently and rigidly, as if they had no interest in the content, and are not in the least concerned with the consideration of the proper expression or meaning of the words ... as is demonstrated daily by teachers and students. On the other hand, it is quite a favor if they do not gossip with, trifle with or ridicule their neighbors during rests; even if the things of which they sing would be worthy of the highest attention.[32]

---

30 Ibid., I, vi, 11ff.

31 Ibid., I, vi, 15ff.

32 Ibid., I, vi, 18ff.

The true goal for both church and concert performance, Mattheson summarizes, is 'that gesture, words and music form a three-part braid, and should perfectly harmonize with each other toward the goal that the feeling of the listener be stirred.'

Turning to the theater, here, he says, is 'the real college for all sorts of gesticulations.'[33] *Hypocritica*, communication through gesture, is what an actor does. It is in pretending what he is not, notes Mattheson, that we get the origin of 'hypocrite.' Here also one finds the dance, in which *Hypocritica* 'is as indispensable as the feet themselves.' So closely related are the dancer's gestures and the music, that he finds most dancing masters prefer to write their own melodies. If the composer is to compose the dance music, then he must understand dance and in this regard Mattheson points to Lully who 'personally instructed all his actors, actresses, and male and female dancers in this art of gesticulation.'[34]

In conclusion, Mattheson points to the importance of gesture in all the arts of ancient Greece and Rome, including mime and pantomime which he says often moved the spectators to tears. The ancient system of notation of gesture, of which he regrets precise knowledge is now lost, was called *Orchesin* in Greek and *Saltationem* in Latin. As a summary of the importance of these relationships in the ancient world, he quotes a contemporary, Charles Rollin, *Histoire ancienne* (Paris, 1730–1738).

> The art of gesticulation also belongs to music, it illustrates and teaches the steps and postures of dance as well as of the common walk, together with the postures which one uses in a public oration. In short, music comprehends all the art of composing and writing public utterances that have nothing to do with singing, through which annotations the sound of the voice is speech as well as the tempo and movement of the gestures would be ordered: which was a very useful art to the ancients but is completely unknown to us.[35]

With respect to the correspondence of the use of gesture among orators, actors and conductors, we find even more interesting detail in the discussion of the use of specific body members, beginning with the hands. In a long discussion on communication, which includes his interesting perception of animal communication, Michel de Montaigne (1533–1592) reminds us of the rather extraordinary possibilities of non-verbal hand-signal communications, which we perceive by sight alone.

> And what about our hands? With them we request, promise, summon, dismiss, menace, pray, supplicate, refuse, question, show astonishment, count, confess, repent, fear, show shame, doubt, teach, command, incite, encourage, make oaths, bear witness, make accusations, condemn, give absolution,

---

33 Ibid., I, vi, 23ff.

34 Ibid., I, vi, 26.

35 Ibid., I, vi, 35. Mattheson concludes this chapter with an account of the the Imperial composer in Vienna in 1730, Francesso Conti, who, having 'used his art of gesticulation in a most wicked manner,' was placed on bread and water, beaten by a priest and forced to stand before the doors of St. Stefan Cathedral in a long hairy coat holding a black candle for an hour!

insult, despise, defy, provoke, flatter, applaud, bless, humiliate, mock, reconcile, advise, exalt, welcome, rejoice, lament; show sadness, grieve, despair, astonish, cry out, keep silent and what not else, with a variety and multiplicity rivaling the tongue.[36]

Charles Gildon, in his 1710 biography of the famous English actor, Thomas Betterton, provides an extensive survey of the theory of theater gestures in the late Baroque. Regarding the hands, he begins with a similar list of commonly recognized gestures.

> The lifting of one hand upright, or extending it, expresses force, vigor and power. The right hand is also extended upwards as a token of swearing, or taking a solemn oath; and this extension of the hand sometimes signifies pacification, and desire of silence.
> The putting of the hand to the mouth is the habit of one, that is silent and acting modestly; of admiration and consideration. The giving the hand is the gesture of striking a bargain, confirming an alliance, or of delivering ones self into the power of another. To take hold of the hand of another expresses admonition, exhortation, and encouragement. The reaching out of an hand to another implies help and assistance. The lifting up both hands on high is the habit of one who implores, and expresses his misery. And the lifting up of both hands sometimes signifies congratulation to Heaven for a deliverance ...
> The holding the hands in the bosom is the habit of the idle and negligent. Clapping the hands, among the Hebrews signified deriding, insulting, and exploding; but among the Greeks and the Romans it was, on the contrary, the expression of applause.[37]

Gildon warns that one must avoid all affectation in gesture, which he notes will always appear 'commonly ridiculous and odious.' Rather, all gestures should be true and appropriate to the emotions one intends to express.

> To make these motions of the face and hands easily understood, that is, useful in the moving of the passions of the auditors, or rather spectators, they must be properly adapted to the thing you speak of, your thoughts and design; and always resembling the *passion* you would express or excite.[38]

The gestures of the hands are so powerful, he says, that we are even moved when we see them pictured in a painting. Furthermore, they are so universally understood, as to be a kind of international language.

> Gesture has this advantage above mere speaking, that by this we're only understood by those of our own language, but by action and gesture we make our thoughts and passions intelligible to all nations and tongues.[39]

The most interesting rule given by Gildon regarding the gestures of the hands is a warning that unless a careful distinction is made between left and right hand gestures, the actor (or lawyer, or preacher, he says) may offend the viewer. He pauses to observe that the actor's ear will

---

36 Ibid., II, xi, 507.

37 Charles Gildon, *The Life of Mr. Thomas Betterton* [1710] (London: Frank Cass, 1970), 46.

38 Gildon, Ibid., 53.

39 Ibid., 50.

correct mistakes in his voice, but since he cannot see his own gestures, especially those of his face, some actors practice before a mirror. But this is very dangerous, says Gildon, for everything will appear backwards, that is the left hand will appear as the right, etc. His real concern, in this regard, he expresses in the following rule:

> If an action comes to be used by only one hand, that must be by the *right*, it being indecent to make a gesture with the *left* alone.[40]

Indecent?! Why would society consider the use of the left hand alone to be *indecent*? First of all, this brings to mind the fact that throughout the entire history of literature there has been documented a clear preference for the *right* hand. Familiar to us all are the expressions regarding the favorite sitting on the *right* hand of the king and the *left*-handed compliment. At the direction of Jesus, his disciples catch fish on the right side of the boat, but nothing on the left. Morally we claim to be in the right, but no one is ever said to be 'in the left.'

Physiologically, the explanation for this right hand preference has its roots in the dominance of the left hemisphere of the brain (which controls the right hand), which does our speaking and writing for us and which tends to not even acknowledge the existence of the right hemisphere of the brain. On the social level, however, the explanation lies in an ancient hygienic practice. Before the advent of toilet paper, man traditionally performed this specific daily function with his *left* hand. It is for *this* reason that Gildon considers the use of the left hand alone 'indecent,' and it is for this reason why even today we offer *only* the *right* hand to shake hands and why we hold the baton with the right hand.

With regard to movements of the head, Gildon suggests that moving it from one side to the other, 'wantonly and lightly,' reflects folly and inconstancy.[41] Hanging the head down suggests grief and sorrow, while lifting the head or tossing it up conveys the gesture of pride and arrogance. Carrying the head high is a sign of joy, victory and triumph, but a 'hard and bold' forehead suggests obstinacy, contumacy, perfidiousness and impudence. Hanging the head on the breast he finds 'disagreeable to the eye,' while leaving the head in a position of leaning toward the shoulders is 'rustic, affected, a mark of indifference and languidness.'

The eye-brows should for the most part remain in a natural position, not always raised when speaking in earnest and much less one up and one down. Better, he recommends, to save them for moments of passion, 'to contract themselves and frown in sorrow, to smooth and dilate themselves in joy and to hang down in humility.'

Thrusting out the belly or throwing back the head Gildon finds 'unbecoming and indecent.' Shrugging the shoulders he does not admit in oratory, although he finds it is sometimes appropriate in comedy. He relates how a famous ancient orator cured himself of this habit.

---

[40] Ibid., 74.

[41] Ibid., 42–43, 58–59.

> I have read of a pleasant method that Demosthenes took to cure himself of this vice of action, for he at first was mightily given to it. He used to exercise himself in oration in a narrow and straight place, with a dagger hung just over his shoulders, so that as often as he shrugged them up, the point, by pricking his shoulders, put him in mind of his error.[42]

Of course it is the face in which Gildon finds the most powerful gestures are created. To turn the face toward an object conveys one's attention, to bend the face down suggests consciousness and guilt while lifting it up 'is a sign of good conscience or innocence, hope and confidence.'

> The face is changed into many forms and is commonly the most certain index of the passions of the mind. When it is pale it betrays grief, sorrow, and fear, and envy, when it is very strong. A leering and dark visage is the index of misery, labor and vehement agitations of the soul.[43]

As the face reveals the emotions, 'the soul is most visible in the eyes.'

> Eyes lifted on high show arrogance and pride, but cast down express humbleness of mind ...
> Denial, aversion, nauseating, dissimulation, and neglect are expressed by a turning away of the eyes.
> A frequent winking, or tremulous motion of the eyes argues malicious manners, and perverse and noxious thought and inclinations.
> Eyes drowned in tears discovers the most vehement and cruel grief.[44]

If, Gildon suggests, one is sincere in his feelings, his eyes will express the correct emotions and with a power that will move the audience.

> For then Nature, if you obey its summons, will alter your looks and gestures. Thus when a man speaks in anger his imagination is inflamed, and kindles a sort of fire in his eyes, which sparkles from them in such a manner, that a stranger who understood not a word of the language, or a deaf man that could not hear the loudest tone of his voice, would not fail to perceive his fury and indignation. And this fire of his eyes will easily strike those of the audience ... and by a strange sympathetic infection, it will set them on fire too with the very same passion.[45]

This reminds us of a charming passage in Wagner's 'Mementos of Spontini,' where he relates that that conductor attributed his success to his eyes.

> How important it was to him to suffer not the smallest alteration in his habits I clearly saw when he explained to me his method of conducting, for he directed the orchestra—so he said—by a mere glance of his eye: 'my left eye is for the first violins, my right for the second violins; wherefore, to

---

[42] Ibid., 73.

[43] Ibid., 45.

[44] Ibid., 44.

[45] Ibid., 66ff.

work by a glance, one must not wear spectacles as bad conductors do, even if one is short-sighted. I,' he admitted confidentially, 'can't see a step before me, and yet I use my eyes in such a way that everything goes as I wish.'

Gildon, in conclusion, suggests that the real secret to facial gesture is to clearly have the specific emotion in mind, which then allows Nature to create the proper expression in the face. No greater advice, we might add, could ever be given a conductor.

> The orator ought to form in his mind a very strong idea of the subject of his passion, and then the passion itself will not fail to follow, rise into the eyes, and affect both the sense and understanding of the spectators.[46]

Failing this, it is very interesting that he mentions a method by which ancient actors could practice and then produce on demand tears when needed on stage. It turns out again to be the very same method which drama schools today attribute to the nineteenth-century actor, Stanislavsky.

> They kept their own private afflictions in their mind, and bent [their minds] perpetually on real objects, and not on the fable, or fictitious passion of the play which they acted.[47]

Finally, we should not forget that the ancient Greeks used music to train the movements necessary to be a good soldier. The reader will no doubt recall the often quoted comment by Socrates that 'the best dancer makes the best soldier.'[48] One illustration of the use of music by the ancient Greeks to train military movements was in the performance of the dance known as the *pyrrhiche*. This was danced to the aulos and the first part consisted of very fast feet movement, needed to chase the enemy, or escape its pursuit. The second part was a simulated combat and the third part consisted of leaping movements, as might be needed to leap over walls and ditches, etc.[49]

The general absence of literature during the Medieval Period limits our knowledge of this subject, like all subjects. However, because the Arab philosopher, Al-Farabi, in his Latin treatise, *De Ortu Scientiarum*, of ca. 900 AD, still continues to include movement within the definition of music, we might suppose this idea had continued for some time after the ancient Greeks. Al-Farabi writes,

---

[46] Ibid., 70.

[47] Ibid., 68. We might also list the subjects which Gildon states 'the complete actor' must study in the course of his preparation for the stage. They include history, moral philosophy, rhetoric, elocution, painting, sculpture, dance, fencing and the vault.

[48] Athenaeus, *Deipnosophistae*, XIV, 628. In 19th century Hungary army recruitment was done in part through the use of music and dance. The theory being that the best dancer was likely to be the best coordinated and hence was made captain of the village troops.

[49] Georges Kastner, *Manuel General de Musique Militaire* (Paris, 1848), 9ff.

> To this science [of music] are three roots—meter, melody, and gesture. Meter was devised to regulate a rational comprehension of diction. Melody was devised to regulate the parts of acuteness and gravity, and to it two roots have been included in the sense of hearing. Gesture has been included in the sense of seeing which, by coincident motions and corresponding proportions, has been arranged to agree with meter and sound. This art, therefore, is included in two particular senses—hearing and seeing.[50]

This same connection between movement and music explains a compliment which the philosopher, Psellus, paid to his employer, Emperor Michael VII (1071–1078), in praising his graceful movements.

> A musician, who from the nature of his vocation must understand the regulated succession of notes, would praise his movements.[51]

And this same idea we find in the treatise, *De Musica* (ca. 1300), by Johannes de Grocheo.

> An understanding of music is necessary to those who wish to have a complete understanding of bodies moving and moved.[52]

One who shared no enthusiasm for this long observed connection between movement and music was Pope John XXII (1324–1325). In his bull, *Docta Sanctorum*, the Pope outlaws a number of performance practices which he finds an embarrassment to the Church. Among these he includes those singers who 'endeavor to convey by their gestures the sentiment of the music which they utter.' Since we assume he really did not want church music sung with no feeling, he must have observed gestures which he associated with popular music.

We have somewhat of a summary of the state of views on movement and music in 1588 in the famous dancing manual, *Orchesography*, by Thoinot Arbeau. First, we note that in spite of the objections of the Church, such as the one just mentioned, Arbeau reports,

> In the primitive church there was a custom, which has survived into our own times, of dancing and swaying while chanting the hymns of our faith, and it may still be seen in several places.

He regrets that knowledge of the dances of the ancient Greeks has been lost.

> As regards ancient dances all I can tell you is that the passage of time, the indolence of man or the difficulty of describing them as robbed us of any knowledge thereof.

His admitted lack of information on the views of the ancient Greeks perhaps explains why he associates dance movements more with oratory than music.

---

[50] Quoted in Henry George Farmer, *Al-Farabi's Writings on Music* (New York: Hinrichsen, 1934), 49.

[51] Michael Psellus, *Chronographia*, trans. E. R. A. Sewter (Baltimore: Penguin Books, 1966), VII, 5.

[52] Johannes de Garlandia, *De Mensurabili Musica*, trans. Stanley Birnbaum (Colorado Springs: Colorado College Music Press, 1978), 1.

> Most of the authorities hold that dancing is a kind of mute rhetoric by which the orator, without uttering a word, can make himself understood by his movements and persuade the spectators that he is gallant or worthy to be acclaimed, admired and loved.

During the sixteenth century a fundamentalist religious concept began to appear in many parts of Europe, best known in England for the resultant Quakers and Puritans. For many of these people, dance became a new symbol of sin and music was not left untouched due to its association. The German philosopher Henry Agrippa (1486–1536) is a typical example.

> To Music, moreover, belongs the Art of Dancing, very acceptable to maidens and lovers, which they learn with great care, and without tediousness do prolong it until midnight, and with great diligence do devise to dance with framed gestures, and with measurable passes to the sound of the cymbal, harp, or flute, and do, as they think very wisely, and subtly, the fondest thing of all and, little differing from madness, which except that it is tempered with the sound of instruments … There is no sight more ridiculous, taken out of context, than dancing: this is a liberty to wantonness, a friend to wickedness, a provocation to fleshly lust, enemy to chastity, and a pastime unworthy of all honest persons.[53]

In England the literature of the religious right is almost unbelievable. We will quote one as representative of the entire school, Philip Stubbs's *Anatomy of the Abuses in England* (1583).

> Wherefore, if you would have your son become womanish, unclean, smooth mouthed, affected to bawdy, scurrility, filthy thymes, and unseemly talking; briefly, if you would have him, as it were, transformed into a woman, or worse, and inclined to all kinds of whordom and abomination, send him to dancing school, and to learn music, and then shall you not fail of your purpose. And if you would have your daughter whorish, bawdy, and unclean and a filthy speaker, and such like, bring her up in music and dancing, and, my life for your's, you have won the goal.[54]

Even in France, the country we associate with dance, in Voltaire's play, *The Prude* (I, v), when the character, Mme Dorfise, is asked about music and dancing, she answers, 'they are the devil's inventions.'

In Zurich, under the influence of the strict Protestant, Zwingli, public dancing was actually forbidden. A civic ordinance of 1519 reads,

> Let it be announced in the pulpits of the city and written notice sent into the country that since dancing has been forbidden, it is also forbidden to musicians or anyone else to provide dances in courts or other places, whether it be at public weddings or church festivals.[55]

---

[53] Henry Cornelius Agrippa, *Of the Vanitie and Uncertaintie of Arts and Sciences*, ed. Catherine Dunn (Northridge: California State University, Northridge Press, 1974), 69. Interestingly enough, he associates the origin of dance to the movement of the planets and the 'music of the spheres.'

[54] Philip Stubbs, *The Anatomy of the Abuses in England* (1583), ed. Frederick Furnivall (London: The New Shakespeare Society, n.d.), 169ff.

[55] Quoted in Jackson, *Huldreich Zwingli* (New York: Putham, 1901), 24.

At the beginning of the twentieth century, a remarkable educator, named Emile Jaques-Dalcroze, attempted to create a Renaissance in music education with a new system of education called 'Eurhythmics.' While mainstream American music educators pay only token recognition to his ideas, he has had to the present day many fervent individual supporters. It will strike the reader, in the following excerpts of his writings,[56] that Dalcroze attempted to take education full circle back to the beliefs of the ancient Greeks in the unity of music, movement and the emotions.

> The aim of eurhythmics is to enable pupils, at the end of their course, to say, not 'I know,' but 'I have experienced,' and so to create in them the desire to express themselves; for the deep impression of an emotion inspires a longing to communicate it, to the extent of one's powers, to others.
>
> ......
>
> Rhythm is the live essence of feeling, the fundamental impulse of a movement in the form impressed on it by the first emotional reaction.
>
> ......
>
> Gesture must define musical emotion and call up its image.
>
> ......
>
> Gesture itself is nothing—its whole value depends on the emotion that inspires it.

---

[56] 'Rhythm, Time, and Temperament' (1919), 63, 107, 119, 139.

Ancient Views on Music and Oratory

*Music is oratory in tones, and
the ancient orators gleaned their best rules from music.*

Johann Mattheson (1739)

WE MUSICIANS SHARE THE STAGE before the audience with some other people, in particular other vocal performers such as actors, orators, poets and preachers. One thing we share with these fellow public figures is the fact that in each case the art rests on a physiological foundation. That is to say, we have physical things in common.

One thing we have in common with other practitioners of vocal arts we have discussed in the previous chapter. That has to do with the fact that we all have common roots in the remote era of early man before language, when 'musical' sounds, gesture and emotion all came together in the most primitive and earliest form of communication.

Another thing we have in common is the use of the body to communicate emotion. In the case of the face, this follows from the fact that the face expresses the basic emotions, as for example a smile, in the same way in every culture. And since the fetus also makes a smile in the same way, without ever having seen a model to imitate, the implication is that basic facial communications, as well as the basic emotions themselves, are genetic.

In the extant writings of ancient philosophers there is considerable discussion of orators, no doubt because of their political impact on society. In these discussions one finds much reference to music and musicians. Sometimes music is used as a metaphor to explain emotional purpose, but sometimes these early treatises point to musicians as models for orators to study with regard to actual gestures and facial expressions.

These early treatises use music as a mirror to enlighten the orator. But we are presenting this discussion on oratory in the hope that it might also work the other way around. Perhaps in the discussion of oratory, especially in its focus on communicating emotion to the audience, the reader will discover some interesting and ancient reflections about the performance of music.

There are several surviving accounts of a famous ancient Roman orator, Gaius Gracchus, who had a servant with a kind of pitch pipe stand behind him when he spoke. If we can judge from modern experience, apparently the pitches produced by the servant served to control the speakers pitch, preventing it from rising as the speech became more passionate. Here is an account by Cicero (106–43 BC).

> Gracchus made a practice of having a skilled attendant to stand behind him out of sight with a little ivory pipe when he was making a speech, in order promptly to blow a note to rouse him when he was getting slack or to check him from overstraining his voice …

> In every voice there is a mean pitch, but each voice has it own; and for the voice to rise gradually from the mean is not only agreeable (because it is a boorish trick to shout loudly at the beginning) but also beneficial for giving it strength; then there is an extreme point of elevation, which nevertheless falls short of the shrillest possible screech, and from this point the pipe will not allow one to go further, and will begin to call one back from the actual top note; and on the other side there is similarly an extreme point in the lowering of the pitch, the point reached in a sort of descending scale of sounds. This variation and this passage of the voice through all the notes will both safeguard itself and add charm to the delivery. But you will leave the piper at home, and only take with you down to the house the perception that his training gives you.[1]

Julius Caesar, on the other hand, deliberately pitched his voice higher in pleading a cause believing it made a greater impact on his listeners.[2] To this he also added 'impassioned gestures,' something also recommended by Pliny the Younger.

> The orator ought in fact to be roused and heated, sometimes even to boiling-point, and to let his feelings carry him on till he treads the edge of a precipice … It may be safer to keep to the plain, but the road lies too low to be interesting.[3]

The same advice we venture to recommend to classical musicians.

Marcus Fabius Quintilian (35–100 AD), a rhetorician, mentions this orator in his discussion of the importance of the study of music for preparation for oratory. He adds that Gracchus observed this practice even in speeches under the most stressful circumstances and also provides us with the name of the pitch pipe.

> [I] will content myself by citing the example of Gaius Gracchus, the leading orator of his age, who during his speeches had a musician standing behind him with a pitchpipe, or *tonarion* as the Greeks call it, whose duty it was to give him the tones in which his voice was to be pitched. Such was the attention which he paid to this point even in the midst of his most turbulent speeches, when he was terrifying the patrician party and even when he had begun to fear their power.[4]

Plutarch (46–119 AD) also mentions this practice and his account suggests the consideration of texture as well as.

> Wherefore Gaius Gracchus, the orator, being of a rugged disposition and a passionate kind of speaker, had a pipe made for him, such as musicians use to vary their voice higher or lower by degrees; and with this pipe his servant [Licinius] stood behind him while he pronounced, and give him a mild and gentle note, whereby he took him down from his loudness, and took off the harshness and angriness of his voice.[5]

---

[1] Cicero, *De Oratore*, III, lx.

[2] Suetonius, *The Twelve Caesars* (New York: Penguin, 1989), 38.

[3] *The Letters of the Younger Pliny* (New York: Penguin, 1985), 248. Pliny also believed that stage fright, 'our white faces, our trembling, and our nervous glances,' are aided by careful proofreading of one's material. [Ibid., 196]

[4] Quintilian, *The Education of an Orator*, I, x.

[5] 'Concerning the Cure of Anger.'

An ode in honor of Nero, by Calpurnius Siculus, records the kind of wood such a pitch pipe was made of.

> Then please begin; I'm with you. But be careful that
> No high-pitched pipe of frail boxwood blows the notes.
> It's used to voicing for you when you praise Alexis.[6]

Quintilian believed the orator *must* excite the emotions of the listener if he is to be successful. He begins the defense of his contention in a discussion on the difference between *pathos* and *ethos*. This is a particularly valuable passage, not only for its discussion of various emotions, but for comments on the expression of emotions which apply to musical performance as well. He begins by attempting to convey the meaning of these Greek terms to his Latin readers.

> Emotions however, as we learn from ancient authorities, fall into two classes; the one is called *pathos* by the Greeks and is rightly and correctly expressed in Latin by *adfectus* (emotion): the other is called *ethos*, a word for which in my opinion Latin has no equivalent: it is however rendered by *mores* (morals) and consequently the branch of philosophy known as *ethics* is styled *moral* philosophy by us. But close consideration of the nature of the subject leads me to think that in this connection it is not so much *morals* in general that is meant as certain peculiar aspects; for the term *morals* includes every attitude of the mind. The more cautious writers have preferred to give the sense of the term rather than to translate it into Latin. They therefore explain *pathos* as describing the more violent emotions and *ethos* as designating those which are calm and gentle: in the one case the passions are violent, in the other subdued, the former command and disturb, the latter persuade and induce a feeling of goodwill.[7]

He agrees with some authors who maintain that while the *ethos* is continuous, *pathos* is more momentary in character. On the other hand, he points out, *pathos* and *ethos* are sometimes of the same nature, differing only in degree.

> Love for instance comes under the head of *pathos*, affection of *ethos*; sometimes however they differ, a distinction which is important for the peroration, since *ethos* is generally employed to calm the storm aroused by *pathos*.

Quintilian now goes into greater detail in defining *ethos*, with regard to how it is applied by the orator-lawyer. The first kind of *ethos* is calm, mild, ingratiating and courteous, intended to excite pleasure and affection in the listener. This kind of *ethos* is appropriate where the persons are intimately connected and 'the speaker wishes to display no anger or hatred.'

---

[6] Ecloque IV.

[7] Quintilian, *The Education of an Orator* (*Institutio Oratoria*), trans. H. E. Butler (London: Heinemann, 1938), VI, ii, 8 through 36.

Another type is represented by cases dealing with father and son, guardian and ward, or husband and wife. Here the *ethos* must convey the seriousness of the wrongdoing, but not indicate dislike or loss of love. But when an old man has been insulted by a youthful stranger, or a man of high rank by his inferior, then the orator should be 'really deeply moved.'

Closely related, though less violent, is the emotion demonstrated when 'we ask pardon for the errors of the young, or apologize for some youthful amour.' Here one may sometimes use 'gentle raillery' or 'the skillful exercise of feigned emotion or the employment of irony' in making apologies. From the same source comes 'a more powerful method of exciting hatred, when by a feigned submission to our opponents we pass silent censure on their violence.'

The emotion of love and longing for our friends, he calls one of an intermediate character, being stronger than *ethos* and weaker than *pathos*. Also, since *ethos* denotes moral character, Quintilian says it must therefore necessarily be employed when addressing 'rustics, misers, cowards and superstitious persons.'

Finally, if the speaker is to make use of *ethos*, it goes without saying that he himself must be a man of good character.

> For the orator who gives the impression of being a bad man while he is speaking, is actually speaking badly, since his words seem to be insincere owing to the absence of *ethos* which would otherwise have revealed itself.

Now Quintilian defines *pathos* in more detail, beginning with an analogy from the theater.

> The *pathos* of the Greeks, which we correctly translate by *emotion*, is of a different character, and I cannot better indicate the nature of the difference than by saying that *ethos* rather resembles comedy and *pathos* tragedy. For *pathos* is almost entirely concerned with anger, dislike, fear, hatred and pity ...
> I wish to point out that fear is of two kinds, that which we feel and that which we cause in others. Similarly there are two kinds of *invidia* (hatred, envy), to which the two adjectives *invidus* (envious) and *invidiosus* (invidious, hateful) correspond. The first supplies an epithet for persons, the second for things, and it is in this latter connection that the orator's task is even more onerous. For though some things are hateful in themselves such as parricide, murder, poisoning, other things have to be made to seem hateful.

The orator employs *pathos*, or emotion, when he wishes to create empathy in the listener.

> The aim of appeals to the emotion is not merely to show the bitter and grievous nature of ills that actually are so, but also to make ills which are usually regarded as tolerable seem unendurable, as for instance when we represent insulting words as inflicting more grievous injury than an actual blow or represent disgrace as being worse than death.

But how does the orator do this? Quintilian now tells us that he will reveal to us 'secret principles of this art.' What follows is a precursor of Stanislavsky's 'method acting,' through which one learns to re-experience the emotions one had previously experienced to convey from the stage. Among the performing arts only musicians are spared such processes of 'inventing' or reliving emotions, for in music the emotions expressed *are* the real ones. Nevertheless, Quintilian's discussion should remind musicians that genuine emotional communication must be founded on genuine emotions. Just as in the case of the actor, the musician must *feel* the emotions.

> The prime essential for stirring the emotions of others is, in my opinion, first to feel those emotions oneself. It is sometimes positively ridiculous to counterfeit grief, anger and indignation, if we content ourselves with accommodating our words and looks and make no attempt to adapt our own feelings to the emotions to be expressed. What other reason is there for the eloquence with which mourners express their grief, or for the fluency which anger lends even to the uneducated, save the fact that their minds are stirred to power by the depth and sincerity of their feelings? Consequently, if we wish to give our words the appearance of sincerity, we must assimilate ourselves to the emotions of those who are genuinely so affected, and our eloquence must spring from the same feeling that we desire to produce in the mind of the judge. Will he grieve who can find no trace of grief in the words with which I seek to move him to grief? Will he be angry, if the orator who seeks to kindle his anger shows no sign of laboring under the emotion which he demands from his audience? Will he shed tears if the pleader's eyes are dry? It is utterly impossible …
>
> Accordingly, the first essential is that those feelings should prevail with us that we wish to prevail with the judge, and that we should be moved ourselves before we attempt to move others. But how are we to generate these emotions in ourselves, since emotion is not in our own power? I will try to explain as best I may. There are certain experiences which the Greeks call οαvradias, and the Romans *visions*, whereby things absent are presented to our imagination with such extreme vividness that they seem actually to be before our very eyes. It is the man who is really sensitive to such impressions who will have the greatest power over the emotions … It is a power which all may readily acquire if they will.

Finally, Quintilian points to some examples in the theater of those who were skillful in this kind of emotional communication and attributes his own fame to his ability to do this.

> Again, when we desire to awaken pity, we must actually believe that the ills of which we complain have befallen our own selves, and must persuade our minds that this is really the case. We must identify ourselves with the persons of whom we complain that they have suffered grievous, unmerited and bitter misfortune, and must plead their case and for a brief period feel their suffering as though it were our own, while our words must be such as we should use if we stood in their shoes. I have often seen actors, both in tragedy and comedy, leave the theater still drowned in tears after concluding the performance of some moving role …
>
> Suppose we are impersonating an orphan, a shipwrecked man, or one in grave peril. What profit is there in assuming such a role unless we also assume the emotions which it involves? I have thought it necessary not to conceal these considerations from my reader, since they have contributed to the acquisition of such reputation for talent as I possess or once possessed. I have frequently been so much moved while speaking, that I have not merely been wrought upon to tears, but have turned pale and shown all the symptoms of genuine grief.

In another place, Quintilian explains that the ability of the orator to communicate emotions to the audience depends on the use of both the voice and the body. It is interesting that here he recommends to the orator the study of music for learning how this is done.

> Let us discuss the advantages which our future orator may reasonably expect to derive from the study of Music.
>
> Music has two modes of expression in the voice and in the body; for both voice and body require to be controlled by appropriate rules. Aristoxenus divides music, in so far as it concerns the voice, into *rhythm* and *melody*, the one consisting in measure, the latter in sound and song. Now I ask you whether it is not absolutely necessary for the orator to be acquainted with all these methods of expression which are concerned firstly with gesture, secondly with the arrangement of words and thirdly with the inflections of the voice, of which a great variety are required for law practice. Otherwise we must assume that structure and the euphonious combination of sounds are necessary only for poetry, lyric and otherwise, but superfluous in law, or that unlike music, oratory has no interest in the variation of arrangement and sound to suit the demands of the case. But eloquence does vary both tone and rhythm, expressing sublime thoughts with elevation, pleasing thoughts with sweetness, and ordinary with gentle utterance, and in every expression of its art is in sympathy with the emotions of which it is the mouthpiece. It is by the raising, lowering or inflection of the voice that the orator stirs the emotions of his hearers, and the measure, if I may repeat the term, of voice or phrase differs according as we wish to rouse the indignation or the pity of the judge. For, as we know, different emotions are roused even by the various musical instruments, which are incapable of reproducing speech. Further the motion of the body must be suitable and becoming, or as the Greeks call it *eurythmic*, and this can only be secured by the study of music.[8]

In an interesting discussion on the goals of the orator, Cicero (106–43 BC), although he does not specifically mention music, lists goals which would be identical with the performing musician: to instruct, give pleasure, and stir the emotions of the listener. He also mentions here the very important aesthetic topic of Universality. Cicero takes the position that if the fine speaker accomplishes the goals he has listed above, it will always be the masses, and not the experts, who identify the excellent speaker. It is interesting that he begins this discussion with an observation which is almost identical with one Debussy would make twenty centuries later. Debussy noted that an artist is most complimented when he is complimented by the real experts in his field; however, '*fame* is a gift of the masses who know nothing.' Cicero, wrote,

> This discussion about the reasons for esteeming an orator good or bad I much prefer should win the approval of you and of Brutus, but as for my oratory I should wish it rather to win the approval of the public. The truth is that the orator who is approved by the multitude must inevitably be approved by the expert ...
>
> Now there are three things in my opinion which the orator should effect: instruct his listener, give him pleasure, stir his emotions. By what virtues in the orator each one of these is effected, or from what faults the orator fails to attain the desired effect, or in trying even slips and falls, a master of the art will be able to judge. But whether or not the orator succeeds in conveying to his listeners the emotions which he wishes to convey, can only be judged by the assent of the multitude and the approbation of the people. For that reason, as to the question whether an orator is good or bad, there has never been disagreement between experts and the common people ...
>
> When one hears a real orator he believes what is said, thinks it true, assents and approves; the orator's words win conviction. You, sir, critic and expert, what more do you ask? The listening throng is delighted, is carried along by his words, is in a sense bathed deep in delight. What have you here to cavil with? They feel now joy now sorrow, are moved now to laughter now to tears;

---

[8] Ibid., I, x.

they show approbation detestation, scorn aversion; they are drawn to pity to shame to regret; are stirred to anger, wonder, hope fear; and all these come to pass just as the hearers' minds are played upon by word and thought and action. Again, what need to wait for the verdict of some critic? It is plain that what the multitude approves must win the approval of experts ... There have been orators in great number with many varied styles of speaking, but was there ever among them all one who was adjudged preeminent by the verdict of the masses who did not likewise win the approval of the experts?[9]

In particular, Cicero identified emotion as the universal element which captures the appreciation of the large audience, something which he found similar in both music and oratory.

For just as from the sound of the strings on the harp the skill with which they are struck is readily recognized, so what skill the orator has in playing on the minds of his audience is recognized by the emotion produced.[10]

But universality is not the same thing as popularity. Cicero understood this and in his *Tusculan Disputations* he makes it very clear that to actually program at the level of the masses is something quite different and something which the artist does not do.

Can it be that while the aulos players and those who play the lyre use their own judgment, not that of the crowd, to tune their songs and melodies, the wise man, endowed with a far greater skill, searches out not what is most true, but what the crowd wants? Or is anything more foolish than to think that those whom as individuals one despises as mere hacks and hooligans amount to something when taken all together?[11]

On the other hand, Cicero realized that with regard to public speakers the above distinction between what we call universality and popularity are only poles of aesthetic communication. In actual practice other factors make this question somewhat more complicated. Sometimes, for example, the material itself is too complex for the masses to appreciate. He quotes an anecdote in which Demosthenes was reading a long poem and in the midst of his reading all the audience walked out except for Plato. Demosthenes is reported to have said, 'I shall go on reading just the same; for me Plato alone is as good as a hundred thousand.'[12] However, Cicero did not object in principle to the idea that the orator, or artist, might aspire to be successful with his audience.

Ambition is a universal factor in life, and the nobler a man is, the more susceptible is he to the sweets of fame. We should not disclaim this human weakness, which indeed is patent to all; we should rather admit it unabashed. Why, upon the very books in which they bid us scorn ambition, philosophers inscribe their names![13]

---

9   Cicero, *Brutus*, xlix.
10 Ibid., liv. Herodotus, in his *Histories*, V, 98, comments that it is easier to convince a mob than it is an individual.
11 Cicero, *Tusculan Disputations*, V, 104.
12 Cicero, *Brutus*, li.
13 Cicero, *Pro Archia Poeta*, x.

Cicero began to associate oratory with music more when he pointed to rhythm as the element which made the orator an 'artist.' The development of this style, he points out, has its origin in music.

> Who then is the man who gives people a thrill? Whom do they stare at in amazement when he speaks? Who is interrupted by applause? Who is thought to be so to say a god among men? It is those whose speeches are clear, explicit and full, perspicuous in matter and in language, and who in the actual delivery achieve a sort of rhythm and cadence—that is, those whose style is what I call artistic.[14]
>
> ......
>
> After attention to [syntax] comes also the consideration to the rhythm and shape of the words, a point which I am afraid Catulus here may consider childish; for the old Greek masters held the view that in this prose style it is proper for us to use something almost amounting to versification, that is, certain definite rhythms. For they thought that in speeches the close of the period ought to come not when we are tired out but where we may take breath ... It is said that Isocrates first introduced the practice ... by means of an element of rhythm, designed to give pleasure to the ear. For two contrivances to give pleasure were devised by the musicians, who in the old days were also the poets, verse and melody, with the intention of overcoming satiety in the hearer by delighting the ear with the rhythm of the words and the mode of the notes ...
>
> In this matter an extremely important point is, that although it is a fault in oratory if the connection of the words produces verse, nevertheless we at the same time desire the word-order to resemble verse in having a rhythmical cadence ... [Nothing] more distinguishes him from an inexperienced and ignorant speaker.[15]

Finally, Cicero, mentions rhythm again with respect to the accommodations a public performer made for age.

> As we are taking from a single artist a number of details for our likeness of an orator, that same Roscius is fond of saying, that, the older he grows, the slower he will make the aulos player's rhythms and the lighter the music.[16]

Cicero also discusses in some detail the use of pitch as an important aspect of vocal delivery, once observing 'that nature herself modulates the voice to gratify the ear of mankind.'[17] In another place he discusses this in more detail with respect to the orator.

> Manner of speech falls into two sections, delivery and use of language. For delivery is a sort of language of the body, since it consists of movement or gesture as well as of voice or speech. There are as many variations in the tones of the voice as there are in feelings, which are especially aroused by the voice. Accordingly the perfect orator ... will use certain tones according as he wishes to seem

---

[14] *De Oratore*, III, xiv.

[15] Ibid., III, xliv.

[16] Ibid., I, lx.

[17] Ibid., III, xlviii.

himself to be moved and to sway the minds of his audience ... I might also speak about gestures, which include facial expression. The way in which the orator uses these makes a difference which can scarcely be described ...

Demosthenes was right, therefore, in considering delivery to be in the first, second and third in importance ... Therefore the one who seeks supremacy in eloquence will strive to speak intensely with a vehement tone, and gently with lowered voice, and to show dignity in a deep voice, and wretchedness by a plaintive tone. For the voice possesses a marvelous quality, so that from merely three registers, high, low and intermediate, it produces such a rich and pleasing variety in song. There is, moreover, even in speech, a sort of singing ... which Demosthenes and Aeschines mean when they accuse each other of vocal modulations ... Here I ought to emphasize a point which is of importance in attaining an agreeable voice: nature herself, as if to modulate human speech, has placed an accent, and only one, on every word ... Therefore let art follow the leadership of nature in pleasing the ear ... The superior orator will therefore vary and modulate his voice; now raising and now lowering it, he will run through the whole scale of tones.[18]

For all this comparison with music, Cicero makes it clear that in his view music can never compare to oratory. 'Can any music be composed,' he asks, 'that is sweeter than a well-balanced speech?'[19]

One of the greatest frustrations for any writer working with ancient materials is the loss of so many valuable books. One of these was an ancient Greek treatise on gesture called, *Orchesin*, which is mentioned by Johann Mattheson (1681–1764) in one of the earliest discussions on gesture and movement among musicians.[20]

Mattheson's discussion is found under the heading, 'On the Art of Gesticulation.' The proper term he gives for this art is *Hypocritica*, which Mattheson says Cassiodorus defined as 'silent music.' Quintillian defined it as 'the science of hand gesticulation,' but used the term *chironomy*.

But the word Hypocritica, for Mattheson, means more than chironomy, for *Hypo* (under) and *Crisis* (criticism) suggests the submission of one's thoughts for judgment. This should be thought of in a positive sense, as a form of stimulation, and not in the ill-meant 'hypocrisy.' The origin, and source of its power, of gesture is found in its universality. First, Mattheson points out that language itself only developed as a shadow of action.[21] Second, he touches on a very important point.

Words do not move a person who does not understand the language; discriminating words are good only for discriminating minds; but everyone understands the well-used facial expression, even young children with whom neither words nor beatings have as much effect as a glance.[22]

---

18 Ibid., xvii.

19 Ibid., II, viii.

20 Johann Mattheson, *Der vollkommene Capellmeister* (1739), trans. Ernest Harriss (Ann Arbor: UMI Research Press, 1981), I, vi.

21 Ibid., I, vi, 5.

22 Ibid. I, vi, 6.

This observation is more important than Matteson realized, with respect to universality, for modern research has shown that both facial expressions and the basic emotions are universal and the latter are formed before birth and are thus not learned, but genetic.

Matteson classifies this subject under *oratorical*, which directs the movement of the body; the *histrionic*, which belongs to plays and requires much stronger gesturing than the first; and the *saltatorial*, which deals with all kinds of steps and leaps.

The oratorical is closely related to music, he says, for music is 'an oratory in tones' and the ancient orators 'gleaned their best rules from music.'

A comment by Ammianus Marcellinus (mid fourth century AD) suggests that the great age of the Roman orator had come to an end at the same time as the decline of the Roman Empire itself. When he complains that orators have been replaced by actors, we take it to mean that serious orations have been replaced by entertainment.

> The few houses that were formerly famed for devotion to serious pursuits now teem with the sports of sluggish indolence, re-echoing to the sound of singing and the tinkling of flutes and lyres. In short, in place of the philosopher the singer is called in, and in place of the orator the teacher of stagecraft, and while the libraries are shut up forever like tombs, water-organs are manufactured and lyres as large as carriages, and flutes and huge instruments for gesticulating actors.[23]

Before leaving our discussion of the ancient orator, we should mention that Desiderius Erasmus (1469–1536), in 'The Right Way of Speaking Latin and Greek' makes some interesting observations regarding pitch and speech. In particular it is interesting that he touches on what conductors today call the 'pyramid principle,' which means playing lower tones louder than upper tones to counteract the tendency of the brain to emphasize higher partials.

> BEAR. Do you not often find yourself making a low note long or a high note short as well as the other way round?
> LION. Yes. Though the contrast is still more marked with wind instruments.
> BEAR. So why should we be so crude and unmusical when we talk, making every syllable that is accented high long and all the others short? Even donkeys could have taught us better. When they bray they take longer over the low note than over the high one.
> LION. The cuckoo does much the same.[24]

Erasmus suggests that in speaking a distinction be made between high, accented syllables, and lower sounds which might be as much as a fourth, fifth or even an octave (!)—although he admits this might be 'ungraceful.'[25] Erasmus continues his comparison of speech to music by mentioning that a speaker often begins slowly and then accelerates, as happens in music. When

---

[23] Ammianus Marcellinus, *Constantius et Gallus*, trans. John C. Rolfe (London: Heinemann, 1935), I, 47.

[24] 'The Right Way of Speaking Latin and Greek,' [1528] in *The Collected Works of Erasmus* (Toronto: University of Toronto Press, 1992), XXVI, 422ff.

[25] Ibid., 428.

the question is raised regarding the relationship of short to long in syllables, the answer is given as one to two, although 'in ordinary speech there is no need to keep the ratio so exactly as there would be in choral singing or in dancing to a guitar.'[26]

The interest Erasmus had in the tessitura of the voice was shared by several other Renaissance writers. Vincenzo Galilei (1533–1591) recommended to singers that they go to the theater to study the wide variety of contour of the voice and to observe,

> when one quiet gentleman speaks with another, in what manner he speaks, how high or low his voice is pitched, with what volume of sound, with what sort of accents and gestures, and with what rapidity or slowness his words are uttered. Mark what difference obtains in all these things when one of them speaks with one of his servants, or one of these with another; observe the prince when he chances to be conversing with one of his subjects and vassals; when the petitioner who is entreating his favor; how the man infuriated or excited speaks; the married woman, the girl, the mere child, the clever harlot, the lover speaking to his mistress as he seeks to persuade her to grant his wishes, the man who laments, the one who cries out, the timid man, the man exultant with joy …
>
> When the ancient musician sang any poem whatever, he first considered very diligently the character of the person speaking: his age, his sex, with whom he was speaking, and the effect he sought to produce by this means; and these conceptions, previously clothed by the poet in chosen words suited to such a need, the musician then expressed in the tone [*tono*] and with the accents and gestures, the quantity and quality of sound, and the rhythm appropriate to that action and to such a person.[27]

A Baroque writer who also discussed this subject was François Fenelon (1651–1715), who introduces the analogy of music when he contends that an effective orator must have a vocal range with much variety.

> It is a kind of music: all its beauty consists in the variety of its tones as they rise or fall according to the things which they have to express.[28]

If this is not the case, if his voice is not naturally melodious, or is badly managed, it fails to please.

> It does not make any striking impression upon the mind such as it would if it had all the inflections which express feeling. His tones are beautiful bells which should be clear, full, sweet, and pleasant.

One who seems to have disagreed with the importance of a wide vocal tessitura was Marin Mersenne (1588–1648). In the first proposition of the second book of his third treatise of his great *Harmonie universelle* (1636), Mersenne first provides a definition of music which focuses on the emotions.

---

[26] Ibid., XXVI, 424.

[27] Quoted in Oliver Strunk, *Source Readings in Music History* (New York: Norton, 1950), 318. His fellow Italian theorist, Zarlino, was quite upset by this recommendation:
> He bids us [musicians] go to hear the zanies in tragedies and comedies and to become out-and-out actors and buffoons. [*Sopplimenti*, VIII, xi.]

[28] *Fenelon's Dialogues on Eloquence*, trans. Wilbur Howell (Princeton: Princeton University Press, 1951), 102ff.

> The song, or air, is a derivation of the voice, or of other sounds, by certain intervals either natural or artificial, which are agreeable to the ear and to the spirit, and which signify joy, or sadness, or some other passion by their movements.[29]

Having written this, it is interesting that he seems compelled to clarify the distinction between song and the vocal qualities of speakers and actors. In this regard he seems to suggest that speakers, and preachers in particular, lose effectiveness if they have too wide a tessitura.

> Experience has shown us how preachers use the half tone, the tone, the major third, the minor third, the fourth and the fifth, according to their accents or movements which they employ. From this it can be seen that several excellent musicians state that the discourse made by such men form a *Faux-Bordon*. This is verified by the preachers who speak as if they sang. That is why their discourse is less agreeable, and less profitable.

As the emotions became an obsession with musicians during the Baroque Period, it is no surprise to find that philosophers now also declare that what matters most in oration is moving the emotions of the listeners. The English philosopher, Thomas Hobbes (1588–1679) goes so far as to say that in certain cases Truth does not matter, only passion.

> In raising an opinion from passion, any premises are good enough to enforce the desired conclusion; so, in raising passion from opinion, it is no matter whether the opinion be true or false, or the narration historical or fabulous; for, not the truth, but the image, makes passion.[30]

He goes further:

> Speakers do not endeavor so much to fit their speech to the nature of things, as to the passions of the minds to whom they speak; whence it happens, that opinions are delivered not by right reason, but by a certain violence of mind. Nor is this fault in the man, but in the nature itself of eloquence, whose end, as all the masters of rhetoric teach us, is not truth (except by chance), but victory; and whose property is not to inform, but to allure.[31]

The great English writer, David Hume (1711–1776) criticizes his fellow English orators for not having enough passion. His answer was to follow the model of the ancients, to first find the emotion in themselves.

> Perhaps it may be acknowledged, that our modern customs, or our superior good sense, if you will, should make our orators more cautious and reserved than the ancient, in attempting to inflame the passions, or elevate the imagination of their audience. But, I see no reason, why it should make them despair absolutely of succeeding in that attempt. It should make them redouble their art, not abandon it entirely. The ancient orators seem also to have been on their guard against this jealousy of their audience; but they took a different way of eluding it. They hurried away with such a torrent of sub-

---

[29] Marin Mersenne, Treatise Three, Book Two ('Second Book of Songs') of the *Traitez de la Voix et des Chants ...*, trans. Wilbur F. Russell (Princeton: Westminster Choir College, unpublished dissertation, 1952), III, ii, 1.

[30] 'Human Nature,' XIII, vii.

[31] *Philosophical Rudiments Concerning Government and Society*, X, xi. See also *Leviathan*, II, xxv.

lime and pathetic, that they left their hearers no leisure to perceive the artifice, by which they were deceived. Nay, to consider the matter aright, they were not deceived by any artifice. The orator, by force of his own genius and eloquence, first inflamed himself with anger, indignation, pity, sorrow; and then communicated those impetuous movements to this audience.[32]

The French writer, La Rochefoucauld, also emphasizes the important of passion:

> The simplest man, endowed with passion, persuades better than the most eloquent man who lacks it.[33]

Another Frenchman, Fenelon, goes further and stresses the importance of the orator personally feeling the emotion he expresses.

> It is necessary to feel passion in order to paint it well. Art, however great it be, does not speak as does actual passion. Hence, you will always be a very imperfect orator if you are not affected by the feelings which you wish to portray and to inspire in others.[34]

Fenelon also argues of simplifying the language as an aid in doing this.

> B. You would strictly banish all frivolous ornaments from discourse. But tell me by concrete examples how to distinguish them from those which are serious and natural.
> A. Do you like flourishes in music? Don't you prefer animated notes which objectify realities and expressing feelings?
> B. Yes indeed. Flourishes serve only to please the ear; they mean nothing; they arouse no feeling. Formerly our music was full of them; and therefore it was very confused and weak. Then musicians began to discover ancient music. It is a kind of passionate declamation; it acts powerfully upon the soul.
> A. I knew that music, to which you are very sensitive, would serve me in making you understand what concerns eloquence. There must then be a kind of eloquence even in music; and we must eliminate flourishes from eloquence even in music; and we must eliminate flourishes from eloquence as from music. Do you not understand now what I call verbal flourishes—appointed conceits which always return like a refrain, appointed murmurings of languid and uniform periods? There you have false eloquence, and it resembles bad music.[35]

Fenelon also mentions the use of the movement of the body to express emotion, giving us a wonderful phrase, equally valid for musicians, that 'the movement of the body is a painting of the thoughts of the soul.'

> A. For what purpose does the action of the body serve? Does it not serve to express the sentiments and the passions which occupy the soul?
> B. I believe that.
> A. The movement of the body is then a painting of the thoughts of the soul.

---

32 'On Eloquence,' in David Hume, *The Philosophical Works* (Aalen: Scientia Verlag, 1964 reprint), III, 169.
33 *The Maxims of La Rochefoucauld*, Nr. 8, trans. Louis Kronenberger (New York: Random House, 1959).
34 Fenelon, *Fenelon's Dialogues on Eloquence*, 104ff.
35 Ibid., 114ff.

B. Yes.

A. And that painting ought to be a genuine likeness. It is necessary that everything in it represent vividly and naturally the sentiments of him who is speaking and the nature of the things he speaks of. I mean that he must not, of course, go to the point where his representation becomes trivial and ludicrous.[36]

Certainly philosophers of all ages have agreed that the face is a painting of the soul. Yet, when it came to analyzing this more specifically, philosophers have long disagreed on whether it is the eyes or the face which communicates emotion. Consider, for example, the following brief survey of those voting either for the eyes or face:

THE EYES

Cicero (106–43 BC)

> But everything depends on the face, while the face itself is entirely dominated by the eyes; hence our older generation were better critics, who used not to applaud even Roscius very much when he wore a mask. For delivery is wholly the concern of the feelings, and these are mirrored by the face and expressed by the eyes; for this is the only part of the body capable of producing as many indications and variations as there are emotions, and there is nobody who can produce the same effect with the eyes shut.[37]

Pliny the Elder (23–79 AD)

> No other part of the body supplies greater indications of the mind—this is so with all animals alike, but specially with man—that is, indications of self-restraint, mercy, pity, hatred, love, sorrow, joy. The eyes are also very varied in their look—fierce, stern, sparkling, sedate, leering, askance, downcast, kindly: in fact the eyes are the abode of the mind. They glow, stare, moisten, wink; from them flows the tear of compassion, when we kiss them we seem to reach the mind itself, they are the source of tears and of the stream that bedews the cheek. What is the nature of this moisture that at a moment of sorrow flows so copiously and so promptly? Or where is it in the remaining time? In point of fact it is the mind that is the real instrument of sight and of observation; the eyes act as a sort of vessel receiving and transmitting the visible portion of the consciousness. This explains why deep thought blinds the eyes by withdrawing the vision inward.[38]

Rene Descartes (1596–1650)

> There is no passion which some particular expression of the eyes does not reveal. For some passions this is quite obvious: even the most stupid servants can tell from their master's eye whether he is angry with them. But although it is easy to perceive such expressions of the eyes and to know what they signify, it is not easy to describe them. For each consists of many changes in the movement and shape of the eye, and these are so special and slight that we cannot perceive each of them separately, though we can easily observe the result of their conjunction. Almost the same can be said of the facial expressions which also accompany passions. For although more extensive than those of the eyes, they

---

[36] Ibid., 99.

[37] Cicero, *De Oratore*, III, lix.

[38] *Natural History*, XI, liv.

are still hard to discern. They differ so little that some people make almost the same face when they weep as others do when they laugh … [Also] the soul is able to change facial expressions, as well as expressions of the eyes, by vividly feigning a passion which is contrary to one it wishes to conceal. Thus we may use such expressions to hide our passions as well as to reveal them.[39]

Don Pedro Calderon (1600–1681)

My feelings seek to break their bonds;
My poor heart dissolves in tears
And rushes to appear at
The windows of my soul, which are
My eyes.[40]

George Herbert (1593–1633)

The eyes have one language everywhere.[41]

Charles Gildon (flourished late sixteenth century)

To express Nature justly, one must be master of Nature in all its appearances, which can only be drawn from observation, which will tell us, that the passions and habits of the mind discover themselves in our looks, actions and gestures.

Thus we find a rolling eye that is quick and inconstant in its motion, argues a quick but light wit; a hot and choleric complexion, with an inconstant and impatient mind; and in a woman it gives a strong proof of wantonness and immodesty. Heavy dull eyes a dull mind, and difficulty of conception. For this reason we observe, that all or most people in years, sick men, and persons of a flegmatic constitution are slow in the turning of their eyes.

That extreme propensity to winking in some eyes, proceed from a soul very subject to fear, arguing a weakness of spirit, and a feeble disposition of the eye-lids.

A bold staring eye, that fixes on a man, proceeds either from a blockish stupidity, as in rustics; impudence, as in malicious persons; prudence, as in those in authority, or incontinence as in lewd women.

Eyes inflamed and fiery are the genuine effect of choler and anger; eyes quiet, and calm with a secret kind of grace and pleasantness are the offspring of love and friendship …

Eyes lifted on high show arrogance and pride, but cast down express humbleness of mind. Yet we lift up our eyes when we address ourselves in prayer to God, and ask anything of him.[42]

---

39 'The Passions of the Soul,' in *The Philosophical Writings of Descartes*, trans. John Cottingham, Robert Stoothoff and Dugald Murdoch (Cambridge: Cambridge University Press, 1985), 412ff.

40 *The Surgeon of Honor* (Act II).

41 'Jacula Prudentum,' in *The Poems of George Herbert*, ed. Ernest Rhys (London: Walter Scott, 1885), 249.

42 Charles Gildon, *The Life of Mr. Thomas Betterton, the Late Eminent Tragedian* [1710] (London: Frank Cass Reprint, 1970), 41ff..

Richard Wagner (1813–1883)

Wagner recalls a conversation with Spontini in which the then famous composer attributed all his success as a conductor to his use of his eyes.

> 'One must not wear spectacles as bad conductors do, even if one is short-sighted. I,' he admitted confidentially, 'can't see a step before me, and yet I use my eyes in such a way that everything goes as I wish.'[43]

THE FACE

Francesco Petrarch (1304–1374)

> Thus, when these fictions and contours in feckless colors delight you too much, turn your eyes to Him, who painted feelings on the face of man.[44]

Pierre de Ronsard (1524–1585)

> Mine eyes do fear to meet [thine eyes],
> My soul doth tremble neath those rays divine,
> Nor tongue nor voice can to its function move.
>
> Only my sighs, only my tear-stained face
> Must do their office, speaking in their place,
> And bear sufficing witness of my love.[45]

William Shakespeare (1564–1616)

> There's no art,
> To find the mind's construction in the face.[46]
>
> ......
>
> Now good sweet Nurse—O Lord, why look'st thou sad?
> Though news be sad, yet tell them merrily;
> If good, thou sham'st the music of sweet news
> By playing it to me with so sour a face.[47]

---

43 'Mementos of Spontini.'
44 'Remedies,' I, xl, 125ff.
45 Quoted in *Songs and Sonnets of Pierre de Ronsard*, trans. Curtis Page (Westport: Hyperion Press, 1924), 7.
46 *Macbeth*, I, iv.
47 *Romeo and Juliet*, II, iv.

Earl of Chesterfield

> I have often guessed, by people's faces, what they were saying, though I could not hear one word they said.[48]

The answer is, as the reader will perceive with a moment's thought, that the eyes express nothing at all, it is the parts of the face around the eyes which convey emotion. Even tears, which the eyes do produce, can be tears of sadness, tears of happiness, tears of compassion and many other emotions according to the rest of the face.

Only one important early philosopher commented on the possibility that the emotions in the face may not be true. Michel Montaigne (1533–1592) observed,

> I want to be enriched by me not by borrowings from others. Those outside us only see events and external appearances: anyone can put on a good outward show while inside he is full of fever and fright. They do not see my mind: they only see the looks on my face.[49]

Montaigne also contributed a fascinating list of the range of emotion and expressions communicated by the hands alone.

> And what about our hands? With them we request, promise, summon, dismiss, menace, pray, supplicate, refuse, question, show astonishment, count, confess, repent, fear, show shame, doubt, teach, command, incite, encourage, make oaths, bear witness, make accusations, condemn, give absolution, insult, despise, defy, provoke, flatter, applaud, bless, humiliate, mock, reconcile, advise, exalt, welcome, rejoice, lament; show sadness, grieve, despair, astonish, cry out, keep silent and what not else, with a variety and multiplicity rivaling the tongue.[50]

Charles Gildon, in his early (1710) study on the gestures of the actor, also includes a wide variety of communications available in the hands.

> The lifting of one hand upright, or extending it, expresses force, vigor and power. The right hand is also extended upwards as a token of swearing, or taking a solemn oath; and this extension of the hand sometimes signifies pacification, and desire of silence.
>
> The putting of the hand to the mouth is the habit of one, that is silent and acting modestly; of admiration and consideration. The giving the hand is the gesture of striking a bargain, confirming an alliance, or of delivering ones self into the power of another. To take hold of the hand of another expresses admonition, exhortation, and encouragement. The reaching out of an hand to another implies help and assistance. The lifting up both hands on high is the habit of one who implores, and expresses his misery. And the lifting up of both hands sometimes signifies congratulation to Heaven for a deliverance …

---

48 Earl of Chesterfield, letter to his son, March 10, 1746.

49 Michel de Montaigne, *Essays*, trans. M. A. Screech (London: Penguin, 1993), II, xvi, 710. In another place, however, he observes that in speaking, facial expressions and the voice 'lend value to things which in themselves are hardly worth more than chatter.' [Ibid., II, xvii, 726]

50 Ibid., II, xi, 507.

> The holding the hands in the bosom is the habit of the idle and negligent. Clapping the hands, among the Hebrews signified deriding, insulting, and exploding; but among the Greeks and the Romans it was, on the contrary, the expression of applause.[51]

He also makes one very strong warning regarding the use of the hands by the orator or actor.

> If an action comes to be used by only one hand, that must be the right, it being indecent to make a gesture with the left alone … When you speak of your self, the right and not the left hand must be applied to the bosom, declaring your own faculties, and passions; your heart, your soul, or your conscience, but this action generally speaking, should be only applied or expressed by laying the hand gently on the breast.[52]

Gildon also warns that moving the head from side to side, 'wantonly and lightly,' reflects folly and inconstancy.[53] Hanging the head down suggests grief and sorrow, while lifting the head or tossing it up conveys the gesture of pride and arrogance. Carrying the head high is a sign of joy, victory and triumph, but an 'hard and bold' forehead suggests obstinacy, contumacy, perfidiousness and impudence. Handing the head on the breast he finds 'disagreeable to the eye,' while leaving the head in a position of leaning toward the shoulders is 'rustic, affected, a mark of indifference and languidness.'

Thrusting out the belly or throwing back the head he finds 'unbecoming and indecent.' Shrugging the shoulders he does not admit in oratory and he relates a story about Demosthenes who attempted to cure himself of this bad habit by having a dagger hung just above his shoulder.

In the end, however, emotions originate in the mind, not in the external physical features. The mind works the body. Thus the orator, or musician, who tries to convey through gesture, or his face, an emotion which is not genuine will always fail to impress the audience. This is because the basic emotions, like music, are genetic and the audience is endowed genetically to read both emotions and music. Thus Gildon's parting advice:

> The orator ought to form in his mind a very strong idea of the subject of his passion, and then the passion itself will not fail to follow … and affect both the sense and understanding of the spectators.[54]

---

[51] Gildon, *The Life of Mr. Thomas Betterton*, 46.

[52] Ibid., 74ff. This is not unrelated to the historical preference in favor of the right hand and why we shake hands with the right hand today. The left hand, in ancient times, was used for sanitary purposes.

[53] Ibid., 42–43, 58–59. To be a 'complete' actor, Gildon's course of study includes history, moral philosophy, rhetoric, elocution, painting, sculpture, dance, fencing and the vault.

[54] Ibid., 70.

Ancient Voices Wonder: Are Musicians Born or Made?

For nearly two thousand years philosophers have wondered whether artists are born or made. For a very long time it has been a common observation that some musicians seem to have been born with a great natural talent and others not. It would seem, therefore, that musicians are born and not made.

But the question is more complicated. Since everyone is born with a significant amount of genetic information regarding music, what is it that causes one to advance rapidly in musical development and be called 'talented,' whereas another fails to advance beyond the level of a craftsman? From this perspective it would seem the quality of education, environment and experience makes the difference, thus musicians are made and not born.

The existence of thousands of music schools would seem to argue that musicians can be made, like engineers. Arguing against the importance of all that activity are the curious exceptions: famous musicians who cannot even read music. The latter include the most famous male pop singer of the twentieth century and one of that century's most famous orchestral conductors.

The earliest important discussion of this question presents the problem well, found in a treatise, 'On the Sublime,' by a first century AD writer named Longinus. Nothing else can be documented about the man, but this treatise was well-known through the Renaissance and deeply influenced such writers as Dryden and Pope. Longinus begins by emphasizing the importance of learning.

> First of all, we must raise the question whether there is such a thing as an art [craft] of the sublime or lofty. Some hold that those are entirely in error who would bring such matters under the precepts of art. A lofty tone, says one, is innate, and does not come by teaching; nature is the only art that can compass it. Works of nature are, they think, made worse and altogether feebler when wizened by the rules of art.
>
> But I maintain that this will be found to be otherwise if it be observed that, while nature as a rule is free and independent in matters of passion and elevation, yet is she wont not to act at random and utterly without system … Moreover, the expression of the sublime is more exposed to danger when it goes its own way without the guidance of knowledge,—when it is suffered to be unstable and unballasted,—when it is left at the mercy of mere momentum and ignorant audacity. It is true that it often needs the spur, but it is also true that it often needs the curb.[1]

However, in another place, when he is thinking of the great gifts of the orator, Demosthenes, he wonders if such a great performer can be the result of learning. There are some, he seems to conclude, whose success can be explained only by a God-given ability.

---

[1] Longinus, *On the Sublime*, trans. W. Rhys Roberts (Cambridge: University Press, 1935), II, 1.

> But Demosthenes draws—as from a store—excellences allied to the highest sublimity and perfected to the utmost, the tone of lofty speech, living passions, copiousness, readiness, speed (where it is legitimate), and that power and vehemence of his which forbid approach. Having, I say, absorbed bodily within himself these mighty gifts which we may deem heaven-sent (for it would not be right to term them *human*), he thus with the noble qualities which are his own routs all comers even where the qualities he does not possess are concerned, and overpowers with thunder and with lightening the orators of every age. One could sooner face with unflinching eyes a descending thunderbolt than meet with steady gaze his bursts of passion in their swift succession.

In the end Longinus retreats from having to make a choice between a studied craft, which he calls 'art,' and that talent which is a gift of nature. The highest achievement, he reasons, requires both.

> Since freedom from failings is for the most part the successful result of art, and excellence (though it may be unevenly sustained) the result of sublimity, the employment of art is in every way a fitting aid to nature; for it is the conjunction of the two which tends to ensure perfection.[2]

When the Church defeated Rome and began its process of reinventing, so to speak, the Roman citizen, it began by attempting to eliminate as much of the pagan world as possible, in the process burning the books of Plato, Aristotle, Cicero, etc. The church also attempted to remove emotion from the life of the Christian and as a subordinate part of that idea they warned the Christian about being enthusiastic about art. The rationale of the Church was: God created the artist, therefore you should love God and not the artist, much less the art object. Because of this position, during the long Church dominated period we call the 'Dark Ages,' books which discuss art and the artist are rare.

With the Renaissance, however, this subject is widely discussed, beginning with the important sixteenth-century treatise, the *Dodecachordon* of 1547, by Heinrich Glarean. Glarean (1488–1563) of Switzerland was a man of many talents as is testified to in numerous letters by Erasmus, who gives the impression that he was unusually proficient in all the Liberal Arts. In letters of recommendation, Erasmus calls Glarean a mathematician, meaning four branches of the Liberal Arts. It was from this perspective that Glarean was interested in music[3] and our guess is that he probably did not think of himself as a performing musician, although on one occasion he so impressed Maximilian I by his singing of a poem that he was made poet laureate. Such a widely talented man is never universally popular and in the fictitious, satirical 'Letters of Obscure Men,' of 1515, by Crotus Rubeanus and Ulrich von Hutten, Glarean is described as,

---

[2] Ibid., XXXVI, 3.

[3] Glarean does say, in his prefatory letter to Cardinal von Waldburg, that he had spent 20 years thinking about the musical problems presented in his book. See Glarean, *Dodecachordon*, trans. Clement Miller (American Institute of Musicology, 1965), I, 39.

very headstrong man ... A terrible man, a choleric, forever threatening fights—and he must be possessed of a devil.[4]

Glarean first clearly frames the question: who should receive the higher praise, the composer who has his gift through birth or the man who has studied counterpoint and who composes multi-part music upon the original melody?

> As we were hastening to the end of this very toilsome book, this not entirely inconsequential thought came to our mind about a matter which I say has been considered in doubt a long time now among men of our times, that is, which is more deserving of praise, the invention of a theme or the addition of several voices; namely, so that the uninitiated may also understand, whether it is of more value if one can invent a natural tenor, which affects all minds, which takes hold of a man's heart, in short, which so clings to our memory that it often steals upon us without our even thinking, and into which we break as if awakened from sleep, as we commonly see concerning many tenors; or if one adds three or more voices to the tenor invented in the aforementioned way, which voices, so to speak, embellish it with imitations, canons, changes of modus, tempus, and prolatio ...

Having presented the question, Glarean's own view seems to be that talent comes with birth, not study. It is interesting that he mentions the factor we have pointed out at the beginning, the success of untrained artists. He concludes by presenting the subordinate questions which he implies are necessary to answering the main question.

> Here is an example of this matter, so that one may comprehend so much the better what we say. Whoever first invented the tenor *Te Deum laudamus* or any other as *Pange lingua*, may he not be preferred in talent to one who afterwards composed a complete Mass according to it? First, indeed, to say as a preface, we cannot deny that this happens to each through the power of his talent, and through a certain natural and native capacity rather than through art. The reason for this seems to be that very frequently those who are untrained in music are also surprisingly proficient in inventing tenors in our vernacular, whether Celtic or German, and further, that many who are proficient in adding voices likewise have learned music badly, to say nothing of other disciplines. Therefore, it is clear that neither talent is really possible for a man unless he is born to it, and, as it is commonly said, unless he received it from his mother. This is likewise true of painters, also of sculptors, and preachers ..., in short, of all works dedicated to Minerva ...
>
> But indeed, if as Aristotle asserts, a man is truly deserving of praise who discovers the principles of any discipline, for it is very easy to add the rest (he says), I do not see why the first artist, the simple creator of a simple melody (now called a tenor) ought to be inferior to one who does not invent as easily as he adds to what has already been invented. Indeed, we see in the various disciplines that the first inventors always have merited the most praise. Thus Hippocrates is considered superior to Galen, even though Galen surpassed him with a thousand books ... Let everyone direct his attention to the following points as the most worthy of our consideration, namely, which of the two is older, which is more useful, and, finally, which yields to the other.[5]

---

4 Letter of 'Demetrius Phalerius to Ortwin Gratius,' in Francis Stokes, trans., *On the Eve of the Reformation* (New York: Harper & Row, 1909), 183.

5 Glarean, *Dodecachordon*, I, 205ff.

Giraldi Cinthio, in a letter sent to his publisher,[6] indicated that he wrote his treatise, *Discorso intorno al comporre dei romanzi* of 1549, to refute attacks on Ariosto's *Orlando Furioso*, which he considered a great heroic poem. While his treatise is thus about the sixteenth-century heroic poem in general, which he calls the Romance, Giraldi is equally concerned with establishing poetry as an art. In so doing, he presents one of the most important treatises on Beauty to be found in the sixteenth century.[7]

He begins by stating that all men have the genetic materials necessary to fine writing. But, he follows this by writing that 'Nature produces the poets, but art makes the orators,'[8] His point apparently is in attempting to make a distinction between genius and (learned) skill. By 'elocution,' Giraldi means the manner of expressing with fitting words to the thought which the poet has in mind. Here he presents a unique and curious analogy.

> Since elocution has the same place in composition as the skin does in the human body, the poet ought to put his effort on this part, under which stand all the others, as nature does on the skin of the body. Just as nature, a judicious creatress (by virtue of the intelligence which rules her) of that which she produces, took great care to make the skin soft, pliable, and delicate, and to give it the grace of proper colors so that it appears pleasing to our eyes and makes delightful all that is under it, so the poet should put much talent and study on everything pertaining to words. Since they clothe our ideas and carry them from the intellect to the eyes, they ought to be adorned with all the beauty that the industry of the writer can give them. Although in this, no less than in other particulars, one ought to shun such superfluous diligence, lest what one would make good becomes bad, and lest excessive desire to embellish results in fastidiousness. Negligence neatly practiced is sometimes better than too much diligence.[9]

This last sentence requires a note of explanation. For the Italian Renaissance (upper class) man, one of the personal characteristics held to be important was that he never exhibit effort. 'Studied negligence' was the goal. This can be easily understood in the example of chess playing, where it was held that the gentleman could play but that he should not appear to be very good, for if he were good it implied study, practice and work, all of which were not appropriate to a gentleman.

Giraldi contends that epic poetry must be in rhyme. This is only fitting for heroic matter and 'it carries in itself the sweetness of sound and gravity with measure and with the other qualities that belong to the sublime.'[10] Later he adds that words must not only convey thoughts, but in themselves, 'pleasurable beauty.' It is interesting that he warns the poet to remember that his goal is to find words for the thoughts, and not thoughts for the words.

---

6   He is known by his first name.

7   Giraldi Cinthio, *Discorso intorno al comporre dei romanzi*, trans. in Henry Snuggs, *Giraldi Cinthio On Romances* (Lexington: University of Kentucky Press, 1968), 7.

8   Ibid., 66.

9   Ibid., 72ff.

10   Ibid., 78.

He pauses to comment on the ancient question of the relationship of learned Art and genius which is a gift of Nature. Here concludes that both are necessary.

> Of these two, however, the one so needs the other that each is of little value alone. Indeed, art without nature produces such impoverished verses that they seem to have suffered for ten years from the hectic fever. Nature without art makes them like fat peasants who are of good color and health but withal have no gentility.[11]

Therefore, he concludes, that a poet who has as his guide both Nature and Art cannot help but succeed. His definition of Art, which follows consequently, focuses on both Beauty and Nature.

> By art I mean here not the intricacies and the entanglements of which I spoke above, which with metaphors, enigmas, and monstrosities would turn authors into alchemists; which precepts can make it appear that a man has seen and read much, but are not likely to teach; but that which gives us light, not shadow; makes our way pleasant, not painful; easy, not intricate; level, not steep; that which leads us not through briars but through flowering meadows; that which teaches us without so much tortuousness and such monstrosities of words and images. Like arranged flowers, after we have chosen them from the green fields of poesy, our compositions ought to be set in order with marvelous beauty.[12]

Marco Girolamo Vida was born in Cremona some time before the beginning of the sixteenth century, at which time his first poems appear, and died in 1566. His poem on chess (*Scacchiae Ludus*) brought him to the attention of Leo X. After the death of Leo X, Vida remained in the papal court of Clement VII, who made him Bishop of Alba in 1532. Holding this office, Vida participated in the council of Trent.

In his treatise on poetry, *De Arte Poetica*, of 1561, Vida has observed that there are some who fervently desire to be poets, yet, in spite of all, are not successful. They, apparently, have the training, but not the gift. These men, he recommends, might find a suitable career as lawyers!

> How oft the youth, who wants the sacred fire,
> Fondly mistakes for genius his desire,
> Courts the coy Muses, though rejected still,
> Nor Nature seconds his misguided will!
> He strives, he toils with unavailing care,
> Nor Heaven relents, nor Phoebus hears his prayer.
> He with success, perhaps, may plead a cause,
> Shine at the bar, and flourish by the laws.[13]

---

[11] Ibid., 93.

[12] Ibid., 94.

[13] Marco Vida, *The Art of Poetry*, trans. Pitt, in Albert Cook, *The Poetical Treatises of Horace, Vida, and Boileau* (Boston: Ginn, 1892), I, 354ff.

One of the important Italian Renaissance writers, Pietro Aretino (1492–1556), was much concerned with respect to the character of the artist. He also considered the question of the nature of Art and the artist and concluded that the essential gift is one of genetics and not instruction.

> The truth is that art is an innate gift for considering the excellencies of nature that comes to us when we are babes in swaddling clothes. That which is learned later may be called art, but it is not legitimate, whereas you could not call that art bastard which the spider uses in weaving his web.[14]

We might add that to another correspondent he states that neither the gift nor the skill is of any importance without heart.[15]

To Giorgio Vasari (1511–1574) we are indebted for his revised *Lives* of 1568, which provides important biographical information regarding sixteenth-century artists. Vasari summarizes his views on our subject of whether the artist is born or taught by declaring,

> Very great is the obligation that is owed to Heaven and to Nature by those who bring their works to birth without effort and with a certain grace which others cannot give to their creations either by study or by imitation.[16]

With the Baroque Period we begin to find German commentary which is related to our question, that is are musicians the product of training or Nature? One philosopher that we appreciate was Johann David Heinichen (1683–1729), a composer in Dresden. In his mind, there was a natural connection between the learned rules of music and the talent which comes from Nature, for he believed the important rules were all drawn from Nature herself.

> All arts and sciences have rules and must be learned through rules, if we do not wish to remain simple naturalists, i.e., half-ignorant. But we must not err excessively on the side of rules; furthermore, we should not accept so crudely the equivocal word: Rule, as if we would serve as high sounding rule makers, prescribing laws even to Nature, according to which she must limit herself to *auctoritate nostra*. No! All of our useful rules must be derived from Nature; and we must investigate on all levels the will, preference, and character of this mistress and learn from her *cum submissione*.[17]

Heinichen conceded the importance of that which is learned about music, believing that the essential abilities needed for successful composition include natural aptitude and diligence, as well, of course, as knowledge of the basic conceptual information on writing music. However, as he quotes Andreas Werkmeister, rules alone do not suffice.[18]

---

[14] Letter to Coccio, in Thomas Chubb, *The Letters of Pietro Aretino* (New Haven: Shoe String Press [Archon Books], 236.

[15] Letter to Massiminiano Stampa, in Ibid., 39.

[16] Quoted in Anthony Blunt, *Artistic Theory in Italy, 1450–1600* (Oxford: Clarendon Press, 1959), 96.

[17] Johann David Heinichen, *General-Bass Treatise* [1711], quoted in George Buelow, *Thorough-Bass Accompaniment according to Johann David Heinichen* (Ann Arbor: UMI Research Press, 1986), 315ff.

[18] Ibid.

> If one has no musical aptitude 1,000 rules could be illustrated with 10,000 examples and still the purpose would not be achieved.[19]

We have seen above Heinichen's contention that all useful rules must be derived from Nature. But he seems hesitant to take on the burden of discussing the full dimension of Nature's contribution. For one reason, while he finds Nature's gifts unquestionably important, he finds that these gifts vary from composer to composer.

> One can as little describe the differences in musical talent as one can describe the differences between all ingenuities. Generally, however, one can say that the good talents of composers differ only in degree. For Nature gives to one an animated, clear, burning spirit, but to another a tempered, modest, or even affective nature. The latter is better suited to to the devout church style, the former, however, more to the theatrical.[20]

Another very important German writer took a similar position. Johann Mattheson (1681–1764) not only found that the gifts of Nature varied from man to man, but that sometimes Nature left her gifts incomplete!

> One sometimes encounters fine minds without true desire and love for it; thus one encounters nothing more seldom than the required diligence and necessary, untiring industry, joined together with these two things, natural ability and real desire: because commonly not a little laziness and idleness, lasciviousness, comfortableness, and the like, tend to go side by side with innate gifts and inclinations.
> A so-called natural disposition without ambition or love is like a buried treasure … Desire and diligence without natural ability is really the worst of all.[21]

This partiality which Nature demonstrates in passing out her talents led Mattheson, in another place, to comment on the treatment of students.

> Natural stupidity or innate simplicity is among the failures of the intellect which no one can rightfully punish, though it can be deplored or at best ridiculed. Desiring to make youngsters intelligent with thrashing is not only futile, but godless. Many examples verify that beatings make heads ten times more dumb than they were previously. This is and remains abysmally characteristic of education in almost every guild and apprenticeship.[22]

The great German composer, Georg Telemann (1681–1767), found that of the poets he worked with, some were talented but lacked the learning to successfully complete their assignment.

---

[19] Andreas Werckmeister, *Nothwendigsten Anmerckungen*, 40ff.

[20] Johann David Heinichen, *General-Bass Treatise*, 285.

[21] Johann Mattheson, *Der vollkommene Capellmeister* (1739), trans. Ernest Harriss (Ann Arbor: UMI Research Press, 1981), II, ii, 59ff.

[22] Ibid., II, ii, 30.

> Just as not everyone is born a poet, so every poet cannot write texts adaptable to music, and especially sacred music. It would be desirable for experts to explore this question.[23]

Another German writer of the Baroque, Johann Birnbaum, placed more importance on the learned facet of the artist. Indeed, his was a rather unique opinion that one of the fundamental roles of the artist was to perfect and shape Nature into its most ideal state.

> If art imitates Nature, then indisputably the natural element must everywhere shine through the works of art. Accordingly it is impossible that art should take away the natural element from those things in which it imitates Nature—including music. If art aids Nature, then its aim is only to preserve it, and to improve its condition; certainly not to destroy it. Many things are delivered to us by Nature in the most misshapen states, which, however, acquire the most beautiful appearance when they have been formed by art. Thus art lends Nature a beauty it lacks, and increases the beauty it possesses. Now, the greater the art is—that is, the more industriously and painstakingly it works at the improvement of Nature—the more brilliantly shines the beauty thus brought into being.[24]

The opposite view was taken by the great French philosopher, Marin Mersenne (1588–1648). He studied mathematics, physics, the classics and metaphysics at the Jesuit College of Le Mans. After becoming a Jesuit priest, and a member of the Minorite friars, Mersenne began teaching Hebrew, philosophy and theology at the Sorbonne in Paris in 1619. His residence became a required stopping place for every intellectual visiting Paris, which, together with his correspondence with persons throughout Europe, including Galilei, Huygens and Descartes, made him a virtual one-man academy. His studies and experimentation in music resulted in his *Harmonie universelle* (1636), a work of encyclopedia proportion organized in five treatises.

It was the conclusion by Mersenne that composers are born and not made through 'Art.'

> Whatever rules we could give for composing fine and beautiful melodies on all kinds of subjects and texts, it appears that they cannot bring this to pass until we are induced by the favorable genius and natural inclination of those who write excellent ones without having learned or established any other rules than those which their imagination furnishes …
>
> I shall be of the opinion of those who say that the genius of music is like that of the poet, the painter, the orator, and of several other craftsmen, to whom nature, or rather the Master of Nature, has dispensed certain gifts to which art cannot attain.[25]

He was also of the opinion that to some degree the beautiful singer is born and not made.

> This should be ascribed to the order of Divine Providence, which makes use of all kinds of conditions, as it does of as many voices, to compose the great concert of this universe, whose beauties and charms we will never understand except in Heaven.[26]

---

23 Georg Philipp Telemann, preface to T. E. Schubart, *Fortsetzung des harmonischen Gottesdienstes* (1731), quoted in Sam Morgenstern, *Composers on Music* (New York: Pantheon, 1956), 39.

24 Johann Birnbaum, 'Impartial Comments on … Der Critische Musicus,' quoted in Hans T. David and Arthur Mendel, *The Bach Reader* (New York: Norton, 1966), 244ff.

25 *Harmonie universelle*, IV, vi, 9.

26 Ibid., IV, vi, 6.

François Marie Arouet (1694–1778), known as Voltaire,[27] was the son of a successful attorney and a lively and intelligent woman who hosted a minor salon in Paris. His father advised him, 'Literature is the profession of the man who wishes to be useless to society and a burden to his relatives, and to die of hunger.' The son responded by becoming one of the most read writers of the Baroque, supporting his family and dying wealthy.

Voltaire arrived in Paris in 1715 as France was in transition from the era of Louis XIV to the regency for the young Louis XV. His brilliant wit, and sharp tongue, soon brought him to the attention of high society and earned him several visits to the Bastille. One comment remembered from this time followed an announcement that the regent, for reasons of the economy, had sold half the horses of the royal stables. Voltaire suggested it might have been better if he dismissed half the asses at court!

In one place Voltaire seems to take the position that learning must be everything in the artist, for the reason that Nature has rendered all men equal physically.

> Yet all nations …, even the Hottentots and Kaffirs, pronounce the vowels and consonants as we do, because the larynx in them is essentially the same as in us—just as the throat of the rudest boor is made like that of the finest opera-singer, the difference, which makes of one a rough, discordant, insupportable bass, and of the other a voice sweeter than the nightingale's, being imperceptible to the most acute anatomist; or, as the brain of a fool is for all the world like the brain of a great genius.[28]

In another place, however, he takes the position that those with real individual genius in the arts possessed something beyond learning or emulation.

> It must be confessed that in the arts having genius as their basis, everything is the product of instinct.[29]

By 'instinct' here, Voltaire apparently meant that the true genius is born and not made. Here he seems to suggest that 'learning' is replaced by 'taste.'

> We use the word 'genius' indifferently in speaking of … an artist, or a musician … Now an artist, however perfect he may be in his profession, if he have no invention, if he be not original, is not considered a genius. He is only inspired by the artists his predecessors, even when he surpasses them …
>
> Poussin, who was a great painter before he had seen any good pictures, had a genius for painting. Lully, who never heard any good musicians in France, had a genius for music …
>
> Genius, conducted by taste, will never commit a gross fault … Genius, without taste, will often commit enormous errors; and, what is worse, it will not be sensible of them.[30]

---

27 He took the name Voltaire, a name which had been in his mother's family, while in the Bastille.
28 *Philosophical Dictionary*, 'The Alphabet,' in *The Works of Voltaire* (New York: St. Hubert Guild, 1901).
29 Letter to Denis Diderot (April, 1773), in *The Selected Letters of Voltaire*, trans. Richard Brooks (New York: New York University Press, 1973), 298.
30 *Philosophical Dictionary*, 'Genius,' in *The Works of Voltaire*, IX, 194.

In another place, he adds,

> The gift of nature is an imagination inventive in the arts—in the disposition of a picture, in the structure of a poem. It cannot exist without memory, but it uses memory as an instrument with which it produces all its performances.[31]

The primary characteristic of this 'gift of nature,' that the artist is born with, Voltaire finds to be the quality of his imagination.

> Active imagination, which constitutes men poets, confers on them enthusiasm, according to the true meaning of the Greek word, that internal emotion which in reality agitates the mind and transforms the author into the personage whom he introduces as the speaker; for such is the true enthusiasm, which consists in emotion and imagery …
>
> In general, the imaginations of painters when they are merely ingenious, contribute more to exhibit the learning in the artist than to increase the beauty of the art …
>
> In all the arts, the most beautiful imagination is always the most natural.[32]

Two examples from English literature take the position that the successful artist is the product of *both* birth and art (learning). We have an interesting poem in honor of Shakespeare by Ben Jonson, in which the poet observes that 'though the matter of poets be Nature,' it is the art of the poet which must shape it. In a reflection on Shakespeare's own labor, Jonson notes,

> For a good poet's made, as well as born.
> And such wert thou.[33]

A similar reflection is made by Robert Herrick (1591–1674):

> Man is composed here of a two-fold part;
> The first of Nature, and the next of Art:
> Art presupposes Nature.[34]

And now, it might be interesting to consider what some of the great composers have written on this subject. First, there are some isolated thoughts from the diary of Robert Schumann, which has been dated about 1833.

> It is the curse of talent that, although it labors more steadily and perseveringly than genius, it does not reach a goal; while genius, floating on the summit of the ideal, grazes from above, serenely smiling.
>
> ……
>
> It is not a good thing to have acquired too much facility in any occupation.
>
> ……

---

[31] *Philosophical Dictionary*, 'Imagination,' in Ibid., X, 162.
[32] Ibid., 164ff.
[33] *The Complete Poetry of Ben Jonson*, ed. William Hunter (New York: Norton, 1963), 373ff.
[34] *The Poetical Works of Robert Herrick*, ed. L. C. Martin (Oxford: Clarendon Press, 1963), 153.

> The youthful works of masters who have become great, are looked upon with very different eyes than are the works of composers who promised as much, but did not keep their word.
>
> ……
>
> Dare talent permit itself to take the same liberties as genius?
>
> ……
>
> Talent labors, genius creates.
>
> ……
>
> Few strikingly original works of genius have become popular.

These comments on talent as opposed to genius by Schumann remind us of one of Wagner's essays where he quotes Schopenhauer:

> Talent hits a mark we all can see, but cannot lightly reach; whilst Genius attains a goal we others do not even see.[35]

Our original question was, 'Are musicians born or made?' When you look at the sketch books of Beethoven, it is perfectly obvious that even so great a composer as he had to go to great efforts to 'make' his compositions. In looking at these sketches one sometimes feels that if he had a gift, it was the gift of knowing what to reject. His birth gift was Taste, not counterpoint.

Mozart is another matter. As Schumann pointed out one time, the only way you can be a Mozart is to be born a Mozart.[36]

But, if you have to be *born* a Mozart, then what is going on in all those thousands of music schools around the world? It is an interesting question. It reminds us of a comment by Beethoven when a young composer was exclaiming the benefits of the new invented metronome for making it possible for a composer to designate at the beginning of a movement exactly what tempo he had in mind. Yes, said Beethoven, but it is only good for the first couple of measures. 'After that,' said the great musician, 'feeling has its own tempo.' This simple truth that tempo is determined by feeling, something practiced by every artist in the world, is not a subject of instruction in the music schools.

What then *is* being taught in all those music schools? In our view most of this activity is centered in two areas:

[1] A great amount of time is spent by music schools in the teaching of grammar. In no other field and in none of the other arts is such a disproportionate amount of time spent on grammar as opposed to meaning, purpose and creativity. Can one imagine, for example, Marlon Brando, Jack Nicholson, Marilyn Monroe and Jane Fonda at the Lee Strasberg Actors Studio in New York sitting around discussing grammar?

---

35 'Pubic and Popularity.'

36 'Chamber Music,' in *Neue Zeitschrift für Musik*, 1837.

In what music school is there even one comprehensive course in aesthetics? In what music school is there discussion on what music *meant* to Beethoven? Who will talk about music and character development?

Who tells students why classical music is important and popular music is not? Who explains to students the difference between inspired music and educational music? Who takes on the responsibility for explaining to students that music education is about commerce, but not art?

[2] The other great field of activity in music schools is the instruction of students on how to become players of instruments, including the vocal instrument. But what studio teacher, as a part of the necessary technique, explains to the student how to move the emotions of the listener? In how many studios is the word 'listener' even mentioned?

What studio teacher brings up the subject of earning a living? One day students will ask that question and the house of cards will collapse.

To conclude, surely everyone understands that one cannot learn, in any music school anywhere, how to become a Mozart. That is not only a gift of God, but a gift God rarely dispenses. But there are other gifts, some of which are genetic, gifts of God to everyman. First and foremost among these is the ability to understand music as a listener without going to those music schools.

And then there are the gifts which come from participation in music. Surely anyone whose means of making a living includes the performance of music, whether professional, community or school, must feel a recipient of a gift of the gods. You *could* be a dentist! How much would they have to pay you to stand and look into other people's mouths all day?

And finally there are those people who may not have the opportunity to perform, but understand the importance of music to society and give of themselves to make it happen. It was of them that Mendelssohn once wrote,

> The smallest real service to art … seems a blessing sent by God.[37]

---

[37] Letter to Karl Klingemann, Jan. 17, 1843.

Ancient Voices Wonder: Is Music Genetic?

*Infants before age one
can distinguish whether particular chords
contain a wrong note.*[1]

*Infants two days old
demonstrate specific behavioral responses to
music heard as fetuses.*[2]

HOW OLD IS MUSIC? In the oldest literature, the surviving ancient Greek literature, the Old Testament and the Egyptian tomb paintings, we see the same instruments used in the same functions. Music was already international in use and what we find here is little different from the use of music today.

Far older are some of the surviving instruments, one of which, a 43,000 to 82,000 year old flute made from a bear bone, has holes cut to create a diatonic scale. The oldest instruments are all made from natural objects: flutes from branches, percussion from turtle shells and trumpet-types from conches. Since only the most primitive technology was necessary, such instruments could extend back to a very remote age.

And then there are the cave paintings of Spain and France, the estimates of age for which vary from 10,000 to 90,000 years BC. Here we see pictures of musicians performing as part of an organized ritual. It has been observed that the most resonant caves have the most painting. The quest for better concert halls acoustics had begun!

Far older, ca. 250,000 years BC, evolutionary changes in the skull occurred making possible modern speech. Before this was possible, all philologists agree that man communicated by vocal sounds. Since the basic five vowel sounds are genetically common to every language on earth,[3] they were probably also the basic emotional sounds known to early man. Some of these sounds would have been fundamental for security and for recognizing a stranger at a time when no one wore clothes. Since the basic emotions are also universal and genetically carried forward in all men, Charles Darwin was quite correct when he observed, 'Music has a wonderful power … of recalling … those strong emotions which were felt during long-past ages.'[4]

---

[1] Research by Sandra Trehub, University of Toronto.

[2] Research by Peter Hepper, 'An examination of fetal learning before and after birth,' *Irish Journal of Psychology* 12 (1991): 95–107.

[3] First pointed out, we believe, by John of Salisbury, first half of the twelfth century, in *The Metalogicon*, trans. Daniel McGarry (Berkeley: University of California Press, 1955), 36. Born of humble parents in southern England, John went to Paris in 1136, where he studied with Peter Abelard. With the aid of Bernard of Clairvaux he became Archbishop of Canterbury, where he became an intimate counselor of, and witnessed the murder of, Thomas Becket.

[4] *The Expression of Emotions in Man and Animals* [1872] (New York: St. Martin's Press, 1979), 219; also see *The Descent of Man*, II, 336.

On the darker side, Darwin also believed that so slight a symptom as a snarl or sneer, the one-sided uncovering of the upper teeth, is something carried forward from the time when our ancestors had large canines and exposed them (as dogs now do) for attack.[5] It is beyond question that we carry genetic musical contributions from this early man, foremost among which are the melodic contours of our speaking voice and its tendency to rise when we are excited.

But music may be older still. Some modern research relative to the physiological nature of music leaves open the possibility that sound may have influenced the development of the species. The French doctor, Alfred Tomatis, who studied the impact of chant in various societies has concluded that music is a kind of 'food' for the brain, that 'warms it up' for enhanced activity. A similar comment was made in the nineteenth century by Disraeli, who said that 'Music is a stimulant to mental exertion.' There is clinical evidence for this as listening to music can cause the pleasant release of endorphins. And then there is a group of physicists, including Dr. Hans Jenny of Switzerland, who are working with the vibrations of molecules in human organs, which has promise for medical cures by 'tuning' the ill organs. A member of this group concludes that the species looks as it does due to the twin influences of this internal 'harmony' and gravity.

Before that, the elements of music must have been present near the creation. The overtone series, of course, would have been heard by the first creature with ears. And one physicist, Richard Voss of the IBM Thomas J. Watson Research Center, has found simple mathematical relationships which describe the rise and fall of pitches in a composition which are similar to natural patterns in the electrical patterns of brain cells, the fluctuations in sunspots and in the growing of tree rings. Whatever vibration stirred that original primordial 'soup' and began the chain of evolution also began music.

Modern clinical research has identified more specific elements of music which appear to be genetic. But, before considering this research, let us survey some of the intuitive speculation on the subject by ancient philosophers.

The ancient philosophers did not need modern physiological research to suspect that music was somehow genetic with man. First, it would have been obvious to them, as to us, that all men respond to music. 'Why,' asks Aristotle, 'do all men love music?'

> Is it because we naturally rejoice in natural movements? This is shown by the fact that children rejoice in [rhythm and melody] as soon as they are born.[6]

Aristotle also noticed that the ability to be a fine player was not related to [noble] birth or wealth.[7]

What we call genetic information which is included at birth could only be explained by Cicero (106–43 BC) as a kind of proof of our divine connection.

---

[5] Quoted in *The Works of William James*, ed. Frederick Burkhardt, et. al. *The Principles of Psychology*, II (Cambridge: Harvard University Press, 1981), 1092.

[6] *Problemata*, 920b.28.

[7] *Politica*, 1283a.

> The human soul is in some degree derived and drawn from a source exterior to itself. Hence we understand that outside the human soul there is a divine soul from which the human soul is sprung.[8]

The earliest philosophers must also have observed the response of newly born infants to lullabies. From this observation alone the first century AD philosopher, Philodemus of Gadara, concluded music was both universal and genetic.

> We have an innate affinity with the Muses, one which does not have to be learned. This is clearly shown by the way infants are lulled to sleep with wordless singing.[9]

Erasmus (1469–1536) also observed this response and, as a very rational man, was particularly fascinated that a lullaby could have this effect when the infants 'have no idea what music is.'[10]

These early ideas are found again in a famous treatise, 'On the Sublime,' by the first century AD philosopher, Longinus, a man of whom otherwise virtually nothing is known. In addition, he contends that the genetic elements of music which we arrive with at birth also prepare man for understanding more complex communications, such as that of the orator.

> For does not the flute instill certain emotions into its hearers and as it were make them beside themselves and full of frenzy, and supplying a rhythmical movement constrain the listener to move rhythmically in accordance therewith and to conform himself to the melody, although he may be utterly ignorant of music? ...
>
> Are we not, then, to hold that composition (being a harmony of that language which is implanted by nature in man and which appeals not to the hearing only but to the soul itself), since it calls forth manifold shapes of words, thoughts, deeds, beauty, melody, all of them born at our birth and growing with our growth, and since by means of the blending and variation of its own tones it seeks to introduce into the minds of those who are present the emotion which affects the speaker and since it always brings the audience to share in it and by the building of phrase upon phrase raises a sublime and harmonious structure: are we not, I say, to hold that harmony by these selfsame means allures us and invariably disposes us to stateliness and dignity and elevation and every emotion which it contains within itself, gaining absolute mastery over our minds? But it is folly to dispute concerning matters which are generally admitted, since experience is proof sufficient.[11]

Several of the early Christian fathers also commented on the fact that music must be genetic. St. John Chrysostom (ca. 345–407 AD) wrote that music 'is thoroughly innate to our mind.'[12] His younger contemporary, St. Augustine (354–430 AD), observed that the appreciation of fine performance is genetically present in the listener, not just the musician.

---

8   Cicero, *De Divinatione*, xxxii, 70 and xxxvii.

9   Quoted in Warren D. Anderson, *Ethos and Education in Greek Music* (Cambridge: Harvard University Press, 1966), 173.

10 'Adages,' in *The Complete Works of Erasmus* (Toronto: University of Toronto Press, 1992), XXXI, 167. He could have said the same thing for many adults.

11 Longinus, *On the Sublime*, trans. W. Rhys Roberts, (Cambridge: University Press, 1935), XXXIX, 2.

12 'Exposition of Psalm XLI.'

AUGUSTINE. How do you explain the fact that an ignorant crowd hisses off a flute player letting out futile sounds, and on the other hand applauds one who sings well, and finally that the more agreeably one sings the more fully and intensely it is moved? For it isn't possible to believe the crowd does all this by the art of music, is it?
STUDENT. No.
AUGUSTINE. How then?
STUDENT. I think it is done by nature giving everyone a sense of hearing by which such things are judged.
AUGUSTINE. You are right.[13]

The fourteenth-century English writer, Chaucer, also believed that man comes with certain genetic information. Since the understanding of genetics was far in the future, for him it was sufficient to attribute it to the goddess of Nature, the 'vicaire of the almyghty Lord.'[14] In 'The Squire's Tale,' for example, he writes,

That Nature in youre principles hath set.[15]

Marsilio Ficino, the fifteenth-century founder of the Florentine Academy, was a philosopher who was an active musician in his leisure, playing the lyre for his own relaxation, but also in concerts in the Medici palace.[16] His combined interests in music and philosophy resulted in some very interesting conclusions on the virtues of music. Music, he believed, served man's 'spirit' in the same way medicine serves the body and theology the soul. In his view, what we call the genetic aspects of music were to him a memory in the soul of the divine music found in the mind of God and in the music of the spheres.[17] The great Italian Renaissance theorist, Zarlino, agreed and thought it was the genetic memory of the music of angels which impels man to sing as a means of easing labor.

Many were of the opinion that in this life every soul is won by music, and, although the soul is imprisoned by the body, it still remembers and is conscious of the music of the heavens, forgetting every hard and annoying labor.[18]

We should not be surprised to find that Renaissance philosophers also pointed to Love as an example of an emotion which is natural to man. Giambattista Guarini (1538–1612), a diplomat in the courts of Florence and Urbino, for example, wrote,

---

[13] *On Music*, trans., Robert Taliaferro in Writings of Saint Augustine (New York: Fathers of the Church), v.

[14] 'The Parliament of Birds,' 379.

[15] 'The Squire's Tale,' 487. See also 'The House of Fame,' I, 490 and III, 276; 'The Legend of Good Women,' 975; and 'The Complaint of Venus,' 14.

[16] Paul Kristeller, 'Music and Learning in the Early Italian Renaissance,' *The Journal of Renaissance and Baroque Music* 1, no. 4 (1947): 269ff.

[17] Ficino carries his belief in the 'music of the spheres' to an association of the signs of the zodiac with the tones of the scale.

[18] 'Le Istitutioni harmoniche,' quoted in Claude V. Palisca, *Humanism in Italian Renaissance Musical Thought* (New Haven: Yale University Press, 1985), 179.

> [Love] is born with us, and it grows up as fast
> As we do, Amarillis; 'tis not writ,
> Nor taught by masters—nature printed it
> In human hearts with her own powerful hand.[19]

The greatest French essay writer of the sixteenth century was unquestionably Michel Montaigne (1533–1592). After an education in law at Toulouse, he became in turn a soldier, courtier, traveler and mayor of Bordeaux. He gave great credit to what Nature has provided and urged man to follow her teachings.

> You cannot extirpate the qualities we are originally born with: you can cover them over and you can hide them …
> Just take a little look at what our own experience shows. Provided that he listen to himself there is no one who does not discover in himself a form entirely his own, a master-form which struggles against his education as well as against the storm of emotions which would gainsay it.[20]

A master of ironic phrases, there is one related to our topic which we especially like:

> No man is poor by Nature's standards, but by opinion's standards, every man is.

Rene Descartes (1596–1650) wanted to rid himself of possible error in all prior learning by starting over, educating himself from the beginning. In setting out on this course, he wanted to find some universal beginning point which could not be questioned and thus he formulated the most single famous sentence in philosophy, *Cogito ergo sum* [I think, therefore I am]. This concept of starting with the individual, conscious self was in itself a revolution in France, where there was still preserved in the universities a Scholastic tradition one thousand years old which emphasized God before self.

In a letter to Pierre Chanut, French ambassador to Sweden, Descartes acknowledges the genetic nature of the emotions, but contends that the prenatal fetus has only four 'passions': joy, love, sadness and hatred. It was the unconscious retention of the confused prenatal emotions which complicated our judgments of the passions in later life, Descartes suggested.

> Those four passions, I think, were the first we felt, and the only ones we felt before our birth. I think they were then only sensations or very confused thoughts, because the soul was so attached to matter that it could not do anything except receive impressions from the body … Before birth love was caused only by suitable nourishment, which entered in abundance into the liver, heart, and lungs and produced an increase of heat: this is the reason why similar heat still always accompanies love, even though it comes from other very different causes … The other bodily conditions which at the

---

[19] Giambattista Guarini, *The Faithful Shepherd* [*Il Pastor Fido*], in *Five Italian Renaissance Comedies* (New York: Penguin Books, 1978), III, 354. Giraldi Cinthio, in *Discorso intorno al comporre dei romanzi*, trans. in Henry Snuggs, *Giraldi Cinthio On Romances* (Lexington: University of Kentucky Press, 1968), 27 and 64ff, argues (correctly) that the elements of language are also genetic.

[20] *Essays*, trans. M. A. Screech (London: Penguin, 1993), II, xxxvii, 866. In Ibid., III, ii, 914, he adds here that because we are made by God as we are, the idea of repenting for our actions seems foreign to him.

beginning of our life occurred with these four passions still accompany them. It is because of these confused sensations of our childhood, which continue connected to the rational thoughts by which we love what we judge worthy of love, that the nature of love is difficult for us to understand.[21]

The brilliant composer and theorist, Jean-Philippe Rameau (1683–1764) was absorbed for years with the idea that man is born with a genetic pitch template. He was pondering observations which he had made along these lines in 1734, when he wrote,

> In music the ear obeys only nature. It takes account of neither measure nor range. Instinct alone leads it.
>
> Whether a novice or the most experienced person in music, the moment one sings an improvisation, one ordinarily places the first tone in the middle register of the voice and then continues up, even though the voice range above or below this first tone is about equal; this is completely consistent with the resonance of any sounding body from which all emanating overtones are above its fundamental tone which one thinks one is hearing alone.
>
> On the other hand, inexperienced as one may be, one hardly ever fails, when improvising on an instrument, immediately to play, ever ascending, the perfect chord made up of the overtones of the sounding body, the major form of which is always preferred to the minor, unless the latter is suggested by some reminiscence.[22]

Twenty-five years later he was still struggling with this idea. He begins by discounting the ancient explanations based on faith and wonders why these early philosophers did not pursue natural rules, that is, understanding based on Nature.

> [The ancient writers] found the relationships between sounds in divinely inspired order; they discoursed a great deal on that subject, and every reason they were able to advance evaporated like a wisp of smoke. Finally the geometricians and the philosophers became disheartened. Can it be true that up to the present time man has always been so enthralled by this single inspiration that it never occurred to anyone to seek the reason why, despite ourselves, we should be compelled to prefer certain intervals to others after certain sounds, especially after the first sound? Allow your natural feelings to operate in yourself with no preconceived expectation and then try to see if you can ever ascend a semitone after a given semitone, and whether you can do the same thing after two successive tones. Why was this suggested to me in this way? Whence this sensation? What could have given rise to this sensation in me, if it was not in the moment itself? It was necessary to test the effect of the sound, and from it three sounds would have been distinguished which form that enchanting harmony, and from there one would have proceeded with certainty, as I believe I have done.
>
> The principle is inexhaustible and holds true for theology as well as geometry and physics. Anyone more enlightened than myself should be able to draw the most far-reaching conclusions from this and already I can envision the origin of that final knowledge which cannot be denied without denying the phenomenon from which it is derived.[23]

---

[21] Letter to Chanut, February 1, 1647, quoted in *Descartes Philosophical Letters*, trans. Anthony Kenny (Oxford: Clarendon Press, 1970), 210ff.

[22] Jean Philippe Rameau, *Observations sur notre instinct pour la musique et sur son principe* (1734), quoted in Sam Morgenstern, *Composers on Music* (New York: Pantheon, 1956), 44.

[23] Letter to A. M. Beguillet, October 6, 1762, quoted in Gertrude Norman and Miriam Shrifte, *Letters of Composers*, 20.

The French musician, Michel de Saint-Lambert, in his *Les Principes du Clavecin* of 1702, was certain that we carry genetically into birth specific information of a musical nature, in particular rhythm. After briefly mentioning some of the abilities needed in performance, he says,

> Though this at first sight may appear a large order, it is nevertheless sure that this extreme accuracy in intonation and rhythm is a gift given to almost all men, like sight and speech. There are very few who do not sing and dance naturally; if it is not with the delicacy and correctness that Art has sought, it is at least with the correctness which Art dictates and which Art itself has derived from Nature. It is already a great asset for those who want to learn music or to play some instrument that they know they have discernment of the ear by nature, that is, the first and most important of these aptitudes.[24]

The nineteenth-century German philosopher, Friedrich Schelling (1775–1854) also believed that man had a genetic instinct for rhythm, which caused him to attempt to infuse rhythm into his daily activities.

> The human being, driven by an impulse of nature, seeks through rhythm to impose variety or diversity onto everything that in and for itself constitutes a pure identity of activity. In every activity that is by nature meaningless, such as counting, we do not endure long within that uniformity. We divide it into units. Most mechanical workers make their work easier this way. The inner pleasure of that—not really conscious, but rather unconscious—counting enables them to forget the work.[25]

The French philosopher, Charles Batteaux (1713–1780), in reference to the innate character of music, believed it was melody which was genetic, quoting, without source, a Latin expression, 'We are led to melody by natural instinct.'[26]

Gottfried Wilhelm Leibniz (1646–1716) was reared in a highly educated family, his father being a professor at Leipzig University. Leibniz also entered Leipzig University, receiving a bachelor's degree in philosophy at age sixteen and two doctorates by age twenty-one. Leibniz was a brilliant mathematician, having discovered the foundations of differential and integral calculus.

Leibniz was a great believer of genetic knowledge in general, writing, for example,

> Nothing can be taught us the idea of which is not already in our minds, as the matter out of which our thought is formed.[27]

Leibniz's most extensive writings on the general subject of genetic knowledge is found in his *New Essays on Human Understanding* (1704) which was written in refutation of John Locke's (1632–1704) *Essay Concerning Human Understanding* (1690). Locke had gone to some length to

---

[24] Michel de Saint-Lambert, *Les Principes du Clavecin* (1702), quoted in Carol MacClintock, *Readings in the History of Music in Performance* (Bloomington: Indiana University Press, 1979), 212.

[25] Friedrich von Schelling, *The Philosophy of Art* (Minneapolis: University of Minnesota Press, 1989), 110.

[26] *Les beaux-arts reduits a un meme principe* [Paris 1746], quoted in Peter le Huray and James Day, *Music and Aesthetics in the Eighteenth and Early-Nineteenth Centuries* (Cambridge: Cambridge University Press, 1981), 50ff.

[27] Leibniz, 'Discourse on Metaphysics' (1686), xxvi, in 'A New Method for Learning and Teaching Jurisprudence' (1667), I, xxxiv, in Leroy Loemker, *Philosophical Papers and Letters* (Dordrecht: Reidel, 1956), 320.

contend that man is born with no innate ideas.²⁸ For him it was sufficient proof that there is no such thing as universal, genetic knowledge that one found no such things in children and idiots.²⁹

In the preface to his own work, Leibniz associates Locke with those who believed man is born a 'blank slate,' whereas he finds a passage in the New Testament to prove this is not true.

> Our differences are upon subjects of some importance. The question is to know whether the soul in itself is entirely empty as the tablets upon which as yet nothing has been written (tabula rasa) according to Aristotle, and the author of the Essay [Locke], and whether all that is traced thereon comes solely from the senses and from experience; or whether the soul contains originally the principles of many ideas and doctrines which external objects merely call up on occasion, as I believe with Plato, and even with the schoolmen, and with all those who interpret in this way the passage of St. Paul where he states that the law of God is written in the heart.³⁰

Leibniz continues by contending that the Stoics called this genetic knowledge, 'fundamental assumptions,' while contemporary mathematicians call it 'general notions.'

> Julius Scaliger in particular named them *semina aeternitatis*, also *zopyra*, i.e., living fires, luminous flashes, concealed within us, but which the encounter of the senses makes appear like the sparks which the blow makes spring from the steel. And the belief is not without reason, that these glitterings indicate something divine and eternal which appears especially in the necessary truths ... The senses, although necessary for all our actual knowledge, are not sufficient to give it all to us, since the senses never give us anything but examples, i.e., particular or individual truths.

In this same preface, Leibniz also points to some inconsistencies in Locke, for the purpose of suggesting that perhaps Locke believed in some form of genetic knowledge but did not recognize it as such.

> Perhaps our clever author will not wholly differ from my view. For after having employed the whole of his first book in rejecting innate intelligence, taken in a certain sense, then nevertheless, at the beginning of the second and in the sequel, admits that ideas, which do not originate in sensation, come from reflection. Now reflection is nothing else than attention to what is in us, and the senses do not give us what we already carry with us.

Six years later, Leibniz retreated from the idea of rational knowledge being genetic by contending that this genetic knowledge is not actual reason, but only its components.

---

28 'Essay on Human Understanding,' in *The Works of John Locke* (London, 1823; reprinted in Aalen: Scientia Verlag, 1963), I, ii, ¤1ff.

29 Ibid., I, ii, 5.

30 Leibniz, *New Essays Concerning Human Understanding* (1704), trans. Alfred Langley (La Salle: The Open Court Publishing Company, 1949), Preface. The St. Paul reference is found in Romans 2:15.

> They show that what the law requires is written on their hearts, while their conscience also bears witness and their conflicting thoughts accuse or perhaps excuse them on that day when, according to my gospel, God judges the secrets of men by Christ Jesus.

> I do not affirm the preexistence of rationality. Yet one may believe that in the preexisting germs there has been already prepared and pre-established by divine grace what at some future time is to issue there from, namely, not only the human organism, but also rationality itself, contained in a sealed blueprint to be carried out later.[31]

Since Leibniz was a great believer of genetic knowledge in general, we notice two passages which seem to suggest that perhaps he was thinking of this with respect to music as well. In the first passage he speaks of the unconscious memory of music, in the context of a discussion of genetic knowledge.

> It seems that our clever author claims that there is nothing *virtual* in us, and indeed nothing of which we are not always actually conscious; but he cannot take this rigorously, otherwise his opinion would be too paradoxical; since, moreover, acquired habits and the stores of our memory are not always perceived and do not even always come to our aid at need, although we often easily recall them to the mind upon some slight occasion which makes us remember them, just as we need only the beginning of a song to remember it.[32]

Leibniz also believed that the average man often dreamed of music, although if he were awake he would find it difficult to recreate this music.

> Noteworthy, too, is what Colomesius tells in his lesser works about a song which Gaulminus dreamed about the immortality of the soul. I do not believe that there is a mortal man who would not confess to me that there have often occurred to him while he dreamed, spontaneously and as if made in a moment, elegant visions and skillfully fashioned songs, verses, books, melodies, houses, gardens, depending upon his interests—visions which he could not have formed without effort while awake. Even such unnatural things as flying men and innumerable other monstrosities can be pictured more skillfully than a waking person can do, except with much thought. They are sought by the waker; they offer themselves to the sleeper.[33]

On the other hand, music heard live he thought seemed to create a 'sympathetic echo in us.'[34]

John Dryden (1631–1700), who has been called the greatest literary man of his age,[35] was buried next to Chaucer in Westminster Abbey. In the introduction of his translation of Ovid's *Epistles*, he emphasizes the universality and genetic nature of the emotions.

> If the imitation of Nature be the business of a poet, I know no author who can justly be compared [to Ovid], especially in the description of the passions. And to prove this, I shall need no other judges than the generality of his readers: for all passions being inborn with us, we are almost equally judges when we are concerned in the representation of them.[36]

---

31 Leibniz, 'A Vindication of God's Justice Reconciled with His Other Perfections and All His Actions' (1710), lxxxii, in Paul Schrecker, trans., *Monadology and Other Philosophical Essays* (Indianapolis: Bobbs-Merrill, 1965), 132.

32 Leibniz, *New Essays Concerning Human Understanding*.

33 Leibniz, 'A Fragment on Dreams' (ca. 1666–1676), in Loemker, *Philosophical Papers and Letters*, 115.

34 'On Wisdom' (ca. 1690–1698), in Loemker, *Philosophical Papers and Letters*, 425ff.

35 Bernard Grebanier, *English Literature* (Great Neck: Barron, 1959), 249.

36 *The Works of John Dryden*, ed. Edward Hooker (Berkeley: University of California Press, 1956), I, 111.

William Wotton (1666–1727), chaplain to the Earl of Nottingham, published his *Reflections upon Ancient and Modern Learning* (1694) as a rebuttal to William Temple's essay, 'Of Ancient and Modern Learning,' which had suggested that little insight had been added to those of the ancient writers. Wotton discounts any idea of universal genetic information, much less ability. If it has to do with Nature, he wonders,

> Why have we heard of no orators among the inhabitants of the Bay of Soldania, or eminent poets in Peru?

Anthony Cooper, Earl of Shaftesbury (1671–1713), known simply as Shaftesbury, was a student of Locke, but as a wealthy and cultured gentleman, he was comfortable in discussing the arts, which was a subject rarely mentioned by Locke. In a footnote in his 'Miscellaneous Reflections,' Shaftesbury indicates he believes the emotions are genetic.[37] But if the emotions are in some sense genetic, Shaftesbury still recognized an inequality in their strength among individual men. It is interesting that he uses music, which is the very expression of emotions, as a metaphor to describe his views on this subject.

> Upon the whole, it may be said properly to be the same with the affections or passions in an animal constitution as with the strings of a musical instrument. If these, though in ever so just proportion one to another, are strained beyond a certain degree, it is more than the instrument will bear: the lute or lyre is abused, and its effect lost. On the other hand, if while some of the strings are duly strained, others are not wound up to their due proportion, then is the instrument still in disorder, and its part ill performed. The several species of creatures are like different sorts of instruments; and even in the same species of creatures (as in the same sort of instrument) one is not entirely like the other, nor will the same strings fit each. The same degree of strength which winds up one, and fits the several strings to a just harmony and consort, may in another burst both the strings and instrument itself. Thus men who have the liveliest sense, and are the easiest affected with pain or pleasure, have need of the strongest influence or force of other affections, such as tenderness, love, sociableness, compassion, in order to preserve a right balance within, and to maintain them in their duty, and in the just performance of their part, whilst others, who are of a cooler blood, or lower key, need not the same allay or counter-part, nor are made by Nature to feel those tender and endearing affections in so exquisite a degree.[38]

David Hume (1711–1776), born into a Scottish Presbyterian family, studied at the University of Edinburgh, but left before graduation to pursue philosophy and indeed wrote his great *Treatise on Human Nature* at age twenty-six. He tried law briefly, but found it 'nauseous.' He traveled and worked at various jobs, never quite having a career although he became one of the great representatives of the Enlightenment in philosophy. He knocked the foundation out from under Christianity, not to mention traditional metaphysics, of which he said 'commit it to the flames, for it is nothing but sophistry and illusion.'[39]

---

37 'Miscellaneous Reflections,' in *Characteristics of Men, Manners, Opinions, Times*, IV, ii, fn.
38 Ibid., 'Concerning Virtue or Merit,' II, iii.
39 Royce, *The Spirit of Modern Philosophy* (Boston, 1892), 98.

Hume raises the entire subject of the emotions to a higher level than any former philosopher, even going so far as to make feeling dominant over rational ideas. No one had ever before written anything so extraordinary as the following:

> All probable reasoning is nothing but a species of sensation. It is not solely in poetry and music, we must follow our taste and sentiment, but likewise in philosophy. When I am convinced of any principle, it is only an idea, which strikes more strongly upon me. When I give the preference to one set of arguments above another, I do nothing but decide from my feeling concerning the superiority of their influence.[40]

Hume also seemed to be aware of the universality of the basic emotions.

> The minds of all men are similar in their feelings and operations; nor can any one be actuated by an affection, of which all others are not, in some degree, susceptible.[41]

As we pointed out above, earlier philosophers, beginning with Aristotle, probably felt inclined to assume there was something genetic about music simply on the basis of its universality. But they were like those early astronomers who had to speculate on the organization of the solar system without the benefit of a telescope. It has only been during the past 50 years that breakthroughs in medical research have for the first time thrown some genuine light on this subject, offering physical proof to support earlier philosophical speculation. Thus far we have seen many individual scientists studying a wide variety of aspects of music perception which seem to point toward genetic foundations. It is too early for a unified theory, but these individual findings are remarkable. Consider the following:

ITEM: Dennis Molfese of the University of Pennsylvania has found an affinity for musical language in infants less than forty-eight hours after birth.[42]

ITEM: Psychologist Jerome Kagan of Harvard University in a study for infants four months old found an apparent genetic predilection to consonance over dissonance.[43]

ITEM: University of California researchers believe that infants are born with a genetic ability to recognize and respond to music, even before language.[44]

ITEM: Research at UCLA with newborns before they left the hospital establish bicameral patterns for speech versus musical sounds. Furthermore the brain adds amplification: to the left ear for music (right brain) and to the right ear for speech.[45]

---

[40] *A Treatise of Human Nature*, I, iii, 8.
[41] Ibid., III, iii, 1.
[42] Reported in Craig Buck, 'Knowing the LEFT from the RIGHT,' *Human Behavior* (June, 1976).
[43] Reported in the *Los Angeles Times*, Dec. 2, 1996.
[44] Reported in the Associated Press, January 23, 1992.
[45] UCLA Press Release, Sept. 10, 2004.

ITEM: Psychologists have found that even before age one infants can detect errors in music.[46]

ITEM: There is evidence that almost all musicians who began their training before the age of six possess absolute pitch, compared with none of those who began after the age of eleven.[47] Some believe absolute pitch may be a vestigial talent of our primate ancestors.

ITEM: Research by Dr. Jamshed Bharucha, of Dartmouth College, has found that we have a genetic preference for certain kinds of melodic patterns.

ITEM: A study by Stewart Hulse of Johns Hopkins University found that starlings have the ability to recognize a simple melody in different keys. In another experiment, pigeons were trained to distinguish random excerpts of music by J. S. Bach from excerpts by Stravinsky and were able to correctly categorize music by other composers as being either 'Bach-like' or 'Stravinsky-like.'[48]

ITEM: Jay Dowling, of the University of Texas at Dallas, has found clinical evidence to suggest that ordinary people perceive melodic patterns on the basis of the relationship between the notes themselves, and not on the basis of precise pitches. Hence almost everybody can sing 'Happy Birthday' beginning from any note on the piano.[49]

ITEM: John Pierce of Stanford has demonstrated that the brain has little ability to recognize melodic patterns played backwards. For example, most people do not realize that the sound of the word *we* is the reverse of the sound of the word *you*.[50]

ITEM: In 1974, physician and researcher, Dr. Thomas wrote, 'The need to make music, and to listen to it, is universally expressed by human beings … It is like speech, a dominant aspect of human biology.'[51]

A great deal of additional research has been done in the past ten years and it seems clear that we come into this world with some elements of music. It is because the basic emotions and elements of music are universal and genetic in character that the expression about music being the international language is true.

Music teachers therefore have an unbelievable advantage. Suppose you were a geology teacher and someone told you, 'every student loves geology and every student has the basics of geology implanted genetically before he enters the school.' That would be a happy geology teacher, he would suddenly feel his teaching area was fundamental and important to mankind.

---

46 Reported in 'The Musical Brain,' *U. S. News & World Report*, June 11, 1990.

47 D. Sergeant, 'Experimental Investigation of Absolute Pitch,' *Journal of Research in Musical Education* 17, no. 1 (Spring 1969): 135–143.

48 Reported in 'The Musical Brain.'

49 Reported in Ibid.

50 Reported in Buck, 'Knowing the LEFT from the RIGHT.' This is unwelcome news for twelve-tone composers.

51 Jacqueline Schmidt Peters, *Music Therapy, an Introduction* (Springfield: Charles Thomas, 1987), 49.

Music teachers actually have these two advantages but they do not capitalize on them. Our grandchildren will be hard pressed to explain why the music educators of today have failed to base music education on these two pregnant characteristics of music and instead have constructed an educational edifice built on conceptual information *about* music, an edifice no child has any interest in visiting.

Suppose you were a young person who wanted to learn to play golf. You love watching golf; you feel instinctively that you have what it takes to play golf. So you take a course called, 'Introduction to Golf.' What do you do when you find it is not a course in playing golf at all, but a course *about* golf, the history of golf and every imaginable concept relating to golf. You don't return and you go off and teach yourself golf.

And that is the same reason why the majority of school children are not in our music classes. And all those students who are *not* in our classes, every single one of them, are involved in music on their own, utterly unsupervised.

Ancient Views on Geography and Music

> *As climates are distinguished by degrees of latitude, we might distinguish them also in some measure by those of sensibility. I have been at the opera in England and in Italy, where I have seen the same pieces and the same performers: and yet the same music produces such different effects on the two nations: one is so cold and phlegmatic, and the other so lively and enraptured, that it seems almost inconceivable.*
>
> 'Of the Difference of Men in different climates'[1]
> Montesquieu (1689–1755)

HAVING BEEN A RESIDENT OF LOS ANGELES for nearly forty years, I can attest to the fact that among the residents of California there is a very strong prejudice between 'Northern Californians' and 'Southern Californians.' No one can say, exactly, where the geographical line of demarcation lies, but we have never met a Californian who did not fervently believe the line existed.

But since Northern and Southern California share a common Spanish heritage and are thought of as one by most of the rest of the world in their rejection of its culture, one has to wonder if climate can really be the determining factor between north and south. Montesquieu, as part of his discussion on climate and men from which we have drawn the quotation above, believed there is indeed a physical, and hence physiological difference. He writes,

> Cold air constringes the extremities of the external fibres of the body; this increases their elasticity, and favors the return of the blood from the extreme parts of the heart. It contracts those very fibres; consequently it increases also their force. On the contrary, warm air relaxes and lengthens the extremes of the fibres; of course it diminishes their force and elasticity.
>
> People are therefore more vigorous in cold climates. Here the action of the heart and the reaction of the extremities of the fibres are better performed, the temperature of the humors is greater, the blood moves more freely towards the heart, and reciprocally the heart has more power.

William Temple (1628–1699), an English philosopher, agreed that climate had an adverse influence on English character.

> Our country must be confessed to be what a great foreign physician called it, the region of spleen, which may arise a good deal from the great uncertainty and many sudden changes of our weather in all seasons of the year. And how much these affect the heads and hearts, especially of the finest tempers, is hard to be believed by men whose thoughts are not turned to such speculations. This makes us unequal in our humors, inconstant in our passions, uncertain in our ends, and even in our desires.[2]

---

[1] Charles de Secondat, Baron de Montesquieu (1689–1755), *The Spirit of Laws* (1748), trans. Thomas Nugent in *Great Books*, XXXVIII (Chicago: Encyclopedia Britannica, 1952), 102ff.

[2] *Five Miscellaneous Essays by Sir William Temple*, ed. Samuel Monk (Ann Arbor: University of Michigan Press, 1963), 200.

Montesquieu, we might add, seems to agree. In the work we have cited above, he concludes that the English have a 'disrelish of everything' and an 'impatience of temper' which makes concentration difficult.

Our interest in this question is, of course, whether the physiological impact of climate affects national character and, in turn, national predilections in music. One can find many observations such as the following conclusion by Robert Greene (1560–1592), an important English playwright and observer of manners.

> In Crete you must learn to lie, in Paphos to be a lover, in Greece a dissembler, you must bring home pride from Spain, lasciviousness from Italy, gluttony from England and carousing from the Danes.[3]

This reminds us of a letter the young Mendelssohn wrote to his sister, Rebecca.

> In Italy I was lazy, in Switzerland a wild student, in Munich a consumer of cheese and beer and in Paris I must talk politics.[4]

With respect to music, such generalizations are particularly prevalent when the subject is the vocal characteristics of different nations. Thus one finds these sweeping conclusions by two German philosophers of the Renaissance. First, Henry Agrippa (1486–1536), in his discussion of moral philosophy, provides amusing characterizations of the men of various nations. After with comparing them as lovers, in their speech and dress, he adds,

> We know moreover that the Italians do bleat in their singing, the Spaniards wail, the Germans howl and the French sing with pleasant tone and accent.[5]

Similarly, Andreas Ornithoparchus, in his *Musice active micrologus* of 1517, observes,

> Various nations have diverse fashions and differ in clothes, diet, studies, speech and song. Hence it is that the English carol, the French sing, the Spaniards weep, the Italians caper with their voices and others bark. But the Germans, I am ashamed to say, howl like wolves.[6]

Perhaps we should pause to consider what is being described in these comparisons of music in various countries. The great contribution of the medieval minstrels as they crossed back and forth across Europe was that they created a common European music language. It is true we still hear differences in the music between, say, France and Germany, but those differences are not nearly as dramatic as the differences in language and food, etc. And, as time went on, there were certainly changes in music itself, but the biggest difference between nations was in

---

[3] Robert Greene, *Mourning Garment* (ca. 1590), in *The Life and Complete Works of Robert Greene*, ed. Alexander Grosart (New York: Russell & Russell, 1964), IX, 136. His romance, *Pandosto* (1588) was the source of Shakespeare's *Winter's Tale*.

[4] Letter of December 20, 1831.

[5] Henry Cornelius Agrippa, *Of the Vanitie and Uncertaintie of Arts and Sciences*, ed. Catherine Dunn (Northridge: California State University, Northridge Press, 1974), 161.

[6] Ornithoparchus, *Musicae active mirologus* and Dowland, *Introduction: Containing the Art of Singing* (New York: Dover, 1973), 208ff.

performance practice and performance values. This remains very strongly felt today, as, for example, in the difference between the French oboe sound and the German oboe sound. And for those who have lived and worked in Europe, the very phrases 'German orchestras,' 'French orchestras' and 'Italian orchestras' bring to mind powerfully different memories.

Above, we have quoted some surveys of national vocal styles. Now we would like to present two more, both by Johann Mattheson, for we believe they demonstrate how material such as this can throw valuable light on the values of the societies they reflect. First, in a book published in 1713 (*Das Neu-Eroffnete Orchestre*), Mattheson pays tribute to the Italians above the French. However, in a book published in 1739 (*Der vollkommene Capellmeister*) he now finds the French more satisfying than the Italians. Part of his change of opinion reflects the change which had occurred in French values during this thirty-five year period. This period saw a number of philosophical papers which argued over the values of the 'French style' (formalistic and objective) as opposed to the 'Italian style' (emphasis on the communication of feeling). Lying at the foundation of this dialog was a supreme irony which no one seems to have noticed. Lully, *an Italian*, was regarded as the exponent of the official *French* style, whereas Rameau, *a Frenchman*, was regarded as a representative of the *Italian* style. In any case, there *was* an important change taking place. French performers who had previously most often been described as being satisfied with merely pleasing the ears of the listener were now placing much greater emphasis on moving the emotions of the listener. It was this change, this adoption of the values of the Italians, which made Mattheson come to appreciate the French singers in the second, and later, of these two national surveys.

In his *Das Neu-Eroffnete Orchestre*, Mattheson finds in the compositions of the Italians the most beauty, due in part to 'their polished and *insinuante* artistic ideas.' There is no question, he concludes, that all nations who desire to be distinguished in music 'have borrowed nearly everything from the Italians, and have imitated them completely in all things.'

The fame of the French, he writes, lies not so much in their composition as in their execution, especially in dance music where they are the masters. The English style he characterizes as a 'flat-footed imitation of the Italian style.' And as for the music of his own country,

> Among the educated Germans the esteem for music has never been really small or thoroughly prosperous either. In fact, this noble art ... has come to be treated somewhat sleepily and indifferently; hence the great revolution in musical affairs has not come to my countrymen as it has to those in other lands ... Our German virtuosi, who are—to speak dispassionately—altogether worthy to bear such a title with honor, are much more deserving of esteem than whole bands of foreigners ... But a contemptible custom affecting these matters has come to pass; we prefer anything that is foreign, not necessarily because of its beauty and value, but merely because it is foreign to our own people, and things which are not bad or simple in themselves suffer the odium of being merely native.[7]

---

7 Johann Mattheson, *Das Neu-Eroffnete Orchestre* (Hamburg, 1713), 200ff.

In his later book, Mattheson writes,

> If we turn from playing to singing, oh! that is when the misery really begins. Look at the fervor with which the French men and women singers present their pieces, and how they almost always seem really to feel what they are singing. Hence the reason that they strongly stir the emotions of the listeners, particularly their countrymen, and replace through gesticulation and mannerisms what they lack in thorough instruction, in strength, or in vocal ability.
>
> The Italians carry this even further than the French; indeed, sometimes they even go a little too far: As in almost all their undertakings they frequently overstep the limits and love the extremes. Meanwhile they frequently have tears in their eyes when they perform something that is melancholy; and on the other hand, their heart is overjoyed when there is something enjoyable: for they are very emotional by nature ...
>
> Only the cool Germans, although they have revealed to the Italians their great musical abilities through the three great H's, namely Handel, Heinichen and Hasse, on the one hand place their greatest merit in the fact that they look just as stiff and unemotional with the sad as well as the cheerful affections with which their music deals ... they sing very decently and rigidly, as if they had no interest in the content, and are not in the least concerned with the consideration of the proper expression or meaning of the words ... as is demonstrated daily by teachers and students. On the other hand, it is quite a favor if they do not gossip with, trifle with or ridicule their neighbors during rests; even if the things of which they sing would be worthy of the highest attention.[8]

Some of the most interesting discussions of musical style during the Baroque Period center on the differences between French and Italian singing. For the French, especially, there was real tension on this subject during the seventeenth century. On one hand, the court of Louis XIV was universally recognized as the model aristocratic court and was imitated by nobles even in Germany. The French, therefore, thought of themselves as the cultural leaders of Europe. At the same time a powerful new musical medium had been born in Italy and was, at the very same time, sweeping across Europe, dominating everything in its path. Because of the popularity of this new medium courts in Northern Europe were seeking to hire Italian composers in residence and young composers were going to Italy to study. Italian singers and instrumentalists were also being transported throughout Europe. This vastly popular new medium was opera, or as they called it, Italian opera. The source of the popularity of late seventeenth-century Italian opera was the same as daytime television: stories of a young lady, weeping and wailing, caught up in an impossibly complicated plot. It was the emotional singing which caused the crisis in French music and engendered so much debate. Let us sample some of these views.

A very influential French philosopher, who commented early in this debate, was Marin Mersenne (1588–1648) in his *Harmonie universelle* of 1636. He was a brilliant, influential and widely known man and he clearly saw what was coming.

---

[8] Johann Mattheson, *Der vollkommene Capellmeister* (1739), trans. Ernest Harriss (Ann Arbor: UMI Research Press, 1981), I, vi, 18ff.

> The Italian [singers] observe several things in their solos of which ours are deprived, since they represent as much as they can the passions and the affections of the soul and the mind, for example, choler, wrath, spite, rage, lapses of the heart, and several passions, with a violence so peculiar that one would almost judge that they felt the same affections which they represent when singing, whereas we French are content with charming the ear, and use a constant mildness in our songs, which hinders their vigors.[9]

In another place, he makes the same point:

> As to the Italians, they … represent as much as they can the passions and the feelings of the soul and spirit; for example, anger, fury, spleen, rage, faintheartedness, and many other passions, with a violence so strange, that one judges them as if they were touched with the same affects as they represent in singing; in place of which our Frenchmen are content to caress the ear, and use nothing but a perpetual sweetness in their songs; which hinders their energy.[10]

Another Frenchman who clearly understood the revolution emanating from Italy was Andre Maugars, a violist and secretary attached to Cardinal Richelieu. Sent to Rome in 1639 on a diplomatic mission, he reported back on the more interesting church music and came to understand how rule-bound the French composers were.

> In the first place, I find that [the Italian] composers of church music have more artistry, more knowledge, and more variety than ours; but also that they have more freedom. And for me, since I could not disapprove of this freedom, when it is used discreetly and with skill, which insensibly deceives our feelings, so I cannot approve of the stubbornness of our composers who keep themselves religiously limited in pedantic categories and who feel that they would commit solecisms against the rules of the art if they wrote two successive fifths or if they departed even a little bit from their modes. No doubt it is in these very agreeable departures that the secret of the art consists—since music has figures of speech just like rhetoric, which all tend to charm the listener and deceive him insensibly. To tell the truth, it is not so necessary to amuse ourselves by observing the rules so rigorously that it makes us lose track of a fugue or the beauty of a song, in view of the fact these rules have been invented only to keep young schoolboys under control and prevent them from emancipating themselves before they have reached years of discretion. That is why a judicious man, with full knowledge of the science, is not condemned, by absolute fiat, to stay eternally in this narrow prison and can always soar according as his caprice carries him into some fine experiment, wherever the power of the words and the beauty of the parts shall lead him. This is what the Italians practice to perfection, and as they are much more refined than we in musical matters, they sneer at our musical regularity, and thus they write their Motets with more art, more knowledge, more variety, and more skill than we do ours …
>
> As for our composers, if they were willing to emancipate themselves a little more from their pedantic rules and take a few journeys to observe foreign music, my feeling is that they would succeed much better than they are doing now.[11]

---

9 *Harmonie universelle*, IV, vi, 6.

10 Ibid., II, vi, 356.

11 Andre Maugars, 'Response faite a un curieux sur le Sentiment de la Musique d'Italie, Ecrite a Rome le premier Octobre 1639,' quoted in Carol MacClintock, *Readings in the History of Music in Performance* (Bloomington: Indiana University Press, 1979), 117ff, 124ff.

Maugars also attended the opera in Rome and was full of admiration of this new form which as yet had not had much influence in France.

> There are a large number of castrati for the Dessus and the Haute-Contre, very beautiful and natural Tenors, and very few deep Basses. They are very certain of their technique and sing the most difficult music at sight. In addition, they are almost all actors by nature, and it is for this reason that they succeed so perfectly in their musical comedies. I have seen them play three or four this last winter, but I must admit that in truth they are incomparable and inimitable in music for the stage, not only for their singing but also for the expression of the words, the postures, and the gestures of the characters they play naturally and very well.
>
> As for their manner of singing, it is much more animated than ours; they have certain inflections of the voice that we do not possess. It is true that they perform their *passages* with more roughness, but today they are beginning to correct that.[12]

By the end of the seventeenth century Italian opera had made its full impact across Europe and could not be ignored by the French. A strong complaint against his contemporaries' absorption with the old rules was made by François Raguenet, in his famous 'Parallele des Italiens et des Français,' of 1702.

> It is not to be wondered that the Italians think our music dull and stupefying, that according to their taste it appears flat and insipid, if we consider the nature of the French airs compared to those of the Italian. The French, in their airs, aim at the soft, the easy, the flowing and coherent; the whole air is of the same key, or, if sometimes they venture to vary it, they do it with so many preparations, they so qualify it, that still the air seems to be as natural and consistent as if they had attempted no change at all; there is nothing bold and adventurous in it; it is all equal and of one piece. But the Italians pass boldly and in an instant from B-natural to B-flat to B-natural; they venture the boldest cadences and the most irregular dissonance; and their airs are so out of the way that they resemble the compositions of no other nation in the world.
>
> The French would think themselves undone if they offended in the least against the rules; they flatter, tickle, and court the ear and are still doubtful of success, though everything be done with an exact regularity. The more hardy Italian changes the tone and the mode without any awe or hesitation; he makes double or treble cadences of seven or eight bars together upon tones we should think incapable of the least division. He will make a swelling of so prodigious a length they they who are unacquainted with it can't choose but be offended at first to see him so adventurous, but before he has done it they will think they can't sufficiently admire him. He will have *passages* of such an extent as will perfectly confound his auditors at first, and upon such irregular tones as shall instill a terror as well as surprise into the audience, who will immediately conclude that the whole concert is degenerating into a dreadful dissonance; and betraying them by that means into a concern for the music, which seems to be upon the brink of ruin, he immediately reconciles them by such regular cadences that everyone is surprised to see harmony rising again, in a manner, out of discord itself and owing its greatest beauties to those irregularities which seemed to threaten it with destruction. The Italians venture at everything that is harsh and out of the way, but then they do it like people that have a right to venture and are sure of success. Under a notion of being the greatest and most absolute masters of music in the world, like despotic sovereigns they dispense with its rules in hardy but fortunate

---

[12] Ibid., 122.

sallies; they exert themselves above the art, but, like masters of that art whose laws they follow or transgress at pleasure, they insult the niceness of the ear which others court; they master and conquer it with charms which owe their irresistible force to the boldness of the adventurous composer.[13]

After a visit to Italy, he was equally impressed with the instrumental music he heard there.

As for the accompaniments of the violin [in France], they are, for the most part, nothing but single strokes of the bow, heard by intervals, without any uniform coherent music, serving only to express, from time to time, a few accords. Whereas in Italy, the first and second upper part, the thorough bass, and all the other parts that concur to the composition of the fullest pieces, are equally finished. The parts for the violins are usually as beautiful as the melody itself. So that after we have been entertained with something very charming in the melody, we are insensibly captivated by the parts that accompany it, which are equally engaging and make us quit the subject to listen to them. Everything is so exactly beautiful that it is difficult to find out the principal part … It is too much for one soul to taste the several beauties of so many parts. She must multiply herself before she can relish and digest three or four delights at once which are all beautiful alike; it is transport, enchantment, and ecstasy of pleasure; her faculties are upon so great a stretch, she is forced to ease herself by exclamations; she waits impatiently for the end of the air that she may have a breathing space …

To conclude, the Italians are inexhaustible in their productions of such pieces as are composed of several parts, in which on the other side the French are extremely limited. In France, the composer thinks he has done his business if he can diversify the subject; as for the accompaniments you find nothing like it in them; without any variety or surprise. The French composers steal from one another or copy from their own works so that all their compositions are much alike.[14]

There seems no doubt that Raguenet understood that the driving principle in Italian music was a new emphasis on the expression of the emotions.

As the Italians are much more brisk than the French, so are they more sensible of the passions and consequently express them more lively in all their productions. If a storm or rage is to be described in a symphony, their notes give us so natural an idea of it that our souls can hardly receive a stronger impression from the reality than they do from the description; everything is so brisk and piercing, so impetuous and affecting, that the imagination, the senses, the soul, and the body itself are all betrayed into a general transport; it is impossible not to be borne down with the rapidity of these movements. A symphony of furies shakes the soul; it undermines and overthrows it in spite of all its care; the artist himself, whilst he is performing it, is seized with an unavoidable agony; he tortures his violin; he racks his body; he is no longer master of himself, but is agitated like one possessed with an irresistible motion.

If, on the other side, the symphony is to express a calm and tranquility, which requires a quite different style, they however execute it with an equal success. Here the notes descend so low that the soul is swallowed with them in the profound abyss. Every string of the bow is of an infinite length, lingering on a dying sound which decays gradually until at last it absolutely expires. Their symphonies of sleep insensibly steal the soul from the body and so suspend its faculties and operations that, being bound up, as it were, in the harmony that entirely possesses and enchants it, it is as dead to everything else as if all its powers were captivated by a real sleep.[15]

---

[13] François Raguenet, 'Parallele des Italiens et des Francais,' (1702), quoted in Oliver Strunk, *Source Readings in Music History* (New York: Norton, 1950), 477ff.

[14] Ibid., 480ff.

[15] Ibid., 478ff.

Raguenet, who took his own life in 1722, would not live long enough to see that Italian opera was an idiom which would lead to the emotionally expressive German and Austrian music of the Classical Period. In the following passage we find him trying hard to make a case for the old French opera style.

> Our operas are written much better than the Italian; they are regular, coherent designs; and, though repeated without the music, they are as entertaining as any of our other pieces that are purely dramatic. Nothing can be more natural and lively than their dialogues; the gods are made to speak with a dignity suitable to their character, kings with all the majesty their rank requires, and the nymphs and shepherds with a softness and innocent mirth peculiar to the plains. Love, jealousy, anger, and the rest of the passions are touched with the greatest art and nicety, and there are few of our tragedies or comedies that appear more beautiful than [the librettist] Quinault's operas.
>
> On the other hand, the Italian operas are poor, incoherent rhapsodies without any connection or design; all their pieces, properly speaking, are patched up with thin, insipid scraps; their scenes consist of some trivial dialogues or soliloquy, at the end of which they foist in one of their best airs, which concludes the scene …
>
> Besides, our operas have a further advantage over the Italian in respect of the voice, and that is the bass, which is so frequent among us and so rarely to be met with in Italy. For every man that has an ear will witness with me that nothing can be more charming than a good bass; the simple sound of these basses, which sometimes seems to sink into a profound abyss, has something wonderfully charming in it. The air receives a stronger concussion from these deep voices than it does from those that are higher and is consequently filled with a more agreeable and extensive harmony. When the persons of gods or kings, a Jupiter, Neptune, Priam, or Agamemnon, are brought on the stage, our actors, with their deep voices, give them an air of majesty, quite different from that of the feigned bases among the Italians, which have neither depth nor strength. Besides, the interfering of the basses with the upper parts forms an agreeable contrast and makes us perceive the beauties of the one from the opposition they meet with from the other, a pleasure to which the Italians are perfect strangers, the voices of their singers, who are for the most part castrati, being perfectly like those of their women.[16]

When it came to the music, however, Raguenet could not help but admire many aspects of Italian singing.

> There is no weak part in any of the Italian operas, where no sense is preferable to the rest of its peculiar beauties; all the songs are of an equal force and are sure to be crowned with applause, whereas in our operas there are I know not how many languishing scenes and insipid airs with which nobody can be pleased or diverted.
>
> It must be confessed that our recitative is much better than that of the Italians, which is too close and simple; it is the same throughout and cannot properly be called singing. Their recitative is little better than downright speaking, without any inflection or modulation of the voice, and yet there is this to be admired in it—the parts that accompany this psalmody are incomparable, for they have such an extraordinary genius for composition that they know how to adapt charming concords, even to a voice that does little more than speak, a thing to be met with in no other part of the world whatsoever.

---

[16] Ibid., 474ff.

> I observed in the beginning of this parallel how much we had the advantage over the Italians in our basses, so common with us and so rare to be found in Italy; but how small is this in comparison to the benefit their operas receive from their castrati, who abound without number among them, whereas there is not one to be found in all France. Our women's voices are indeed as soft and agreeable as are those of their castrati, but then they are far from being either so strong or lively. No man or woman in the world can boast of a voice like theirs; they are clear, they are moving, and affect the soul itself …
>
> Add to this that these soft—these charming voices acquire new charms by being in the mouth of a lover; what can be more affecting than the expressions of their sufferings in such tender passionate notes; in this the Italian lovers have a very great advantage over ours, whose hoarse masculine voices ill agree with the fine soft things they are to say to their mistresses. Besides, the Italian voices being equally strong as they are soft, we hear all they sing very distinctly, whereas half of it is lost upon our stage unless we sit close to the stage or have the spirit of divination. Our upper parts are usually performed by girls that have neither lungs nor wind, whereas the same parts in Italy are always performed by men whose firm piercing voices are to be heard clearly in the largest theaters without losing a syllable, sit where you will.
>
> But the greatest advantage the Italians receive from these castrati is that their voices hold good for thirty or forty years together, whereas our women begin to lose the beauty of theirs at ten or twelve years end.[17]

At the dawn of the eighteenth century, other Frenchmen were still finding essentially the same comparison between the Italian and French musicians. The French composer, Sebastien de Brossard, in his *Dictionaire de musique* (1703), concluded,

> The Italian style is sharp, colorful, expressive; the French in contrast, natural, flowing, tender.[18]

The great François Couperin, in thinking of the difference between French and Italian style, observed in 1717,

> The French gladly swallow what is novel, at the expense of losing what is fit and proper, which they believe they understand better than other nations.[19]

There were some loyal Frenchmen, of course, who attempted to defend the old formalistic style of French music. One of these persons was Charles de Saint-Evremond (1610–1703), a man who didn't like opera in the first place. After admitting 'the little esteem the Italians have for our opera, and the great disgust we have for the Italian ones,' he treats the reader to a little tour of national characteristics in opera.[20]

---

[17] Ibid., 482ff..

[18] Quoted in George J. Buelow, 'Music and Society in the Late Baroque Era,' in *The Late Baroque Era* (Englewood Cliffs: Prentice Hall, 1994), 15ff.

[19] François Couperin, *L'Art de toucher*.

[20] Charles de Saint-Evremond, 'Lettre sur les Opera,' quoted in MacClintock, *Readings in the History of Music in Performance*, 253ff.

> As to the manner of singing, what we call the execution in France, I think with no partiality that no nation can rival ours. The Spanish have admirable throats; but with their graces [*fredons*] and their roulades they seem in their singing to be thinking of rivaling the nightingale in the facility of their throats. The expressiveness of the Italians is false or at least exaggerated, because they do not know exactly the nature and degree of the passions. It is bursting out laughing rather than singing when they express some joyous feeling. If they try to sigh one can hear sobs that are formed violently in the throat, not the sighs with which a loving heart gives vent to its passion in secret. Of a sad reflection they make the most powerful exclamations; tears of absence become funeral weeping; sad things become lugubrious in their mouths; they utter cries of pain instead of laments; and sometimes they express the languor due to passion as a weakness of nature. Perhaps there is some change now in their way of singing and they have profited by their contact with us to acquire a clear-cut, polished execution, just as we have profited from them to acquire the beauties of a greater and bolder composition.
>
> I have seen comedies in England where there was much music. But to speak discreetly, I have never been able to grow accustomed to English singing. I came too late to acquire a taste so differently from any other. There is no nation which shows more courage in the men, and more beauty in the women, more wit in both sexes. But you cannot have everything. Where so many good qualities are common it is no great loss that good taste is so rare …
>
> There is no one slower in understanding the sense of the words and entering into the spirit of the composer than the French; there are few who understand quantity less, and who have so much trouble with the pronunciation; but when long study has enabled them to really understand what they are singing, nothing approaches their pleasantness. The same is true for instruments and especially in concerts, where nothing is sure or correct until after an infinity of rehearsals are finished. The Italians, very learned in music, bring their knowledge to our ears with no sweetness whatsoever; the French are not content to rid knowledge of its first roughness, which smacks of the hard work of composing; they find in the secrets of performing something to charm the soul, a *je ne sais quoi* very touching, which they can bring to our very hearts.

We should include the remarks of the French philosopher who made the greatest effort in defense of the old French opera, Jacques Bonnet-Bourdelot.

> One can say that Italian music resembles an amiable coquette, although somewhat painted, full of vivacity, always rushing about seeking to sparkle everywhere without reason, and not knowing why; like a scatter brain who shows her passions in everything she does; when it is a question of tender affection she makes it dance the gavotte or gigue. Would not one say that serious matters become comical in her hands, and that she is more suited to *ariettes* and *chansonettes* than to deal with noble subjects? In that, is she not like to those comedians who having talent only for the comic, succeed very badly, turning tragedy to ridicule when they wish to have a hand in it? One must admit that the majesty of French music treats heroic subjects with greater nobility and is more appropriate to the cothurnus and the theater; whereas in Italian music all the passions appear alike: joy, anger, sorrow, happy love, the lover who fears or hopes—all seem to be painted with the same features and the same character; it is a continual gigue, always sparkling or leaping.[21]

He was particularly suspicious of anything involving technique, for its tendency to detract from the sentiment of the words in the opera.

---

[21] Jacques Bonnet-Bourdelot, *Histoire de la musique et de ses effets depuis son origine, et les progres successifs de cet art jusqu'a esent* (Paris, 1715), quoted in MacClintock, *Readings in the History of Music in Performance*, 242ff.

> We have difficulty to accustom ourselves to the strange intervals in the recitatives of their songs, which sometimes exceed an octave, in which even the most skillful find difficulty with just intonation. Above all, the long *tenutos* make the listener impatient because they are misplaced; these holds, which we also use and which are rarely suitable except on words of repose, they make indifferently on all the words that end with vowels. I do not say there may not be a great deal of art in having a violin and a bass frolic below one of these long fermatas, but what has liberty to do with this sound that lasts a quarter of an hour? Where is the taste and expression in all of that? It very often happens that Italian music expresses something quite different from the words. I hear a Prelude that is fast and furious: I then think that some lover, repelled by the coldness of his lady, is going to give way to spite and abuse Love; not at all: it is a tender lover who praises the price of his constancy, who calls Hope to his aid, or who makes a declaration of love to his mistress.

Another unusually interesting passage regarding opera involves a quotation from St. Augustine which we do not find in the extant works of that Church father.

> But to arrive at perfection in such a fine spectacle, it is necessary to have persons of talent who understand perfectly the principles on which St. Augustine placed the perfection of harmony, arranged in nine degrees: the first in the mind, the second in good judgment, the third in the imagination, the fourth in the emotions, the fifth in the word, the sixth in the melody, the seventh in the sound, the eighth in desire, and the ninth in the composition.
>
> These principles embody also the perfection of the nine Muses, whom the Ancients considered divinities. Thus, to compose a perfect opera it takes at least a poet, a musician, a mathematician, a ballet master, a painter—all of whom excel in their art—and a superintendent of great perception to oversee the construction and execution of the work. Also a great prince, or a republic as powerful as that of Venice, should pay the expenses *a discretion*, for it is necessary that everything be suitable to such a great subject, which is ordinarily drawn from a fable or history or is allegorical.[22]

In summary, he finds,

> One can say also without ostentation that the French operas outdo those of Italy by the size and beauty of the choruses, by the *agrements* of the recitative, as well as by the authority of execution by the instruments of the orchestra, whose symphony is inimitable, as well as by the magnificence of the ballet *entrees* and the *danses élevées*, *danses bases*, or *danses figueres* … executed by dancers who know the art of characterizing the passions through movements of the dance with grace and a nobility worthy of admiration that is not found in Italy.[23]

If French criticism seems somewhat defensive with regard to the Italians, the English are often downright hostile. Henry Peacham (1576–1643), in discussing the education of the noble, includes music as an important subject for study.[24] He begins, however, with a little attack on the Italians, quoting a current proverb 'Whom God loves not, that man loves not music.'

---

[22] Ibid., 249.

[23] Ibid.

[24] Henry Peacham, *The Complete Gentleman*, ed. Virgil Heltzel (Ithaca: Cornell University Press, 1962), 108ff.

> But I am verily persuaded that they are by nature very ill-disposed and of such brutish stupidity that scarce anything else that is good and favorable to virtue is to be found in them.²⁵

Thomas Nashe (1567–1601), in his *Pierce Penilesse His Supplication to the Devil* (1592),²⁶ no doubt had in mind the tradition of English school boys, upon graduation, going to Italy as if to a gentlemen's finishing school, when he calls Italy the 'Academy of man-slaughter, the sporting place of murder, the Apothecary-shop of poison for all Nations.' He makes the claim that Pope Sixtus V (1585–1590) was poisoned by the king of Spain, whom he had invited to dinner. The following pope, according to Nashe, after his election sent someone a note reading '*Sol, Re, Me, Fa,*' which meant *Solus Rex me facit*: 'the king of Spain made me pope.'

The English poet, John Gay (1685–1732), wondered why it was necessary for young Englishmen to travel to Italy to study music. It is not the 'Italian climate' that made that country famous for music, but the financial support for music.

> Why must we climb the Alpine mountain's sides
> To find the seat where Harmony resides?
> Why touch we not so soft the silver lute,
> The cheerful haut-boy, and the mellow flute?
> 'Tis not the Italian clime improves the sound,
> But there the Patrons of her sons are found.²⁷

Roger North, an important English philosopher of music, found, on the other hand, approval for the tradition of young men going to Italy.

> The other circumstance I hinted was the numerous train of young travelers of the best quality & estates, that about this time went over into Italy & resided at Rome & Venice, where they heard the best music and learned from the best masters ... and they came home confirmed in the love of the Italian manner, & some contracted no little skill & proved exquisite performers; then came over Corelli's first consort that cleared the ground of all other sorts of music whatsoever; by degrees the rest of his consorts & at last the concerti came, all of which are to the musicians like the bread of life.²⁸

The great English poet, John Milton (1608–1674) was rather taken by his personal travel to Italy, which he called 'the retreat of civility and of all polite learning.'²⁹

---

25 Of the French, he writes,

   They delight for the most part in horsemanship, fencing, hunting, dancing, and little esteem of learning and gifts of the mind. [Ibid., 163]

26 *The Works of Thomas Nashe*, ed. Ronald McKerrow (Oxford: Blackwell, 1966), I, 186. Nashe is best known for his *The Unfortunate Traveller*, which some consider the first English novel

27 'Epistle IV,' in *The Works of John Gay* (London: Edward Jeffery, 1745), III, 34.

28 Roger North, *The Musicall Gramarian* (Oxford: Oxford University Press, 1925), 37.

29 'A Second Defence of the English People,' in *The Works of John Milton*, ed. Frank Patterson (New York: Columbia University Press, 1931–1938) VIII, 115.

It is also true that one does not find in English literature very much praise for French music. As a representative of English criticism in this regard, we might look at an issue of Addison's famous journal, *Spectator* for 3 April 1711. Here, while he does not refer to climate, he does seem to take for granted that different peoples must appreciate different music.

> For this reason the Italian artists cannot agree with our English musicians, in admiring Purcell's compositions, and thinking his tunes so wonderfully adapted to his words, because both nations do not always express the same passions by the same sounds ...
>
> A composer should fit his Musick to the genius of the people, and consider that the delicacy of hearing, and taste of harmony, has been formed upon those sounds which every country abounds with: In short, that Musick is of a relative nature, and what is harmony to one ear, may be dissonance to another.

Addison then follows with some interesting comments about French and Italian opera.

> Signor Baptist Lully acted like a man of sense in this particular. He found the French Musick extremely defective, and very often barbarous. However, knowing the genius of the people, the humor of their language, and the prejudiced ears he had to deal with, he did not pretend to extirpate the French musick, and plant the Italian in its stead; but only to cultivate and civilize it with innumerable graces and modulations which he borrowed from the Italian. By this means the French Musick is now perfect in its kind; and when you say it is not so good as the Italian, you only mean that it does not please you so well, for there is scarce a Frenchman who would not wonder to hear you give the Italian such a preference. The Musick of the French is indeed very properly adapted to their pronunciation and accent, as their whole opera wonderfully favors the genius of such a gay airy people. The Chorus in which that opera abounds, gives the Parterre frequent opportunities of joining in consort with the stage. This inclination of the audience to sing along with the actors, so prevail with them, that I have sometimes known the performer on the stage do no more in a celebrated song, than the clerk of a parish church, who serves only to raise the psalm, and is afterwards drowned in the Musick of the congregation.

There is also some interesting criticism by English writers who were concerned about their own country's cultural isolation. Robert Greene (1560–1592), for example, had been one of the young Englishmen who had traveled to Italy to absorb culture and he had apparently suffered some criticism for traveling to Italy for this reason. In return, he took some satisfaction in pointing out some of the failures of Englishmen as well.

> I am English born, and I have English thoughts, not a devil incarnate because I am Italianate, but hating the pride of Italy, because I know their peevishness: yet in all the countries where I have traveled, I have not seen more excess of vanity than we English men practice through vain glory: for as our wits be as ripe as any, so our wills are more ready than they all, to put in effect any of their licentious abuses.[30]

---

30 Robert Greene, 'To the Reader,' in *A Notable Discovery of Coosnage* (1591), in *The Life and Complete Works of Robert Greene*, X, 6.

He wrote an entire book on Pride as reflected in the English scene. In this work, *A Quip for an Upstart Courtier* (1592), he says his purpose was to reflect,

> the abuses that Pride had bred in England, how it had infected the Court with aspiring Ennui, the City with griping covetousness, and the country with contempt and disdain. How since men placed their delights in proud looks and brave attire, Hospitality was left off, Neighborhood was exiled, Conscience was laughed at, and Charity lay frozen in the streets.[31]

Some Englishmen went further. Phillip Stubbs wrote of his fellow Englishmen, 'There is not a people more corrupt, wicked, or perverse, living upon the face of the earth.'[32] And John Lyly warns, 'Everyone that shaketh thee by the hand is not joined to thee in heart.'[33]

Today, when we think of Baroque, we tend to first think of Germany because of the great masters, Bach, Handel and Telemann. But they were *late* Baroque and in the first two-thirds of the Baroque what one finds in German criticism is a growing self-confidence as she moved away from the Italian and French traditions.

As with the English, some German young men also traveled to Italy to 'finish' their education by absorbing the culture there. Thus it should be no surprise to find Heinrich Schütz, requesting permission for his second trip to Italy in 1628–1629 to improve his spirit. Indeed, years later Schütz would refer to Italy as 'the true university of music.'[34]

> As from the first I did not come upon this idea prompted by any frivolity, as a mere pleasure jaunt or desire to travel, but through the urge for an improvement in spirit.[35]

After making this trip, Schütz documents his discovery there of a new style of church music, which we know as the church concerti.

> When I arrived in Venice, I cast anchor here where as a youth I had passed the novitiate of my art under the great Gabrieli—Gabrieli, immortal gods, how great a man![36]
>
> ......
>
> Staying in Venice with old friends, I found the manner of musical composition [*modulandi rationem*] somewhat changed. They have partially abandoned the old church modes while seeking to charm modern ears with new titillations.[37]

Some years later, in 1647, Schütz provided an interesting reference to the difficulty in the absorption of Italian style in Germany because of the Thirty Years War.

---

31 Robert Greene, *A Quip for an Upstart Courtier* (1592), in Ibid., XI, 209.

32 *The Anatomy of the Abuses in England* (1583), ed. Frederick Furnivall (London: The New Shakespeare Society, n.d.), 23.

33 *Euphues and his England*, ed. Morris Croll (New York: Russell & Russell, 1964), 226.

34 *Geistliche Chormusik* (1648).

35 Quoted in Hans Moser, *Heinrich Schütz* (St. Louis: Concordia, 1936), 126.

36 Heinrich Schütz, *Symphoniae sacrae*, I, Op. 2, 1629, quoted in Oliver Strunk, *Source Readings*, 433.

37 Schütz, quoted in Hans Moser, *Heinrich Schütz*, 128.

> Until now I have been prevented from sending [the *Symphoniae Sacrae*] to press because of the miserable conditions prevailing in our dear fatherland which adversely affect all the arts, music included; and even more importantly, because the modern Italian style of composition and performance (with which, as the sagacious Signor Claudio Monteverdi remarks in the preface to his *Eighth Book of Madrigals*, music is said finally to have reached its perfection) has remained largely unknown in this country.
>
> Experience has proved that the modern Italian manner of composition and its proper tempo, with its many black notes, does not in most cases lend itself to use by Germans who have not been trained for it. Believing one had composed really good works in this style, one has often found them so violated and corrupted in performance that they offered a sensitive ear nothing but boredom and distaste, and called down unjustified opprobrium on the composer and on the German nation, the inference being that we are entirely unskilled in the noble art of music—and certain foreigners have more than once leveled such accusations at us …
>
> As for others, above all those of us Germans who do not know how properly to perform this modern music, with its black notes and steady, prolonged bowing on the violin, and who, albeit untrained, still wish to play this way I herewith kindly request them not to be ashamed to seek instruction from experts in this style and not to shirk home practice before they undertake a public performance of any of these pieces. Otherwise they and the author—though he be innocent—may receive unexpected ridicule rather than praise.[38]

One German composer who acknowledged his debt to the Italian style was George Muffat. In the Foreword to his *Auserlesene Instrumental-Music* (1701) he explains that, while his earlier music had been under the influence of the French, in the present collection he now presents 'certain profound and unusual affects of the Italian manner, various capricious and artful conceits, and alternations of many sorts, interspersed with special diligence between the [ripieno] and [concertino].' The purpose of this music, as he makes very clear, is to listen to—it is concert music. In this same Foreword, he makes it clear that he was also much impressed by certain performance practices of the Italians.

> In directing the measure or beat, one should for the most part follow the Italians, who are accustomed to proceed much more slowly than we do at the directions *Adagio*, *Grave*, *Largo*, etc., so slowly sometime that one can scarcely wait for them, but, at the directions *Allegro*, *Vivace*, *Presto*, *Piu presto*, and *Prestissimo* much more rapidly and in a more lively manner. For by exactly observing this opposition or rivalry of the slow and the fast, the loud and the soft, the fullness of the [ripieno] and the delicacy of the [concertino], the ear is ravished by a singular astonishment, as is the eye by the opposition of light and shade.

In a comment by Johann Scheibe, in 1737, we can document the growing self-confidence of Germans in their own music.

> Indeed, we [Germans] have finally found in music too the true good taste, which Italy never showed us in its full beauty. Hasse and Graun, who are admired also by the Italians, demonstrate by their richly inventive, natural and moving works how fine it is to possess and practice good taste.[39]

---

38   Heinrich Schütz, *Symphoniae Sacrae*, II (1647.

39   Johann Scheibe, *Critischer musicus* (1737), trans. Claude Palisca in *Baroque Music* (Englewood Cliffs: Prentice Hall, 1981), 281.

As indicated in the comment, above, by Muffat, during the years after the Thirty Years War in the seventeenth century, and corresponding with the height of the influence of the court of Louis XIV, German composers experienced a period of French influence. Georg Muffat, in his *Florilegia* (1695), a collection of pieces which he describes as 'conforming in the main to the French ballet style,' comments on this period.

> In Germany the French style is gradually coming to the fore and becoming the fashion. This same style, which formerly flourished in Paris under the most celebrated Jean Baptiste Lully, I have diligently sought to master, and, returning from France to Alsace, from whence I was driven by the late war, I was perhaps the first to bring this manner, not displeasing to many professional musicians, into Austria and Bohemia and afterwards to Salzburg and Passau. Inasmuch as the ballet compositions of the aforesaid Lully and other things after his manner entirely reject, for the flowing and natural movement, all other artifices—immoderate runs as well as frequent and ill-sounding leaps—they had at first the misfortune, in these countries, to displease many of our violinist, at that time more intent on the variety of unusual conceits and artificialities than on grace; for this reason, when occasionally produced by those ignorant of the French manner or envious of foreign art, they come off badly, robbed of their proper tempo and other ornaments.[40]

Another interesting discussion on the contemporary assessment of German style as opposed to the French style is by Johann David Heinichen (1683–1729) in 1711.

> Experience teaches that ... paper music receives more credit in one nation than in another. One nation [Germany] is industrious in all endeavors; another laughs over useless school work and tends to believe skeptically that the 'Northerners' work like a team of draft horses. One nation [Germany] believes art is only that which is difficult to compose; another nation, however, seeks a lighter style and correctly states that it is difficult to compose light music ... One nation [Germany] seeks its greatest art in nothing but intricate musical 'tiff-taff' and elaborate artificialities of note writing. The other nation applies itself more to good taste, and in this way it takes away the former's universal applause; the paper artists [Germans], on the contrary, with all their witchcraft remain in obscurity and, in addition, are proclaimed barbarians, even though they could imitate the other nations blindfolded if they applied themselves more to good taste and brilliance of music than to fruitless artificialities. An eminent foreign composer once gave his frank opinion ... regarding the differences in music of two nations.
>
>> Our nation, he said, ... is more inclined to *dolcezza* in music, so much so that it must take care not to fall into a kind of indolence. Most 'Northerners,' on the other hand, are almost too inclined to liveliness in music, so that they fall too easily into barbarisms. If they would take pains over adapting our *tendresse* and would mix it together with their usual *vivacite*, then a third style would result that could not fail to please the whole world.
>
> I will not repeat the comments I made at that time, but will say only that this discourse first brought to my mind the thought that a felicitous melange of Italian and French taste would affect the ear most forcefully and must succeed over all other tastes of the world ... Nevertheless, the Germans have the reputation abroad that if they would apply themselves industriously they could usually

---

[40] Quoted in Oliver Strunk, *Source Readings*, 443.

surpass other nations in learning. From this principle I hope that some day our composers will try in general ... to surpass other nations in matters of musical taste as well as they have succeeded long ago in artful counterpoint and theoretical accuracies.[41]

After the beginning of the eighteenth century German self-confidence was rising and occasional comments which were distinctly anti-French in character began to appear. Friedrich Niedt, for example, observed in 1700,

> The final chord must be major regardless of what goes before, except that French composers do the opposite, but everything is not good merely because it comes from France or has a French name.[42]

Telemann, in a letter of ca. 1751 to Carl Graun, makes a comment which was intended as an unfavorable reference to the theories of Rameau, who believed melody came from harmony, instead of the other way around.

> If there is nothing new to be found in melody then we must seek novelty in harmony.[43]

We might quote here two observations by the great German mathematician and philosopher, Gottfried Wilhelm Leibniz (1646–1716), who by the end of the seventeenth century was clearly feeling a distinct sense of German superiority.

> One need not worry about the Italians, who are ready to receive the yoke, and who have degenerated from the virtue of their ancestors.[44]

And the Frenchman, according to Leibniz,

> allows himself no repose, and leaves none to others; the grave and the serious pass for ridiculous, and measure or reason for pedantic; caprice, for something gallant, and inconstancy in one's interactions with other people, for cleverness: everyone meddles with others' affairs in private houses, and pursues people to their very homes, and picks shameful fights. Youth above all glories in its folly and in its disorders ...[45]

---

[41] Johann David Heinichen, *General-Bass Treatise* [1711], quoted in George Buelow, *Thorough-Bass Accompaniment according to Johann David Heinichen* (Ann Arbor: UMI Research Press, 1986), 281ff.

[42] Friedrich Erhard Niedt, *Musicalische Handleitung* (Hamburg, 1700), quoted in Robert Donnington, *The Interpretation of Early Music* (New York, 1964), 141.

[43] Quoted in Sam Morgenstern, *Composers on Music* (New York: Pantheon, 41.

[44] Gottfried Wilhelm Leibniz, 'Mars Christianissimus' (1683), in *The Political Writings of Leibniz*, trans. Patrick Riley (Cambridge: Cambridge University Press, 1972), 133.

[45] Leibniz, 'Manifesto for the Defense of the Rights of Charles III' (1703), in Ibid., 157.

That represents considerable national cultural growth, when one remembers that an earlier German mathematician, Johannes Kepler (1571–1630), writing at the beginning of the seventeenth century, had observed, 'Germany is just as famous for corpulence and gluttony as Spain is for genius, discernment, and temperance.'[46]

Speaking of Spain, after the turn of the eighteenth century, following the marriage of Philip V to Maria Luisa of Savoy, important Italian musicians also began to arrive, notably Domenico Scarlatti and the famous singer, Farinelli. Scarlatti followed his student, Princess Maria Barbara de Braganza to Spain when she married Ferdinand and his only duty seems to have been to produce sonata after sonata.

The influence of the Italian style in Spain was not without protest. In particular the Benedictine Benito Feijoo complained that the Italian music was noisy and lacking in traditional Spanish gravity. He objected that the Spanish had become slaves to a foreign taste. He particularly found the Italian use of harmony to be disturbing. 'Harmony,' he sighed, 'becomes exasperating.'[47]

In view of the rapid rise of China on the world stage today, we might note Voltaire's somewhat condescending view of Chinese culture.[48]

> The Chinese, as well as the rest of the Asiatics, have stopped at the first elements of poetry, eloquence, natural philosophy, astronomy, and painting; all practiced by them so long before they were known to us. They began in everything much sooner than us, but made no progress afterwards; like the ancient Egyptians, who first taught the Greeks, and became at last so ignorant, as not even to be capable of receiving instruction from them.
>
> These people, whom we take so much pains and go so far to visit; from whom, with the utmost difficulty, we have obtained permissions to carry the riches of Europe, and to instruct them, do not to this day know how much we are their superiors; they are not even far enough advanced in knowledge to venture to imitate us, and don't so much as know whether we have any history or not.

Now it might be of interest to the reader if we jump ahead a bit and see how these kinds of national prejudices are reflected in the writings of some of the great nineteenth-century masters. Robert Schumann wrote to his future father-in-law in 1829:

> In the Leipzig concert room I sometimes experienced a thrill of awe in the presence of the genius of music, but Italy has taught me to love it.[49]

In spite of his admiration of the Italians for their love of music, there are hints in his letters that he found their contemporary music somewhat naïve. In 1838 he wrote Clara Wieck:

---

46 Johannes Kepler's (1571–1630) Dream, note 61. See *Kepler's Somnium*, trans. Edward Rosen (Madison: University of Wisconsin Press, 1967), 45.

47 Quoted in Louise K. Stein, 'The Iberian Peninsula,' in *The Late Baroque Era* (Englewood Cliffs: Prentice Hall, 1994), 426.

48 Dedication to Richelieu, of *The Orphan of China*, in *The Works of Voltaire* (New York: St. Hubert Guild, 1901), XV, 180.

49 Letter to Friedrich Wieck, Heidelberg, Nov. 6, 1829.

> I am paying great attention to melody now ... But of course by 'melody' I mean something different from Italian melodies, which always seem to be like the songs of birds,—pretty to listen to, but without any depth or meaning.[50]

And in the same year he makes an analogy of the composition talent of Italy with the fragility of flowers.

> We have lately seen young talent of all sorts of nationalities arising among us: Glinka of Russia, Chopin of Poland, Bennett of England, Berlioz of France, Liszt of Hungary, Hasens of Belgium; in Italy every spring brings forth some, whom the winter destroys.[51]

And finally, we see in Schumann his pride in his fellow German composers in one of his essays for a music journal of which he was the editor.

> One feature separates the masters of the German school from those of the French and Italian—a feature that has made them great—the former use their powers in every mode of construction, while the others usually confine themselves to one branch. When we hear some favorite Parisian opera composer entitled a great artist, we feel inclined to ask, 'Where are his symphonies, quartets, psalms, etc.' How can they be compared to German masters?[52]

The young Mendelssohn left a letter which reflects the strong cultural reputation which was still residual in Paris.

> If I compose indifferent music, it will be quickly forgotten in Germany, but here [in Paris] it would be often performed and extolled, and sent to Germany, and given there on the authority of Paris, as we daily see. But I do not choose this; and if I am not capable of composing good music, I have no wish to be praised for it.[53]

As Mendelssohn became older he also became more critical of others, but one must forgive these great composers if they are guilty of this for you cannot speak of their greatness and then deny their lofty view. In a letter to the family of his teacher in 1840 he complains of 'German petty provincialism'[54] and the following year he accuses the French of insincerity, 'by conjuring tricks and overwrought sentiment.'[55]

Chopin left a vivid description of orchestral discipline in London in mid-century. He is explaining to a friend why he does not want to appear as a soloist there.

---

50   Letter to Clara Wieck, Leipzig, March, 1838.
51   'First Quartet Morning,' in *Neue Zeitschrift für Musik*, 1838.
52   'Trios for Pianoforte, Violin and Violoncello,' in *Neue Zeitschrift für Musik*, 1842.
53   Letter to Karl Immermann, Paris, Feb. 21, 1832.
54   Letter to Charlotte Moscheles, Leipzig, August 8, 1840.
55   Letter to Julius Rietz, Leipzig, April 23, 1841.

> The orchestra is like their roast beef or their turtle soup; excellent, strong, but nothing more. All that I have written is needless as an excuse; there is one impossible thing: they never rehearse, for everyone's time is dear nowadays; there is only one rehearsal, and that is public.[56]

In the summer of this same year, 1848, Chopin makes some general observations on English culture. The reader may find these worthy of reflection, in view of the fact that the English have been by far the most dominant influence on American culture.

> In London, whatever is not boring is not English.[57]
>
> ......
>
> These English are so different from the French, to whom I have grown attached as to my own; they think only in terms of money; they like art because it is a luxury; kind-hearted, but so eccentric that I understand how one can himself grow stiff here, or turn into a machine.[58]

Franz Liszt also found living in England required some adjustment.

> One has to get accustomed to the London atmosphere, and make one's stomach pretty solid with porter and port. For the rest, musical matters are not worse there than elsewhere, and one must even acknowledge some greatness in bestiality. If you can *stand* it, I am convinced that you will make a lucrative and pleasant position for yourself in London.[59]

Liszt, like Mendelssohn, also reports that by the middle of the nineteenth century the cultural influence of Paris was still strong.

> [In the end, Wagner will be] acknowledged as a great *German* composer in Germany, on condition that his works are first heard in Paris or London, following the example of Meyerbeer, to say nothing of Gluck, Weber and Handel![60]

In a letter to a friend, Liszt quotes a nice description of French society:

> A nice remark in Hillebrand's new book: 'The Frenchman likes to pride himself on his feelings for equality: nowhere in the world is there a less well-founded pretension. This feeling exists indeed from bottom to top; each considers himself equal to the one above him, but from top to bottom, it's another matter.'[61]

Although Liszt found Italy somewhat provincial, having attended the very first performance of Beethoven's *Pastoral Symphony* in Rome in 1880[!], he nevertheless reported that the wide appeal of Italian opera still existed.

---

[56] Letter to Wojciech Grzymala, London, May 13, 1848.
[57] Letter to Wojciech Grzymala, London, July 8–17, 1848.
[58] Letter to his Family, August 19, 1848.
[59] Letter to Carl Klindworth, Weimar, July 2, 1854.
[60] Letter to Carl Reinecke, Weimar, may 30, 1849.
[61] Letter to Olga von Meyendorff, November 29, 1872.

> From the aristocrat to the least grocery boy ... everybody takes sides for or against the prima
> donna ... The waiter who froths your chocolate tells you that Francilla Pixis sang the rondo in
> the *Cenerentola* very well; the man who shines your shoes isn't satisfied with the ornamentation of
> Giurameto.[62]

Liszt was enthusiastic about Vienna, recommending it as an intelligent and appreciative audience of great piano playing and who had the ability to raise his own spirits.[63] How different was the assessment by Mendelssohn:

> The people I associated with in Vienna were so dissipated and frivolous ... Moreover, not one of the
> best pianists there, male or female, ever played a note of Beethoven, and when I hinted that he and
> Mozart were not to be despised, they said, 'So you are an admirer of classical music?'[64]

Hector Berlioz was perhaps the most gifted prose writer of any of the great composers. Unfortunately his hundreds of newspaper articles have never been reprinted in any modern language. We will sample some of those here which reflect his views of music making in various countries. There are two such articles we really like, the first on the subject of German music festivals.

> In Germany, where music is honored, festivals are organized with a sort of religion; everything
> happens properly, everything is disposed there in the most perfect and logical order ... We imagine
> in France that all Germans are calm and cold; this is a great error. One only need see the public of
> Vienna and Prague, especially, when a powerful work elevates and illuminates them, when musical
> vertigo seizes them, when the breath of inspiration drags them along, one only need see all those arms
> waving, hear those trembling voices, feel those halls tremble under the tempest of applause, in order
> to conceive an idea of true enthusiasm, and of the joy that the spectacle of the emotions that they can
> cause, gives to the heart of the artists.[65]

Berlioz often wrote about the host of obstacles which the French government placed in the way of musicians in France. On the other hand, he believed that in Germany support for music was found at all levels of government. With this background in mind, the reader will appreciate the following newspaper article which Berlioz wrote, inspired by a notice he found published in a Cologne newspaper.

> Music flowers in Germany because it is respected there, and because the opposite of music generally
> is rejected there. I find a new proof of that German hatred for sonorous horrors in a Police Order
> published recently at Cologne as follows:
>
>> It is forbidden for wandering musicians, organ-grinder players, persons who show exotic
>> animals with musical accompaniment, and in general, for all individuals who make music in
>> the streets or on public squares, *to make use of discordant or untuned instruments*. Violators, if they

---

62 'Lettre d'un bachelier sur La Scala,' *Gazette Musicale*, May 27, 1838.
63 See letter to Simon Lowy, May 20, 1841 and letter to Franz von Schober, March 3, 1845.
64 Letter to Carl Zelter, October 16, 1830.
65 *Journal des Débats*, July 29, 1846.

> are foreigners, will be expelled immediately from the city: if they are natives, they will be deprived of the authorization for themselves obtained from the police; and that authorization will not be given back until after they have replaced their faulty instruments by new instruments in good state or after they have repaired properly the old ones, an operation that, in all cases must be witnessed by means of a certificate delivered by two competent and well-known men of the art.
>
> Fine! That is worthy of a civilized people. In France, that order would seem comical.

Berlioz goes on to point out that if it is considered important to forbid infectious fumes spread by the traffic of vehicles, then it should be important to forbid any public brutalizing of the ears of the people. Perhaps, going further, there should be a ban on any anti-musicality that is being committed in the theaters and churches. Here he includes 'imbecilic singers without a voice, incapable performers,' and,

> conductors who tear apart a masterpiece, break its four members; extinguish its flame, make its physiognomy ignoble and grotesque.

Such music making, Berlioz asserts, is 'incomparably more destructive than if they were spreading infectious odors in the room where they worked.'[66]

Finally, we must quote some observations on the musical culture which Berlioz found in Italy. He complains of their feeble orchestras and choirs and then offers this summary:

> Of all the nations of Europe, I am strongly inclined to think them the most impervious to the evocative, poetic side of music, as well as to any conception at all lofty and out of the common run. Music for the Italians is a sensual pleasure and nothing more. For the noble expression of the mind they have hardly more respect than for the art of cooking. They want a score that, like a plate of macaroni, can be assimilated immediately without their having to think about it or even pay any attention to it.[67]

Richard Wagner, also being a prolific prose writer, has left some colorful reflections on several nations. In a letter to Franz Liszt,[68] Wagner describes his reaction to London.

> I am living here like a damned soul in hell. I did not think I should ever again be obliged to sink so low! ... I have stepped right into a morass of etiquette and custom and am in it up to my ears ... 'Sir, we are not used to that sort of thing here,'—that is all I ever hear, perpetually echoed back at me! Not even the orchestra can offer me any compensation: it consists almost entirely of Englishmen, i.e., skilled machines whom I can never really get going: trade and business stifle every other emotion. Added to this a public which ... sits through the most moving music as it does through the most boring ... And then there is this ridiculous Mendelssohn-cult, the whole brazen hypocrisy of this absurd nation.

---

[66] *Journal des Débats*, January 7, 1852.
[67] *The Memoirs of Hector Berlioz*, ed. David Cairns (London: Gollancz, 1969), 208ff.
[68] London, 16 May 1855.

We should like to conclude our geographical survey of musical taste and performance practices with some additional lines by Wagner. As so often is the case in the prose works of Wagner, we find his thoughts inspiring and reflective of the highest perspective of the art of music.

> Somebody once said: The Italian uses music for love, the Frenchman for society, but the German as science. Perhaps it would be better put: The Italian is a singer, the Frenchman a virtuoso, the German a—musician. The German has a right to be styled by the exclusive name 'Musician,' for of him one may say that he loves Music for herself,—not as a means of charming, of wining gold and admiration, but because he worships her as a divine and lovely art that, if he gives himself to her, becomes his one and all.[69]

---

[69] 'On German Music.'

Weird Science

IN READING OF ANCIENT CIVILIZATIONS one is often amazed at the intellectual progress in many fields without all the modern scientific tools. Consider, for example, those early astronomers who eventually worked out the basic nature of our solar system entirely without telescopes! Since history tends to focus only on those who got it right, we thought the reader might enjoy reading of a few cases where man's intellect led to the wrong answer.

With regard to the natural world, the attribution of everything to the creation by God tended to inhibit logical thinking in science (and still does). Early philosophers were also conflicted by cases where the information gained by the senses seemed in error, as in the case where a straight stick thrust into the water appears bent. Should one trust one's personal observations or one's intellect?

One philosopher of the Alexandrian Period of Greece, Pyrrho (360–270 BC), a representative of the Skeptic School, points out that one cannot really completely trust either one, for 'the senses can deceive, and reason says different [conflicting] things.'[1] It is a good point and certainly one that is reflected in all the incorrect explanations of natural science arrived at by 'Reason' among some of these early philosophers. Lucretius (99–55 BC), for example, concluded there was no such thing as gravity.[2] Pyrrho himself arrived at the conclusion that there is no such thing as motion.[3] Diogenes (ca. 404–323 BC), founder of the Cynic School of philosophy, on hearing a similar statement, answered by simply getting up and walking around the room!

Lucretius, by the way, made a determined effort to explain the nature of sound and hearing, but it would be many centuries before anyone got it right. Lucretius thought that sound must be corporal in nature, as for example shouting gives one a sore throat, caused, he says, by a great number of 'atoms of voice' squeezing through the narrow outlet of the throat.[4] He was an early observer of acoustics in the outdoors. Words, he contends, are utterances from the depths of our body which are forced out and cut up into lengths by the tongue, can be heard at a great distance. But he was at a loss to explain why, if the space were wide, 'the utterance is disjointed by the flight through a long stretch of gusty air,' and the words become jumbled.

He was also confused why a single word, uttered by a crier, could be heard by a great crowd of people.

---

1 Quoted in Diogenes Laertius, *Lives of the Eminent Philosophers*, trans. R. D. Hicks (Cambridge: Harvard University Press, 1950), II, 507.

2 *The Way Things Are*, I, 1051.

3 Ibid., II, 511.

4 Lucretius, *On the Nature of the Universe* (New York: Penguin, 1983), 146 and following.

> Evidently, a single utterance must split up immediately into a multitude of utterances, since it is parceled out among a number of separate ears.

But even with this weird science he could not explain how sound could go where the vision cannot, as for example into a room when the door is closed.

Epicurus (342–270 BC), founder of the Epicurean School of philosophy, on the basis of Reason, gave four possible, and all incorrect, explanations for what causes thunder.

> Thunder may be produced by the rushing about of wind in the hollows of the clouds, as happens in vessels on earth; or by the reverberation of fire filled with wind inside them; or by the rending and tearing of clouds; or by the friction and bursting of clouds when they have been congealed into a form like ice.[5]

And speaking of natural phenomenon, Pliny the Younger (62–113 AD) left us a colorful report of strange music heard on Mt. Atlas:

> It is said that in the day-time none of its inhabitants are seen, and that all is silent with a terrifying silence like that of the desert, so that a speechless awe creeps into the hearts of those who approach it, and also a dread of the peak that soars above the clouds and reaches the neighborhood of the moon's orb; also that at night this peak flashes with frequent fires and swarms with the wanton gambols of Goat-Pans and Satyrs, and echoes with the music of auloi and flutes and the sound of drums and cymbals.[6]

One intellectual property the early philosophers felt confident putting their trust in was numbers. In fact, Nicholas of Cusa (1401–1464 AD) quotes Boethius (480–525 AD) as having written,

> anyone who altogether lacked skill in mathematics could not attain a knowledge of divine matters.[7]

The early Church writers had a particular fascination with the number Seven. Clement of Alexandria (150–215 AD) says, 'the whole world revolves in sevens,' pointing to the seven known planets, seven stars in several constellations, seven phases of the moon, seven lyre strings, and seven (!) senses: two eyes, two ears, two nostrils, and the mouth.[8] Victorinus, Bishop of Petau (third century AD), makes an interesting observation on the frequency of the number seven in the bible, including,

> seven horns of the Lamb *[Revelation 5:6]*,
> seven eyes of God *[Zechariah 4:10]*,

---

5 'Letter to Pythoclea,' in *Epicurus*, trans. Cyril Bailey (Oxford: Clarendon Press, 1926), 69.

6 Tacitus, *The Annals*, V, i, 5ff.

7 Nicholas of Cusa, 'On Learned Ignorance,' trans. Jasper Hopkins (Minneapolis: Banning Press, 1981), I, xi, 31. Will Durant, *The Reformation* (New York: Simon and Schuster, 1957), 257, calls Nicholas of Cusa a great humanist, but he must have been thinking of someone else for Cusa was a pure Church Scholastic philosopher.

8 'The Miscellanies,' trans. Alexander Roberts (Edinburgh: T. & T. Clark, 1869), XII, bk. VI, p. 389.

seven eyes are the seven spirits of the Lamb *[Revelation 4:5]*,
seven torches burning before the throne of God *[Revelation 4:5]*,
seven golden candlesticks *[Revelation 1:13]*,
seven young sheep *[Leviticus 23:18]*,
seven women in Isaiah *[Isaiah 4:1]*,
seven churches in Paul *[Acts 6:3]*,
seven deacons *[Acts 6:3]*,
seven angels *[Revelation]*,
seven trumpets *[Joshua 6, Revelation 8]*,
seven seals to the book, seven periods of seven days and seven weeks in Daniel *[Daniel 9:25]*,
seven of all clean things in the ark *[Genesis 7:2]*,
seven revenges of Cain *[Genesis 4:15]*,
seven years for a debt to be acquitted *[Deuteronomy 15:1]*,
the lamp with seven orifices *[Zechariah 4:2]*,
and the seven pillars of wisdom in the house of Solomon *[Proverbs 9:1]*.[9]

Numbers, according to one famous early English philosopher, Robert Grosseteste (d. 1253), were the key to the explanation of how we hear music. A contemporary, Matthew Paris, tells us Grosseteste was well-grounded in the Quadrivium, which included music.[10] He also paints a rather fierce personal portrait of the man.

> Let no one be disturbed by the violent acts which he did in his life-time ... his treatment of his canons whom he excommunicated and harassed, his savage attacks on monks, and even more savage against nuns ... They arose from zeal.[11]

It was clearly Grosseteste's interest in music which prompted him to attempt to explain the physics of sound production and the nature of hearing. His explanation was all bound up in numbers and the soul, namely that a sound is understood as a number in the ear, which is then compared to numbers stored in the soul-memory, whereupon it is judged harmonious or dissonant. Music, then, was not just a matter of hearing musical tones, but involved a broad range of faculties dealing with numbers, memory and finally Reason.[12]

And speaking of attempting to explain how we hear music, virtually all early writers assumed that the musical sounds they were hearing from instrumentalists were sounds made by the instruments. Actually, although we never tell students, we are hearing vibrations of air, outside and detached from the instrument. The instrument made the vibrations possible, but our ear hears only vibrations of air. It is the miraculous brain, in translating these vibrations, that 'hears' the flute. Focusing on the instrument itself, even Aristotle was led astray into weird science in attempting to define tone production.

---

9   *The Writings of Tertullianus* (Edinburgh: T. & T. Clark, 1895), III, 392. And there are more he missed: seven ears of grain, seven days, seven heads of a dragon, seven plagues, seven rams, seven spirits, seven stars and more.

10 Quoted in R. W. Southern, *Robert Grosseteste* (Oxford: Clarendon, 1992), 11.

11 Ibid., 10.

12 James McEvoy, *The Philosophy of Robert Grosseteste* (Oxford: Clarendon, 1982), 258.

> In the case of oboes and other instruments of the same class, the sounds produced are clear when the breath emitted from them is concentrated and intense. For the impacts on the external air must be of that kind, and it is in this way that they will best travel to the ear in a solid mass.
>
> ......
>
> The reeds of oboes must be solid and smooth and even, so that the breath may pass through smoothly and evenly, without being dispersed. Therefore mouthpieces which have been well steeped and soaked in grease give a pleasant sound, while those which are dry produce less agreeable notes.[13]

Interestingly enough, a clue to the truth about how we hear is a phenomenon which must have been familiar to everyone in the ancient world in the form of the common echo. Ancient singers had used the echo as a surrogate recording device to check on their vocal production. But it had apparently not occurred to anyone to observe that when the echo returns for us to hear, it is a sound accompanied by no instrument and no musician. Therefore, sound is not the instrument or the player.

The man who first discussed this clue about how we hear, in so far as we know, was the great English philosopher, Thomas Hobbes (1588–1679). Hobbes correctly understood sound as being in the mind, not in the instrument. For him, the proof of this was that if the sound we hear is in the instrument which produces it, it would not be possible to 'disconnect' the sound from its original source, as happens in an echo.

> Neither is sound in the thing we hear, but in ourselves. One manifest sign thereof is, that as a man may see, so he may hear double or treble, by multiplication of echoes, which echoes are sounds as well as the original; and not being in one and the same place, cannot be inherent in the body that makes them. Nothing can make anything which is not in itself; the clapper has no sound in it, but motion, and makes motion in the internal parts of the bell; so the bell has motion, and not sound, that imparts motion to the air; and the air has motion, but not sound; the air imparts motion by the ear and nerve unto the brain; and the brain has motion but not sound; from the brain, it rebounds back into the nerves outward, and thence it becomes an apparition [idea] without, which we call sound.[14]

Before leaving topics touching on the natural world, we should note that some ancient philosophers placed much importance on astrology. It was most surprising to us to find that the ranks of the believers included Thomas Aquinas (1224–1274), the most prolific Church writer of the late Middle Ages. Born to a noble family, Aquinas spent five years at the University of Naples where he came under the influence of the recently rediscovered works of the ancient Greek philosophers. Aquinas' admiration for Aristotle is apparent on nearly every page of his many books and he no doubt thought of himself as being one of the people attempting to find a common ground between the world of Aristotelian logic and a Church based on faith. We are confident, however, that Aristotle would not have approved when Aquinas cites the heavenly bodies as being another influence on intelligence.

---

[13] 'De Audibilibus,' 802a.9, and 802b.19.
[14] 'Human Nature,' II, ix.

> We must observe that although heavenly bodies cannot be the direct cause of our knowledge, they can cooperate indirectly towards it ... Thus, even as physicians are able to judge of a man's intelligence from his bodily temperament, as a proximate disposition thereto, so too can an astrologer, from the heavenly movements, as being a remote cause of this disposition. In this sense we can approve of the saying of Ptolemy:
>
>> When Mercury is in one of Saturn's houses at the time of a man's birth, he bestows on him a quick intelligence of the inner nature of things.[15]

Just as surprising is Aquinas' praise of astrologers for their ability to 'foretell the truth in the majority of cases,' regarding whether a man will be carried away by his passions or not.[16] He brings this subject up yet again in the course of trying to discuss the emotions, a subject that probably required some courage in view of the Church's long and official condemnation of emotions. Some of his conclusions still carry the imprint of the Church:

> Emotion leads one towards sin in so far as it is uncontrolled by reason; but in so far as it is rationally controlled, it is part of the virtuous life.[17]
>
> ......
>
> That a man lusts, try not to as he will, is due to a disposition of body which holds up the sensitive appetite from perfect compliance with the command of reason.[18]

Early philosophers could imagine that Reason was housed within the brain, but then where were the emotions housed? Aquinas shared this difficulty and he is contradictory in his statements on where exactly in man the emotions are located. In one place he indicates that the emotions were not located in the cognitive side of man, but instead in the soul.[19] While it was clear to him they were related to the senses, in another place he concludes they must also be related to the intellect, on the basis that the Scriptures also mention love and joy with respect to God and the angels.[20] In yet another place he suggests that emotions exist in the intellect without a corporeal organ, but in the senses with corporeal organs.[21] Having noticed that physiological changes were associated with strong emotions, he incorrectly concludes that the senses themselves also change, for example the eye seeing a bright color becomes that color itself. The physical changes for an emotion such as anger, he attributed to 'the overheating of the blood around the heart.'[22]

---

[15] *Summa Contra Gentiles*, LXXXIV. Further endorsement of astrology can be found in *Commentary on Peri Hermeneias*, 115 (19a12.14.) and 'Letter to Reginald of Piperno,' quoted in *Theological Texts*, trans. Thomas Gilby (London: Oxford University Press, 1955), 243.

[16] Ibid., XV, 107.

[17] *Summa Theologiae*, 37.

[18] Ibid., 199ff.

[19] Ibid., 11.

[20] Ibid., 13.

[21] *Summa Contra Gentiles*, LXXXIII

[22] *Summa Theologiae*, XIX, 13.

Aquinas also arrives at a bit of weird science when he credits an influence on the emotions by the planets.

> We have already noted that emotional feeling is an act of a bodily organ. Consequently there is nothing to prevent us holding that impressions from heavenly bodies render some people more prompt to anger than others, or to concupiscence, or to some such emotion. Indeed they are such by temperamental constitution. Most men follow their passions; only the wise resist. And therefore in the majority of cases astrological predications may well be verified.[23]
>
> ......
>
> [The heavenly bodies] may make impressions on our own body, and when the body is affected movements of the passions arise; either because such impressions make us liable to certain passions; for instance the bilious are prone to anger; or because they produce in us a bodily disposition that occasions a particular choice, thus when we are ill, we choose to take medicine. Sometimes too, the heavenly bodies are a cause of human acts, when through an indisposition of the body a person goes out of his mind, and loses the use of reason.[24]

These views by Acquinas may have influenced Juan Ruiz in writing his famous book, *The Book of True Love* (1330). Ruiz doesn't emphasize it too much, but he seems to be hinting that we should not be punished for any sins that might result from our emotions, since they are caused by the heavenly bodies which God made. It is God's fault.

Ruiz makes a strong argument in favor of astrology, which he suggests provides truths which one can find neither in years of study nor in the Bible. Astrology, he says, cannot be called 'mere accident' and his argument for its validity follows the logic that since God made Nature 'and all happenings therein,' this must presumably include the movements of the stars and planets. He concludes, therefore, that 'believing the laws of nature shape our fates is not a sin.'[25] He also adds that men born under the sign of Venus are consumed with a desire for Love which they can never suppress.[26]

The subject area in which we most frequently find weird science among early philosophers is anatomy, in particular how the brain functions relative to the body and where in the body our various faculties are located. But one has to sympathize for it is only the clinical brain research of the past fifty years which has answered nearly all of their questions. The exception is that creation of the Church, the soul. It has not been found yet.

Lucretius (99–55 BC) was not the only early philosopher who failed to connect the dots between intelligence and the brain. Even so, for us today it is hard to understand how they concluded that intelligence was located in or near the heart, rather than in the brain.

> I maintain
> That mind and spirit are held close together,

---

[23] Ibid., 79.

[24] *Summa Contra Gentiles*, LXXXV.

[25] Juan Ruiz, *The Book of True Love*, trans. Saralyn Daly (University Park: Pennsylvania State University Press, 1978), 123.

[26] Ibid., 152.

> Compose one unity, but the lord and master
> Holding dominion over all the body
> Is purpose, understanding - in our terms
> Mind or intelligence, and this resides
> In the region of the heart.[27]

Another early philosopher, Varro (116–27 BC), as his work was devoted mostly to brief definitions and does not go into philosophical details regarding the workings of the mind, under a discussion of 'Regularity,' outlines the mental process as consisting of the senses, reason, instinct, and speech, all located within eight partitions of a rather complicated 'soul.'

> As [man and woman] are made up of soul and body, are not also the parts of soul and body alike with the same regularity?
> What then of the fact that the souls of men are divided into eight parts—are these parts not mutually alike with regularity? Five [parts] with which we perceive, the sixth with which we think, the seventh with which we procreate, the eighth with which we utter articulate words?[28]

One scholar who did contribute important original thought was the Englishman, Roger Bacon (b. ca. 1214). Bacon studied at Oxford[29] and at the University of Paris, where he received a doctorate in theology and then joined the Franciscan Order in about 1247. Unlike the gentle patron of his Order, St. Francis, Bacon was very outspoken and many who read or heard him must have felt somewhat insulted. Youth, he says, has no interest in the perfection demanded by science, indeed they take pleasure in their imperfection, and older people, 'with the greatest difficulty climb to perfection in anything.'[30] He was even more outspoken in his disrespect for the masses, the 'unenlightened throng,' the 'ignorant multitude,' whom he says can never rise to the perfection of wisdom. For this reason, he maintains, the wise have always been an elite segment of society, separated from the masses. He found this true in religion, 'as with Moses so with Christ the common throng does not ascend the mountain.'

He came very close to figuring out how the brain works as a bicameral organ, but he ventured into weird science when he quotes Aristotle's notion that older persons have poor memory because of excessive dryness of their organs, while the young have poor memories because their organs are too moist.[31]

---

[27] Lucretius, *The Way Things Are*, III, 133.

[28] Varro, *On the Latin Language*, IX, xxiii.29ff.

[29] Bacon is often cited as a student of Grosseteste, but as McEvoy, *The Philosophy of Robert Grosseteste*, 14, points out, there is no foundation for this belief.

[30] Opus Majus, 'Causes of Error,' III, in *The Opus Majus of Roger Bacon*, trans. Robert Burke (New York: Russell & Russell, 1962), 9ff.

[31] 'De Multiplicatione Specierum,' trans. David Lindberg, in *Roger Bacon's Philosophy of Nature* (Oxford: Clarendon, 1983), 195.

Truly objective speculation on the question of man's faculties had always been hindered somewhat by the Church's adherence to the concept of a soul. Where, for example, is Reason? For Bernard of Clairvaux it was in the soul,[32] but for John of Salisbury it was found in the head. Mother Nature, he says, 'has made our head the seat of all sensation, in which citadel she has enthroned reason as queen.'[33]

The Church writer who was most verbose on the subject of the location of man's faculties was Hildegard von Bingen (1098–1179). She associated the senses with the head, understanding and insight with the soul, and the 'humors' with the liver.[34] Her famous book of visions contains a substantial proportion of visions which we have to characterize as weird science, as for example a passage in which she describes how the various faculties work together.

> The soul pours its thoughts into the heart and collects them in the breast. Thence, these thoughts ascend to the head and into all the limbs of the body. They penetrate into the eyes as well; for the eyes are the windows through which the soul knows external nature.[35]

Related to this discussion is another curious vision in which she equates the head with the solar system.

> From the very top of our cranium to the outer edge of our forehead, seven points are found, separated from one another by equal intervals. This symbolizes the planets, which are also separated from one another in the firmament by like intervals. The highest planet is indicated by the top of the cranium. In the most remote part of the forehead there is the moon, while the sun is found right in the midst of the space between the highest planet and the moon. On each side of this spot, the other planets—the two upper ones and the two lower ones—are seen; there is the same interval between them with respect to their distance from the sun and the other planets. For the features on our head are proportionately just as far apart from one another as the planets are from one another in the firmament.[36]

Thomas Aquinas, influenced in his literary style by the step-by-step rational process of Aristotle, became considerably more complicated, in part because he confused 'soul' with functions which belong to the brain. He wrote, 'The specific nature of the human soul [is]

---

[32] 'On Conversion,' quoted in *Sermons on Conversion*, trans. Marie-Bernard Saïd (Kalamazoo: Cistercian Publications, 1981), 45.

[33] *The Metalogicon*, trans. Daniel McGarry (Berkeley: University of California Press, 1955), 229.

[34] *Book of Divine Works*, ed. Matthew Fox (Santa Fe: Bear & Company, 1987), 89, 93, and 68ff.

[35] 'Vision Four: 103,' in Ibid., 126.

[36] 'Vision Four: 22,' in Ibid., 97.

intellectual.'[37] He adds that it is the *soul's* power of sight which is in the eye and whose hearing is in the ear, accomplished through something he calls, 'internal sense power.'[38] Moreover the soul's powers of intellect and will are not said to be anywhere, specifically, in the body![39]

> Now the body plays no part in the activity of the intellect.[40]

Among the animals, he observes that man has the most developed sense of touch, but the poorest sense of smell. The latter he attributes to his theory that the large brain in man is necessary to cool the heat of the heart, and a large brain, 'owing to its moistness, is a hindrance to the sense of smell which requires dryness.'[41] The senses are also hindered during sleep, Aquinas points out, 'by vapors or gases that are released during digestion, and proportionately to their amount.'[42]

It is particularly interesting that when it came to presenting 'divine matters' to the masses, Aquinas believed this could *only* be done through the senses, rather than Reason. This, he said, was the purpose of the ceremonial aspect of religion.[43] This last contention by Thomas Aquinas, that the masses must be reached by the senses, rather than by the intellect, reminds us of a similar statement by Dante (1265–1321 AD). In his *Purgatorio* we meet an unidentified ghost whom we are told was the most talented writer of all, but who was never recognized by the masses and hence enjoyed no fame. The masses, Dante says, followed opinion, 'without first listening to reason or to art.'[44]

There is another place where Dante expresses a lack of faith in the ability of the masses to judge art. Here he observes that most men are so absorbed in their own craft, or the work of the moment, that they never develop a broader sense of discrimination. Thus he agrees with Boethius, whom he quotes as saying, 'popular esteem is worthless.'[45]

But if Dante finds the masses incapable of judging art, he does seem prepared to grant them the ability to judge on matters requiring Reason, quoting Aristotle as saying, 'What most people judge to be true cannot be wholly false.' He goes on to point out how the senses are

---

37 *Summa Theologiae* (London: Blackfriars, 1971), XLIV, 187. For the sixty volumes of the *Summa Theologiae*, we will cite the volume and page number of this complete edition, XI, 23, 49, 147; XX, 123.

38 Ibid., XV, 31.

39 Ibid., 87. See also *Commentary on Peri Hermeneias*, trans. Jean Oesterle (Milwaukee: Marquette University Press, 1962), 115 (19a12.14.) and *Commentary on de Anima*, quoted in *Selected Writings of St. Thomas Aquinas*, ed. M.C. D'Arcy (New York: Dutton, 1950), 68.

40 Ibid., XV, 153. See also *Summa Contra Gentiles*, LXIX ('... since the intellect is not the act of any part of the body').

41 *Summa Theologiae*, XIII, 27.

42 Ibid., XII, 47.

43 *Summa Theologiae*, XXIX, 41.

44 *Purgartorio*, XXVI.

45 *The Banquet*, I, xi, 7.

obviously capable of reporting inaccurate information. Then, in a passage which makes for rather humorous reading today, he intends to demonstrate that Reason never errors—and in the process only documents how it can.

> Where the Philosopher says, then, 'What most people judge to be true cannot be wholly false,' he is not referring to the superficial judgment formed by the senses, but to the interior judgment made by reason. For judgment formed by the senses is, in most people, often quite false, especially with regard to things that are perceived by the several senses together, since in these cases what the senses report is very frequently mistaken. We know, for instance, that to most people the diameter of the sun appears to be one foot across, but this is quite false; human reason, making observations and discoveries with the various skills at its command, has shown that the diameter of the body of the sun is five-and-a-half times that of the earth. Where the earth is 6,500 miles in diameter, the diameter of the sun, which to judgments formed by the senses is one foot across, is in fact 35,750 miles across.[46]

Benedict (originally Baruch) de Spinoza (1632–1677) is generally called the greatest Jewish philosopher of the modern era, but that only reflects his point of origin. The great Jewish history, the Old Testament, Spinoza found to be deliberately metaphorical and allegorical. Perhaps discovering that precision is the death of faith, Spinoza would conclude,

> For my own part, as I confess plainly, and without circumlocution, that I do not understand the Scriptures, though I have spent some years upon them.[47]

This unhappy man was sent away by his father, his sister would attempt to cheat him out of his small inheritance and old friends ignored him. He found refuge in an attic room[48] in a house owned by Mennonite Christians near Amsterdam. Living there, seeing few people and supporting himself grinding optical lenses, he wrote. We see clearly in his work that even by the seventeenth century it was still not understood that the brain directs the work of the body.

> The human mind has no knowledge of the body, and does not know it to exist, save through the ideas of the modifications whereby the body is affected.[49]
>
> ……
>
> The human mind does not involve an adequate knowledge of the parts composing the human body.[50]

In his 'On the Origin and Nature of the Emotions,' Spinoza returns to this idea. The modern reader can hardly believe he means this:

---

[46] Ibid., IV, viii, 6. The actual diameter of the earth is 7,926 miles and that of the sun, 864,930 miles!

[47] Benedict de Spinoza, Letter to William de Bylenbergh, quoted in *Philosophy of Benedict de Spinoza*, trans. R. Ellwes (New York: Tudor Publishing, 1936), 342. Unless otherwise indicated, all English translations are taken from this edition.

[48] Prompting Anatole France's wry comment that if Napoleon had been more brilliant he would have 'lived in a garret and written four books.'

[49] Spinoza, *The Ethics*, 'Of the Power of the Understanding, or of Human Freedom,' Proposition XIX.

[50] Ibid., Proposition XXIV.

> Body cannot determine mind to think, neither can mind determine body to motion or rest or any state different from these, if such there be.[51]

In his following explanation, however, we can see how general was the ignorance of real brain function.

> No one knows how or by what means the mind moves the body, nor how many various degrees of motion it can import to the body, nor how quickly it can move it. Thus, when men say that this or that physical action has its origin in the mind, which latter has dominion over the body, they are using words without meaning, or are confessing in specious phraseology that they are ignorant of the cause of the said action, and do not wonder at it.[52]

The principal evidence that the mind cannot be proven to operate the body, in so far as Spinoza was concerned, came from the observation of sleep-walkers, the assumption being that sleep-walkers do not engage in 'rational' thinking. Similar 'evidence' in support for the presumed inability of the mind to control the body, Spinoza saw in the fact that men are not as prone to keep silence, as they are to speak, and in the non-rational infant who cries for milk.

The French archbishop and philosopher, François Fenelon (1651–1715) mentions the importance of the child's diet and health and allowing the organs to grow strong, but he cautions avoiding 'anything which may excite the passions.' Fenelon was also in possession of some weird science with respect to the child's brain.

> Their brain substance is soft and hardens gradually; as for their mind, it knows nothing and finds everything new. The result of this softness of the brain is that everything is easily impressed on it and the surprise of novelty makes children quickly moved to admiration and extremely curious. It is true also that this moistness and softness of the brain, together with a great heat, give rise to facile and continual movement. This is the cause of that constant activity of children, for they cannot concentrate their attention on any object nor keep their body still in any one place.[53]

He indirectly refers here to a mistaken view still held by many in our century, that the infant is born a 'blank slate' which the process of education fills. Because, therefore, the child's mind is so open to impression, Fenelon advises that the child should be shown failed examples of humanity.

> They should be shown how often one is despised—or worthy of being so, how often one is miserable when one gives way to one's passions and does not cultivate one's reason.[54]

---

[51] Ibid., Proposition II.

[52] Spinoza, *The Ethics*, 'Of the Origin and Nature of the Emotions,' Proposition II.

[53] *Fenelon on Education*, trans. H. Barnard (Cambridge: University Press, 1966), 9ff.

[54] Ibid., 13.

Fenelon, by the way, makes a passing reference to music education in the ancient civilizations:

> The ancients understood this matter far better. It was through the pleasures of poetry and music that the chief branches of knowledge, the maxims of virtue and of civilization, were introduced among the Hebrews, the Egyptians and the Greeks. Uneducated people can scarcely believe that, so far removed is it from our own customs.[55]

We conclude this chapter with René Descartes (1596–1650) who, after losing his mother at an early age, received from his father a financial inheritance which allowed him to spend his life in contemplation, free from the necessity of employment. His education was in Jesuit schools, centered primarily in mathematics, a background which inspired him to attempt to apply a similar step-by-step process to philosophy. In the course of so doing, he felt the necessity to rid himself of possible error in all prior learning by starting over, educating himself from the beginning. This was the background for his famous *Discourse on Method* of 1637.

In setting out on this course, he wanted to find some universal beginning point which could not be questioned and thus he formulated the most single famous sentence in philosophy, *Cogito ergo sum* [I think, therefore I am]. This concept of starting with the individual, conscious self was in itself a revolution. Even though the humanists of the Renaissance had helped rediscover the individual, in the Catholic countries such as France there was still preserved in the universities a Scholastic tradition one thousand years old which emphasized God before self.

Regarding the various actions of the body, Descartes never tired of comparing the body to a machine. He at least understood some connection between brain and body and on one occasion Descartes uses the organ as a metaphor for the basic body mechanism.

> You can think of our machine's heart and arteries, which push the animal spirits into the cavities of its brain, as being like the bellows of an organ, which push air into the wind-chests; and you can think of external objects, which stimulate certain nerves and cause spirits contained in the cavities to pass into some of the pores, as being like the fingers of the organist, which press certain keys and cause the air to pass from the wind-chests into certain pipes. Now the harmony of an organ does not depend on the externally visible arrangement of the pipes or on the shape of the wind-chests or other parts. The functions we are concerned with here does not depend at all on the external shape of the visible parts which anatomists distinguish in the substance of the brain, or on the shape of the brain's cavities, but solely on three factors: the spirits which come from the heart, the pores of the brain through which they pass, and the way in which the spirits are distributed in these pores.[56]

---

55   Ibid., 21.

56   'Treatise on Man,' 166.

The 'animal spirits' referred to here, Descartes defines as,

> The parts of the blood which penetrate as far as the brain serve not only to nourish and sustain its substance, but also and primarily to produce in it a certain very fine wind, or rather a very lively and pure flame, which is called the *animal spirits*.[57]

The real center piece of all his weird science is the pineal gland, a small gland in the brain, to which Descartes assigned nearly everything for which he could not otherwise discover a physical location. To be fair to Descartes, we must note that the medical profession, after two thousand years of research, *still* has no idea what function this gland performs.[58] But, on the other hand, research has proven that several of the functions which Descartes attributes to this gland are incorrect. In various treatises he says this gland is the seat of the imagination and the common sense,[59] the passions as well as the seat of the soul.[60] With regard to the latter, this gland being the seat of the soul, Descartes gives a very precise description of his theory in a letter of 1640 to Lazare Meysonnier, a professor, doctor and astrologer at Lyons. One can see here that Descartes was evidently bothered by the question, that since we have two eyes, two ears, etc., how *two* senses could feed information to the brain which would result in *one* understanding?

> I will answer the question you asked me about the function of the little gland called [pineal]. My view is that this gland is the principal seat of the soul, and the place in which all our thoughts are formed. The reason I believe this is that I cannot find any part of the brain, except for this, which is not double. Since we see only one thing with two eyes, and hear only one voice with two ears, and altogether have only one thought at a time, it must necessarily be the case that the impressions which enter by the two eyes or by the two ears, and so on, unite with each other in some part of the body before being considered by the soul. Now it is impossible to find any such place, in the whole head, except this gland; moreover it is situated in the most suitable possible place for this purpose, in the middle of all the concavities; and it is supported and surrounded by the little branches of the carotid arteries which bring the spirits into the brain.[61]

The centuries of weird science regarding how the brain acquires intelligence and where it is stored must have given men-at-large little self-confidence.. Perhaps this is reflected in the later pitiable and humble comment by Mozart in a letter of 8 November 1777 to his father:

> I beg you to love me just a little … until in my narrow, little brain new pigeon holes can be made, into which I can put intelligence and common sense.

---

57 Ibid., 129.

58 We asked our own physician and he responded, 'Well, it must do something!'

59 'Treatise on Man,' 129 and 'Meditations on First Philosophy,' VI.

60 'Principles of Philosophy,' IV, 316ff.

61 Letter to Meyssonnier, January 29, 1640, quoted in *Descartes Philosophical Letters*, trans. Anthony Kenny (Oxford: Clarendon Press, 1970), 69ff. He discusses this again at some length in a letter to Mersenne of December 24, 1640.

Bibliography

CHAPTER ONE: THE ANCIENT VOICE OF PYTHAGORAS

Barker, Andrew, trans. *Greek Musical Writings*. Cambridge: Cambridge University Press, 1989.
Isacoff, Stuart. *Temperament*. New York: Vintage Books, 2001.
Jones, Leslie. *An Introduction to Divine and Human Readings*. New York, Octagon Books, 1966.
Kirchner, Walther. *Western Civilization to 1500*. New York: Barnes & Noble, 1960.
Lucian. 'Dialogues of the Gods,' in *A Second Century Satirist*. Translated by Winthrop D. Sheldon. Philadelphia: Drexel Biddle, 1901.
Marrou, H. I. *A History of Education in Antiquity*. New York: The New American Library, 1964.
Milton, John. *The Works of John Milton*. Edited by Frank Patterson. New York: Columbia University Press, 1931–1938.
Montaigne, Michel, de. *Essays*. Translated by M. A. Screech. London: Penguin, 1993.
Nahm, Milton C. *Selections from Early Greek Philosophy*. New York: Appleton-Century-Crofts, 1964.
Porphyry. 'Life of Pythagoras,' in Kenneth S. Guthrie, *The Pythagorean Sourcebook*. Grand Rapids: Phanes Press, 1987.
Reale. *A History of Ancient Philosophy*. Albany: State University of New York Press, 1987.
Robinson, T. M. *Heraclitus*. Toronto: University of Toronto Press, 1987.
Sheldon, Winthrop D. *A Second Century Satirist*. Philadelphia: Drexel Biddle.
Stahl, William Harris and Richard Johnson, trans. *Martianus Capella and the Seven Liberal Arts*. New York: Columbia University Press, 1977.

CHAPTER TWO: ON THE MUSIC OF THE SPHERES, "THE SACRED MADNESS"

Agrippa, Henry Cornelius. *De occulta Philosophia*, in Donald Tyson, *Three Books of Occult Philosophy*. St. Paul: Llewellyn Publications, 1993.
Armitage, Angus. *John Kepler*. New York: Roy Publishers, 1966.
Bacon, Francis. *The Works of Francis Bacon*. Edited by James Spedding. Cambridge: Cambridge University Press, 1869.
Capella, Martianus. *Martianus Capella and the Seven Liberal Arts*. Translated by William Harris Stahl and Richard Johnson. New York: Columbia University Press, 1977.
Cassiodorus. *Variae*. Translated by Thomas Hodgkin. London: Frowde, 1886.
Castiglione. *The Courtier*. Translated by George Bull. New York: Penguin Books, 1967.
Dryden, John. *The Works of John Dryden*. Edited by Edward Hooker. Berkeley: University of California Press, 1956.
Glarean, Heinrich. *Dodecachordon*. Translated by Clement Miller. American Institute of Musicology, 1965.

Hildegard. *The Book of Divine Works.* Edited by Matthew Fox. Santa Fe: Bear & Company, 1987.
Hrotswitha of Gandersheim. *The Plays of Hrotswitha of Gandersheim.* Translated by Larissa Bonfante. New York: New York University Press, 1979.
Isacoff, Stuart. *Temperament.* New York: Vintage Books, 2001.
Johannes de Grocheo. *De Musica.* Translated by Albert Seay. Colorado Springs: Colorado College Music Press, 1967.
Kepler, Johannes. *Harmony of the Universe* (1619). Translated by Charles Glenn Wallis, in *Great Books of the Western World.* University of Chicago, 1990.
Lorris, Guillaume de and Jean de Meun, *The Romance of the Rose.* Translated by Harry Robbins. New York: Dutton, 1962.
Lovelace, Richard. *The Poems of Richard Lovelace.* Edited by C. H. Wilkinson. Oxford: Clarendon Press, 1930.
Lydgate, John. *Fall of Princes.* Edited by Henry Bergen. London: Oxford University Press, 1967.
Manniche, Lise. *Music and Musicians in Ancient Egypt.* London: British Museum Press, 1991.
Marino, Giambattista. *L'Adone* (1623). Translated by Harold Priest. Ithaca: Cornell University Press, 1967.
Milton, John. *The Works of John Milton.* Edited by Frank Patterson. New York: Columbia University Press, 1931–1938.
Montaigne. *Essays.* Translated by M. A. Screech. London: Penguin, 1993.
Nahm, Milton C. *Selections from Early Greek Philosophy.* New York: Appleton-Century-Crofts, 1964.
Nashe, Thomas. *The Works of Thomas Nashe.* Edited by Ronald McKerrow. Oxford: Blackwell, 1966.
Palisca, Claude V. *Humanism in Italian Renaissance Musical Thought.* New Haven: Yale University Press, 1985.
Pliny the Elder. *Natural History.*
Porphyry. 'Life of Pythagoras,' in Kenneth S. Guthrie, *The Pythagorean Sourcebook.* Grand Rapids: Phanes Press, 1987.
Quintilian. *The Education of an Orator (Institutio Oratoria).* Translated by H. E. Butler. London: Heinemann, 1938.
Reale, Giovanni. *A History of Ancient Philosophy.* Albany: State University of New York Press, 1987.
Saint Ambrose. *Hexameron, Paradise, and Cain and Abel.* Translated by John J. Savage. New York: Fathers of the Church, 1961.
Simpson, Christopher. *Division-Violist* (1654). London: Curwen, 1965, facsimile of 1665 edition, 1965.
Thomson, James. *The Poetical Works of James Thomson.* London: Bell and Daldy, c. 1860.

Tinctoris. *The Art of Counterpoint*. Translated by Albert Seay. American Institute of Musicology, 1961.

CHAPTER THREE: EARLY VIEWS ON MUSIC THERAPY

Boccaccio. *The Decameron*. Translated by Mark Musa and Peter Bondanella. New York: Norton, 1977.

Bodin, Jean. *Method for the Easy Comprehension of History*. Translated by Beatrice Reynolds. New York: Columbia University Press, 1945.

Browne, Thomas. *Sir Thomas Browne's Works*. Edited by Simon Wilkin. London: Pickering, 1836.

Burton, Robert. *The Anatomy of Melancholy*. Edited by Floyd Dell. New York: Tudor Publishing Company, 1938.

Campanella, Tommaso. *La Citta del Sole*. Translated by Daniel Donno. Berkeley: University of California Press, 1981.

Capella, Martianus. *Martianus Capella and the Seven Liberal Arts*. Translated by William Harris Stahl and Richard Johnson. New York: Columbia University Press, 1977.

Cassiodorus. *Variae*. Translated by Thomas Hodgkin. London: Frowde, 1886.

Cowley, Abraham. *The Complete Works of Abraham Cowley*. Edited by Alexander Grosart. New York: AMS Press, 1967.

Erasmus. *The Collected Works of Erasmus*. Toronto: University of Toronto Press, 1992.

Giustiniani, Vicenzo. *Discorso sopra la Musica* (ca. 1628). Translated by Carol MacClintock. American Institute of Musicology, 1962.

Guthrie, Kenneth. *The Pythagorean Sourcebook*. Grand Rapids: Phanes Press, 1987.

Honegger, Arthur. *I am a Composer*. Faber & Faber, 1966.

Isacoff, Stuart. *Temperament*. New York: Vintage Books, 2001.

Jones, Emrys, ed. *The New Oxford Book of Sixteenth Century Verse*. Oxford: Oxford University Press, 1991.

Mattheson, Johann. *Der vollkommene Capellmeister* (1739). Translated by Ernest Harriss. Ann Arbor: UMI Research Press, 1981.

McEvoy, James. *The Philosophy of Robert Grosseteste*. Oxford: Clarendon, 1982.

Peacham, Henry. *The Complete Gentleman*. Edited by Virgil Heltzel. Ithaca: Cornell University Press, 1962.

Rabelais, Francois. *Pantagruel*. Translated by Donald Frame. Berkeley: University of California Press, 1991.

Steel, Robert, trans. *Medieval Lore*. London: Stock, 1893.

Wycherley, William. *The Complete Works of William Wycherley*. New York: Russell & Russell, 1964.

CHAPTER FOUR: 'TO SOOTHE A SAVAGE BREAST'

Athanassakis, Apostolos N., trans. *Theogony, Works and Days, Shield*. Baltimore: Johns Hopkins University Press, 1983.

Bellay, Joachim. *The Regrets*. Translated by C. H. Sisson. Manchester: Carcanet Press, 1984.

Bernstein, Jane. *French Chansons of the Sixteenth Century*. University Park: Pennsylvania State University Press, 1985.

Boccaccio. *The Decameron*. Translated by Mark Musa and Peter Bondanella. New York: Norton, 1977.

Bodin, Jean. *Colloquium of the Seven*. Translated by Marion Kuntz. Princeton: Princeton University Press, 1975.

Browne, Thomas. *Sir Thomas Browne's Works*. Edited by Simon Wilkin. London: Pickering, 1836.

Buszin, Walter. 'Luther on Music,' *The Musical Quarterly* 32, no. 1 (January, 1946): 80–97.

Carew, Thomas. *The Poems of Thomas Carew*. Edited by Rhodes Dunlap. Oxford: Clarendon Press, 1964.

Cassiodorus. 'On Music.' Translated by Leslie Jones, in *An Introduction to Divine and Human Readings*. New York, Octagon Books, 1966.

Cassiodorus. *Variae*. Translated by Thomas Hodgkin. London: Frowde, 1886.

Cervantes, Miguel. *Don Quijote*. Translated by Burton Raffel. New York: Norton, 1995.

Cowley, Abraham. *The Complete Works of Abraham Cowley*. Edited by Alexander Grosart. New York: AMS Press, 1967.

Dante. *Paradiso*.

Dante. *Purgatorio*.

de Machaut, Guillaume. 'Le Jugement du roy de Behaigne.' Translated by James Wimsatt and William Kibler. Athens: The University of Georgia Press, 1988.

Donne, John. *Five Sermons*. Menston: Scolar Press.

Donnington, Robert. *The Interpretation of Early Music*. New York, 1964.

Farmer, Henry G. 'The Music of Ancient Mesopotamia,' in *The New Oxford History of Music*. London: Oxford University Press, 1966.

Gafurius, Franchius. *The Practica musicae of Franchinus Gafurius*. Translated by Irwin Young. Madison: University of Wisconsin Press, 1969.

Galen. *On the Passions and Errors of the Soul*. Translated by Paul W. Harkins. Columbus: Ohio State University Press.

Galilei, Vincenzo. *Fronimo* (1584). Translated by Carol MacClintock. Neuhasen-Stuttgart: Hanssler-Verlag, 1985.

Galpin, Francis. *Music of the Sumerians*. Westport: Greenwood Press, 1970.

Guthrie, Kenneth. *The Pythagorean Sourcebook*. Grand Rapids: Phanes Press, 1987.

Hall, Joseph. *The Works of Joseph Hall, D.D.* Edited by Philip Wynter. New York: AMS Press, 1969.

Herbert, George. *The Poems of George Herbert*. Edited by Ernest Rhys. London: Walter Scott, 1885.
Hugh of Orleans, in *Vagabond Verse*. Translated by Edwin H. Zeydel. Detroit: Wayne State University Press, 1966.
Jonson, Ben. *The Complete Poetry of Ben Jonson*. Edited by William Hunter. New York: Norton, 1963.
Lang, A., trans. *Theocritus, Bion and Moschus*. London: Macmillan, 1920.
Luther, Martin. *Luther's Works*. St. Louis: Concordia, 1961.
Lydgate, John. *John Lydgate Poems*. Oxford: Clarendon Press, 1966.
Machiavelli, Niccolo. *Machiavelli, the Chief Works*. Translated by Allan Gilbert. Durham: Duke University Press, 1965.
Manniche, Lise. *Music and Musicians in Ancient Egypt*. London: British Museum Press.
Miller, Clement. *Hieronymus Cardanus, Writings on Music*. American Institute of Musicology, 1973.
Palisca, Claude, V. *Humanism in Italian Renaissance Musical Thought*. New Haven: Yale University Press, 1985.
Petrarch. *Petrarch's Lyric Poems*. Translated by Robert Durling. Cambridge: Harvard University Press, 1976.
Petrarch. *Petrarch's Bucolicum Carmen*. Translated by Thomas Bergin. New Haven: Yale University Press, 1974.
Purvis, J. S. *The York Cycle*. London: S.P.C.K, 1957.
Ruiz, Juan. *The Book of True Love*. Translated by Saralyn Daly. University Park: Pennsylvania State University Press, 1978.
Sharman, Ruth. *The Cansos and Sirventes of the Troubadour Giraut de Borneil*. Cambridge: Cambridge University Press, 1989.
St. Basil. *Exegetic Homilies*. Translated by Sister Agnes Way. Washington, D.C.: The Catholic University of America Press.
Saint-Evremond. *The Letters of Saint-Evremond*. Edited by John Hayward. Freeport, NY: Books for Libraries Press, 1971.
Stahl, William Harris and Richard Johnson, trans. *Martianus Capella and the Seven Liberal Arts*. New York: Columbia University Press, 1977.
Symonds, John Addington. *Renaissance in Italy*. New York: Capricorn Books, 1964.
Tasso, Torquato. *Creation of the World*. Translated by Joseph Tusiani. Binghamton: Center for Medieval & Early Renaissance Studies, 1982.
The Greek Anthology.
The Norton Anthology of English Literature. New York: Norton, 1968.
Vesce, Thomas E., trans. *The Knight of the Parrot*. New York: Garland, 1986.
Voltaire. *The Works of Voltaire*. New York: St. Hubert Guild, 1901.
Williams, John, ed. *English Renaissance Poetry*. Fayetteville: The University of Arkansas Press.
Wither, George. *Works of George Wither*. New York: Franklin, 1967.

Chapter Five: Ancient Views on Movement and Music

Agrippa, Henry Cornelius. *Of the Vanitie and Uncertaintie of Arts and Sciences.* Edited by Catherine Dunn. Northridge: California State University, Northridge Press, 1974.

Aristotle. *Problemata.*

Athenaeus. *Deipnosophistae.*

Bacon, Roger. *The Opus Majus of Roger Bacon.* Translated by Robert Burke. New York: Russell & Russell.

Conway, Geoffrey S. *The Odes of Pindar.* London: Dent, 1972.

Farmer, Henry George. *Al-Farabi's Writings on Music.* New York: Hinrichsen, 1934.

Garlandia, Johannes de. *De Mensurabili Musica.* Tranlated by Stanley Birnbaum. Colorado Springs: Colorado College Music Press, 1978.

Gildon, Charles. *The Life of Mr. Thomas Betterton* [1710]. London: Frank Cass, 1970.

Herodotus. *Histories.*

Jackson. *Huldreich Zwingli.* New York: Putham, 1901.

Kastner, Georges. *Manuel General de Musique Militaire.* Paris, 1848.

Liszt, Franz. *The Gipsy in Music* [1859]. London: William Reeves, 1960.

Livy. *The History of Rome.*

Manniche, Lise. *Music and Musicians in Ancient Egypt.* London: British Museum Press, 1991.

Marchant, E. C. *Memorabilia and Oeconomicus.* Cambridge: Harvard University Press, 1953.

Mattheson, Johann. *Der vollkommene Capellmeister* (1739). Translated by Ernest Harriss. Ann Arbor: UMI Research Press, 1981.

Miller, Clement. *Hieronymus Cardanus, Writings on Music.* American Institute of Musicology, 1973.

Palisca, Claude V. *Humanism in Italian Renaissance Musical Thought,* New Haven: Yale University Press, 1985.

Plato. *Philebus.*

Psellus, Michael. *Chronographia.* Translated by E. R. A. Sewter. Baltimore: Penguin Books, 1966.

Sachs, Curt. *World History of the Dance.* New York: Norton, 1937.

Stubbs, Philip. *The Anatomy of the Abuses in England* (1583). Edited by Frederick Furnivall. London: The New Shakespeare Society, n.d.

Thucydides. *The Peloponnesian War.*

Chapter Six: Ancient Views on Music and Oratory

Ammianus Marcellinus. *Constantius et Gallus.* Translated by John C. Rolfe. London: Heinemann, 1935.

Cicero. *Tusculan Disputations.*

Cicero. *Brutus.*

Cicero. *De Oratore.*

Cicero. *Pro Archia Poeta*.
Descartes, Rene. *The Philosophical Writings of Descartes*. Transcribed by John Cottingham, Robert Stoothoff and Dugald Murdoch. Cambridge: Cambridge University Press, 1985.
Erasmus. *The Collected Works of Erasmus*. Toronto: University of Toronto Press, 1992.
Fenelon, François. *Fenelon's Dialogues on Eloquence*. Translated by Wilbur Howell. Princeton: Princeton University Press, 1951.
Gildon, Charles. *The Life of Mr. Thomas Betterton, the Late Eminent Tragedian* [1710]. London: Frank Cass Reprint, 1970.
Herbert, George. *The Poems of George Herbert*. Edited by Ernest Rhys. London: Walter Scott, 1885.
Herodotus. *Histories*.
Hume, David. *David Hume, The Philosophical Works*. Aalen: Scientia Verlag, 1964.
La Rochefoucauld. *The Maxims of La Rochefoucauld*. Translated by Louis Kronenberger. New York: Random House, 1959.
Mattheson, Johann. *Der vollkommene Capellmeister* [1739]. Translated by Ernest Harriss. Ann Arbor: UMI Research Press, 1981
Mersenne, Marin. *Treatise Three, Book Two ("Second Book of Songs") of the Traitez de la Voix et des Chants ...* Translated by Wilbur F. Russell. Princeton: Westminster Choir College, unpublished dissertation, 1952.
Montaigne, Michel de. *Essays*. Translated by M. A. Screech. London: Penguin, 1993.
Pliny the Younger. *The Letters of the Younger Pliny*. New York: Penguin, 1985.
Quintilian. *The Education of an Orator (Institutio Oratoria)*. Translated by E. Butler. London: Heinemann, 1938.
Ronsard, Pierre de. *Songs and Sonnets of Pierre de Ronsard*. Translated by Curtis Page. Westport: Hyperion Press, 1924.
Strunk, Oliver. *Source Readings in Music History*. New York: Norton, 1950.
Suetonius. *The Twelve Caesars*. New York: Penguin, 1989.

CHAPTER SEVEN: ANCIENT VOICES WONDER: ARE MUSICIANS BORN OR MADE?

Birnbaum, Johann. 'Impartial Comments on ... *Der Critische Musicus*,' quoted in Hans T. David and Arthur Mendel, *The Bach Reader*. New York: Norton, 1966.
Blunt, Anthony. *Artistic Theory in Italy, 1450–1600*. Oxford: Clarendon Press, 1959.
Chubb, Thomas. *The Letters of Pietro Aretino*. New Haven: Shoe String Press [Archon Books].
Cook, Albert. *The Poetical Treatises of Horace, Vida, and Boileau*. Boston: Ginn, 1892.
Glarean, Heinrich. *Dodecachordon*. Translated by Clement Miller. American Institute of Musicology, 1965.
Heinichen, Johann David. *General-Bass Treatise* [1711], quoted in George Buelow, *Thorough-Bass Accompaniment according to Johann David Heinichen*. Ann Arbor: UMI Research Press, 1986.

Jonson, Ben. *The Complete Poetry of Ben Jonson*. Edited by William Hunter. New York: Norton, 1963.

Longinus. *On the Sublime*. Translated by W. Rhys Roberts. Cambridge: University Press, 1935.

Martin, L. C. *The Poetical Works of Robert Herrick*. Oxford: Clarendon Press, 1963.

Mattheson, Johann. *Der vollkommene Capellmeister* (1739). Translated by Ernest Harriss. Ann Arbor: UMI Research Press, 1981

Mersenne, Marin. *Harmonie universelle.*

Snuggs, Henry. *Giraldi Cinthio On Romances*. Lexington: University of Kentucky Press, 1968.

Stokes, Francis. *On the Eve of the Reformation*. New York: Harper & Row, 1909.

Telemann, Georg Philipp, T. E. Schubart, *Fortsetzung des harmonischen Gottesdienstes* (1731), quoted in Sam Morgenstern, *Composers on Music*. New York: Pantheon, 1956.

Voltaire. *The Works of Voltaire*. New York: St. Hubert Guild, 1901.

Chapter Eight: Ancient Voices Wonder: Is Music Genetic?

Anderson, Warren D. *Ethos and Education in Greek Music*. Cambridge: Harvard University Press, 1966.

Aristotle. *Politica.*

Aristotle. *Problemata.*

Batteaux, Charles. *Les beaux-arts reduits a un meme principe*. [Paris 1746], quoted in Peter le Huray and James Day, *Music and Aesthetics in the Eighteenth and Early-Nineteenth Centuries*. Cambridge: Cambridge University Press, 1981.

Cicero. *De Divinatione.*

Darwin, Charles. *The Expression of Emotions in Man and Animals* [1872]. New York: St. Martin's Press, 1979.

Descartes, Rene. *Descartes Philosophical Letters*. Translated by Anthony Kenny. Oxford: Clarendon Press, 1970.

Dryden, John. *The Works of John Dryden*. Edited by Edward Hooker. Berkeley: University of California Press, 1956.

Erasmus. *The Complete Works of Erasmus*. Toronto: University of Toronto Press, 1992.

Grebanier, Bernard. *English Literature*. Great Neck: Barron, 1959.

Guarini, Giambattista. *The Faithful Shepherd [Il Pastor Fido]*, in *Five Italian Renaissance Comedies*. New York: Penguin Books, 1978.

Hepper, Peter. 'An examination of fetal learning before and after birth,' *Irish Journal of Psychology* 12 (1991): 95–107.

James, William. *The Works of William James*. Edited by Frederick Burkhardt, et. al., in *The Principles of Psychology*, II. Cambridge: Harvard University Press, 1981.

John of Salisbury. *The Metalogicon*. Translated by Daniel McGarry. Berkeley: University of California Press, 1955.

Kristeller, Paul. 'Music and Learning in the Early Italian Renaissance,' *The Journal of Renaissance and Baroque Music* (1947).

Leibniz, Gottfreid Wilhelm. *New Essays Concerning Human Understanding* (1704). Translated by Alfred Langley. La Salle: The Open Court Publishing Company, 1949.

Leibniz, Gottfried Wilhelm. 'Discourse on Metaphysics' (1686), in 'A New Method for Learning and Teaching Jurisprudence' (1667), I, xxxiv, in Leroy Loemker, *Philosophical Papers and Letters*. Dordrecht: Reidel, 1956.

Locke, John. 'Essay on Human Understanding,' in *The Works of John Locke*. London, 1823.

Longinus. *On the Sublime*. Translated by W. Rhys Roberts. Cambridge: University Press, 1935.

Montaigne, Michel. *Essays*. Translated by M. A. Screech. London: Penguin, 1993.

Rameau, Jean Philippe. *Observations sur notre instinct pour la musique et sur son principe* (1734), quoted in Sam Morgenstern. *Composers on Music*. New York: Pantheon, 1956.

Royce. *The Spirit of Modern Philosophy*. Boston, 1892.

Saint-Lambert, Michel. *Les Principes du Clavecin* (1702), quoted in Carol MacClintock, *Readings in the History of Music in Performance*. Bloomington: Indiana University Press, 1979.

Schelling, Friedrich. *The Philosophy of Art*. Minneapolis: University of Minnesota Press, 1989.

Schrecker, Paul, trans. *Monadology and Other Philosophical Essays*. Indianapolis: Bobbs-Merrill, 1965.

St. Augustine. *On Music*. Translated by Robert Taliaferro, in *Writings of Saint Augustine*. New York: Fathers of the Church.

Zarlino. 'Le Istitutioni harmoniche,' quoted in in Claude V. Palisca, *Humanism in Italian Renaissance Musical Thought*. New Haven: Yale University Press, 1985.

CHAPTER NINE: ANCIENT VIEWS ON GEOGRAPHY AND MUSIC

Agrippa, Henry Cornelius. *Of the Vanitie and Uncertaintie of Arts and Sciences*. Edited by Catherine Dunn. Northridge: California State University, Northridge Press, 1974.

Berlioz, Hector. *The Memoirs of Hector Berlioz*. Edited by David Cairns. London: Gollancz, 1969.

Buelow, George, J. 'Music and Society in the Late Baroque Era,' in *The Late Baroque Era*. Englewood Cliffs: Prentice Hall, 1994.

Couperin, François. *L'Art de toucher*.

Gay, John. *The Works of John Gay*. London: Edward Jeffery, 1745.

Greene, Robert. *The Life and Complete Works of Robert Greene*. Edited by Alexander Grosart. New York: Russell & Russell, 1964.

Heinichen, Johann David. *General-Bass Treatise* [1711], quoted in George Buelow, *Thorough-Bass Accompaniment according to Johann David Heinichen*. Ann Arbor: UMI Research Press, 1986.

Leibniz, Gottfried. *The Political Writings of Leibniz*. Translated by Patrick Riley. Cambridge: Cambridge University Press, 1972.

Lyly, John. *Euphues and his England*. Edited by Morris Croll. New York: Russell & Russell, 1964.

Mattheson, Johann. *Neu-Eroffnete Orchestre*. Hamburg, 1713.

Mattheson, Johann. *Der vollkommene Capellmeister* (1739). Translated by Ernest Harriss. Ann Arbor: UMI Research Press, 1981.

Maugars, André, quoted in Carol MacClintock, *Readings in the History of Music in Performance*. Bloomington: Indiana University Press, 1979.

Milton, John. *The Works of John Milton*. Edited by Frank Patterson. New York: Columbia University Press, 1931–1938.

Montesquieu. *The Spirit of Laws* (1748). Translated by Thomas Nugent in *Great Books*, XXXVIII. Chicago: Encyclopedia Britannica, 1952.

Morgenstern, Sam. *Composers on Music*. New York: Pantheon.

Moser, Hans. *Heinrich Schütz*. St. Louis: Concordia, 1936.

Nashe, Thomas. *The Works of Thomas Nashe*. Edited by Ronald McKerrow. Oxford: Blackwell, 1966.

Niedt, Friedrich. *Musicalische Handleitung* (Hamburg, 1700), quoted in Robert Donnington, *The Interpretation of Early Music*. New York, 1964.

North, Roger. *The Musicall Gramarian*. Oxford: Oxford University Press, 1925.

Ornithoparchus. *Musicae active mirologus* and Dowland, *Introduction: Containing the Art of Singing*. New York: Dover, 1973.

Palisca, Claude. *Baroque Music*. Englewood Cliffs: Prentice Hall, 1981.

Peacham, Henry. *The Complete Gentleman*. Edited by Virgil Heltzel. Ithaca: Cornell University Press, 1962.

Raguenet, François. 'Parallele des Italiens et des Francais,' (1702), quoted in Oliver Strunk. *Source Readings in Music History*. New York: Norton, 1950.

Rosen, Edward, trans. *Kepler's Somnium*. Madison: University of Wisconsin Press, 1967.

Stein, Louise K. 'The Iberian Peninsula,' in *The Late Baroque Era*. Englewood Cliffs: Prentice Hall, 1994.

Stubbs, Phillip. *The Anatomy of the Abuses in England* (1583). Edited by Frederick Furnivall. London: The New Shakespeare Society, n.d.

Temple, William. *Five Miscellaneous Essays by Sir William Temple*. Edited by Samuel Monk. Ann Arbor: University of Michigan Press, 1963.

Voltaire. *The Works of Voltaire*. New York: St. Hubert Guild, 1901.

CHAPTER TEN: WEIRD SCIENCE

Aquinas, Thomas. *Commentary on Peri Hermeneias*.

Aquinas, Thomas. *Summa Contra Gentiles*.

Aquinas, Thomas. *Summa Theologiae*.

Bacon, Roger. *De Multiplicatione Specierum*. Translated by David Lindberg, in *Roger Bacon's Philosophy of Nature*. Oxford: Clarendon.

Bacon, Roger. *The Opus Majus of Roger Bacon*. Translated by Robert Burke. New York: Russell & Russell, 1962.

Bernard of Clairvaux. *Sermons on Conversion*. Translated by Marie-Bernard Said. Kalamazoo: Cistercian Publications, 1981.

Bernard of Clairvaux. *The Metalogicon*. Translated by Daniel McGarry. Berkeley: University of California Press, 1955.

Clement of Alexandria. In *The Miscellanies*. Translated by Alexander Roberts. Edinburgh: T. & T. Clark, 1869.

Dante. *Purgarorio*.

Dante. *The Banquet*.

Descartes. *Descartes Philosophical Letters*. Translated by Anthony Kenny. Oxford: Clarendon Press, 1970.

Descartes. *Meditations on First Philosophy*

Descartes. *Principles of Philosophy*.

Descartes. *Treatise on Man*.

Diogenes Laertius. *Lives of the Eminent Philosophers*. Translated by R. D. Hicks. Cambridge: Harvard University Press, 1950.

Epicurus. *Epicurus*. Translated by Cyril Bailey. Oxford: Clarendon Press.

Fenelon, François. *Fenelon on Education*. Translated by H. Barnard. Cambridge: University Press, 1966.

Hildegard von Bingen. *Book of Divine Works*. Edited by Matthew Fox. Santa Fe: Bear & Company, 1987.

Lucretius. *On the Nature of the Universe*. New York: Penguin, 1983.

McEvoy, James. *The Philosophy of Robert Grosseteste*. Oxford: Clarendon, 1982.

Nicholas of Cusa. *On Learned Ignorance*. Translated by Jasper Hopkins. Minneapolis: Banning Press, 1981.

Ruiz, Juan. *The Book of True Love*. Translated by Saralyn Daly. University Park: Pennsylvania State University Press, 1978.

Southern, R. W. *Robert Grosseteste*. Oxford: Clarendon, 1992.

Spinoza. *Philosophy of Benedict de Spinoza*. Translated by R. Ellwes. New York: Tudor Publishing, 1936.

Tacitus. *The Annals*.

Tertullianus. *The Writings of Tertullianus*. Edinburgh: T. & T. Clark, 1895.

Varro. *On the Latin Language*.

About the Author

Dr. David Whitwell is a graduate ('with distinction') of the University of Michigan and the Catholic University of America, Washington DC (PhD, Musicology, Distinguished Alumni Award, 2000) and has studied conducting with Eugene Ormandy and at the Akademie für Musik, Vienna. Prior to coming to Northridge, Dr. Whitwell participated in concerts throughout the United States and Asia as Associate First Horn in the USAF Band and Orchestra in Washington DC, and in recitals throughout South America in cooperation with the United States State Department.

At the California State University, Northridge, which is in Los Angeles, Dr. Whitwell developed the CSUN Wind Ensemble into an ensemble of international reputation, with international tours to Europe in 1981 and 1989 and to Japan in 1984. The CSUN Wind Ensemble has made professional studio recordings for BBC (London), the Köln Westdeutscher Rundfunk (Germany), NOS National Radio (The Netherlands), Zürich Radio (Switzerland), the Television Broadcasting System (Japan) as well as for the United States State Department for broadcast on its 'Voice of America' program. The CSUN Wind Ensemble's recording with the Mirecourt Trio in 1982 was named the 'Record of the Year' by The Village Voice. Composers who have guest conducted Whitwell's ensembles include Aaron Copland, Ernest Krenek, Alan Hovhaness, Morton Gould, Karel Husa, Frank Erickson and Vaclav Nelhybel.

Dr. Whitwell has been a guest professor in 100 different universities and conservatories throughout the United States and in 23 foreign countries (most recently in China, in an elite school housed in the Forbidden City). Guest conducting experiences have included the Philadelphia Orchestra, Seattle Symphony Orchestra, the Czech Radio Orchestras of Brno and Bratislava, The National Youth Orchestra of Israel, as well as resident wind ensembles in Russia, Israel, Austria, Switzerland, Germany, England, Wales, The Netherlands, Portugal, Peru, Korea, Japan, Taiwan, Canada and the United States.

He is a past president of the College Band Directors National Association, a member of the Prasidium of the International Society for the Promotion of Band Music, and was a member of the founding board of directors of the World Association for Symphonic Bands and Ensembles (WASBE). In 1964 he was made an honorary life member of Kappa Kappa Psi, a national professional music fraternity. In September, 2001, he was a delegate to the UNESCO Conference on Global Music in Tokyo. He has been knighted by sovereign organizations in France, Portugal and Scotland and has been awarded the gold medal of Kerkrade, The Netherlands, and the silver medal of Wangen, Germany, the highest honor given wind conductors in the United States, the medal of the Academy of Wind and Percussion Arts (National Band Association) and the highest honor given wind conductors in Austria, the gold medal of the Austrian Band Association. He is a member of the Hall of Fame of the California Music Educators Association.

Dr. Whitwell's publications include more than 127 articles on wind literature including publications in Music and Letters (London), the London Musical Times, the Mozart-Jahrbuch (Salzburg), and fifty books, among which is his thirteen-volume *History and Literature of the Wind Band and Wind Ensemble* and an eight-volume series on *Aesthetics in Music*. In addition to numerous modern editions of early wind band music his original compositions include five symphonies.

David Whitwell was named as one of six men who have determined the course of American bands during the second half of the twentieth century, in the definitive history, *The Twentieth Century American Wind Band* (Meredith Music).

A doctoral dissertation by German Gonzales (2007, Arizona State University) is dedicated to the life and conducting career of David Whitwell through the year 1977. David Whitwell is one of nine men described by Paula A. Crider in *The Conductor's Legacy* (Chicago: GIA, 2010) as 'the legendary conductors' of the twentieth century.

> 'I can't imagine the 2nd half of the 20th century—without David Whitwell and what he has given to all of the rest of us.' Frederick Fennell (1993)

About the Editor

CRAIG DABELSTEIN began studying the piano at age seven and took up the saxophone at age twelve. Mr Dabelstein has Bachelor of Arts (Music) and Bachelor of Music degrees from the Queensland Conservatorium of Music, where he majored in the performance of classical saxophone repertoire. He also has a Graduate Diploma of Learning and Teaching and a Graduate Certificate in Editing and Publishing from the University of Southern Queensland.

He has held the principal alto and tenor saxophone chairs in the Australian Wind Orchestra and has been an augmenting member of the Queensland Philharmonic Orchestra, the Queensland Symphony Orchestra, and the Queensland Pops Orchestra. For many years he was also a member of the Queensland Saxophone Quartet.

He has been a casual conductor of the Young Conservatorium Symphonic Winds, and has previously been a saxophone teacher at the Queensland Conservatorium of Music. He is a regular conductor of the Queensland Wind Orchestra, having served as their artistic director and chief conductor from 2004 to 2009.

Craig Dabelstein is a research associate for the *Teaching Music Through Performance in Band* series of books, contributing analyses to volumes 7, 8, 1 (rev. edn), and the *Solos with Wind Band Accompaniment* volume. He served as the copyeditor and layout designer of the *Australian Clarinet and Saxophone Magazine* from 2007 to 2009 and he has written many CD and book reviews for *Music Forum* magazine. He is the editor of the second editions of the books by Dr. David Whitwell including *A Concise History of the Wind Band, Foundations of Music Education, Music Education of the Future, The Sousa Oral History Project, Wagner on Bands, Berlioz on Bands, The Art of Musical Conducting,* the *Aesthetics of Music* series (8 volumes) and *The History and Literature of the Wind Band and Wind Ensemble* series (13 volumes). From 1994 to 2012 he was a staff member at Brisbane Girls Grammar School. He now teaches woodwinds and conducts bands at St. Joseph's College, Gregory Terrace, Brisbane, Australia.

www.ingramcontent.com/pod-product-compliance
Lightning Source LLC
Chambersburg PA
CBHW080550230426
43663CB00015B/2776